SEABIRDS
of the Northern Hemisphere

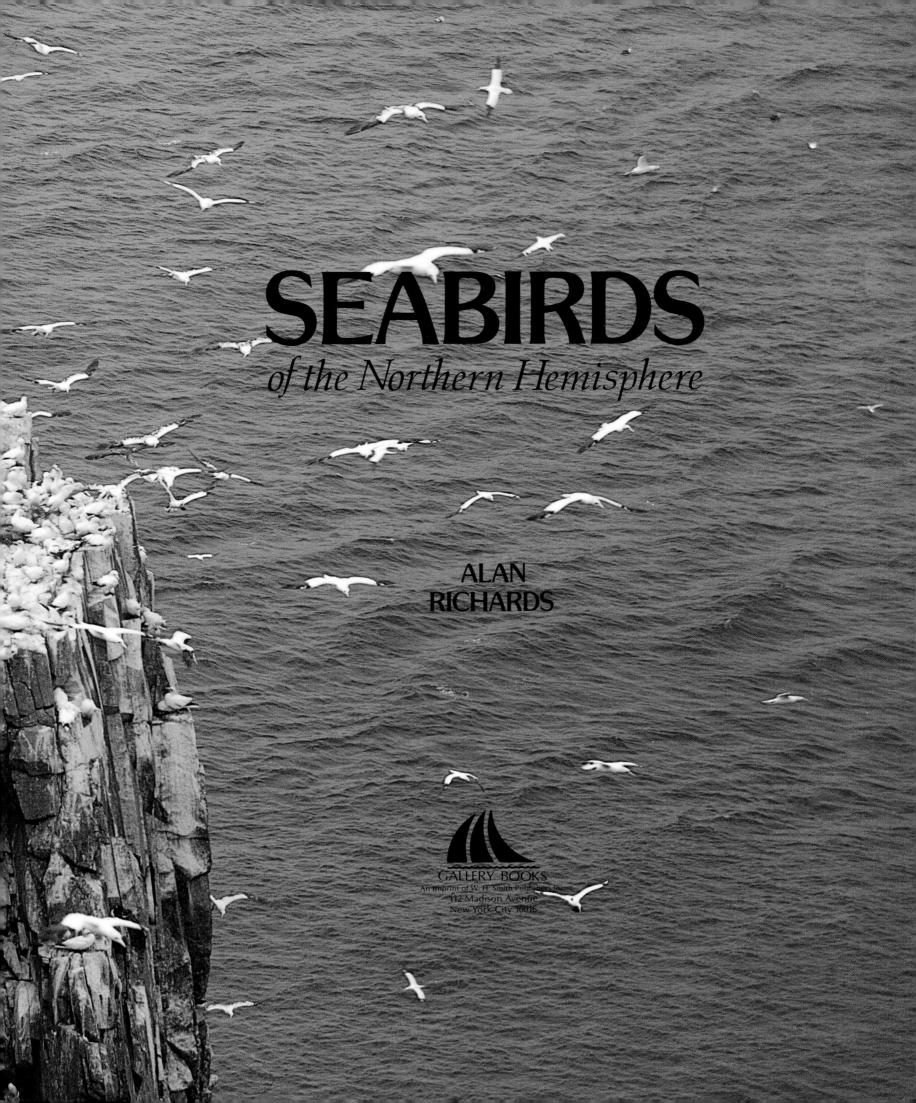

SEABIRDS
of the Northern Hemisphere

ALAN
RICHARDS

GALLERY BOOKS
An imprint of W. H. Smith Publishers Inc.
112 Madison Avenue
New York City 10016

TO THE MEMORY OF MY MOTHER AND FATHER

HALF TITLE
A White Pelican shields its featherless offspring from the searing summer sun

TITLE PAGE
Bass Rock is probably Britain's most famous Gannetry with around 18,000 breeding pairs

KEY TO MAPS
Dark blue = breeding location (area)

Mid blue = range during breeding season

Light blue = migration and winter range

Editor Diana Steedman
Designer Bob Gordon
Editorial Director Pippa Rubinstein

Typeset by Flairplan

Printed in Singapore

This edition first published in 1990 by Gallery Books, an Imprint of W. H. Smith Publishers, Inc., 112 Madison Avenue, New York 10016

Published in England by Dragon's World Ltd, Limpsfield and London

Gallery Books are available for bulk purchase for sales promotions and premium use. For details write or telephone the Manager of Special Sales, W. H. Smith Publishers Inc., 112 Madison Avenue, New York, New York 10016. (212) 532-6600.

ISBN 0 8317 7725 7

CONTENTS

FOREWORD

Allan R. Keith President, American Birding Association

Seabirds are both fascinating and mysterious to amateur and professional bird students alike. But probably less is known about seabirds than almost any other major group of bird families. All must come to land to nest, so what is known about them tends to be data gathered when they are on their breeding grounds. However, many species of petrels and shearwaters only return to their nest sites under cover of darkness, thus their presence may not even be suspected in areas where they actually occur. As an example, in 1973 a Manx Shearwater was discovered, quite by accident, breeding on a little island off the Massachusetts coast. From then it was several years more before other nest sites were located in Newfoundland though the species occurs regularly off nearly the entire east coast of the United States and Canada.

If basic knowledge about where a species breeds is only fragmentary, imagine how little we know about what these birds do and where they go during the part of the year they are not breeding. It is a common misconception that the deep oceans of the world are more or less uniform. In fact, recent studies have shown that many parts of the oceans rarely harbor much bird or aquatic life. Seabirds that live on the open oceans out of sight of land are not distributed randomly or uniformly but concentrate in favored areas where food is more abundant. How do the seabirds know where these areas are? How do they know how to get from one such area to another for different seasons of the year? How widely are seabird populations dispersed? Since the juveniles of many species are thought not to travel with the adults, how do they find their way the first time? We have no good answers to these and many other similar questions.

Another common misconception is that there are many places that seabirds can live or nest. In fact the majority of seabird species are restricted to the coastal zones of the oceans, or only about two percent of all the oceans' surface. For this reason, seabirds are much more vulnerable to pollution or habitat alteration in this narrow zone than most people appreciate. Many breeding sites are ancestral ones, chosen because they may be the best or perhaps the only good ones for many miles in any direction. Build condominiums nearby and the breeding biology of a significant percentage of the population of a species could be disrupted.

One way to appreciate seabirds more is to get better acquainted with them, and this book makes that possible. Its focus is on the species that live in the coastal and immediate offshore waters of North America and, because many of the species are the same there, western Europe. An Appendix also lists some of the less frequent seabird visitors to this area that spend their lives primarily in other parts of the world. The magnificent photographs selected by Alan Richards are a delight to the eye and communicate the grace and physical handsomeness of birds that most observers are fortunate to see so well once or twice in a lifetime. The American Birding Association exists to help enjoy their avocation by learning more about where birds live and what they look like. ABA is very proud to sponsor the publication of this portfolio celebrating this special group of birds. Like the sea itself, the lives of these birds are enigmatic to us, guided by primeval tides we cannot feel, vulnerable and aloof, but possess a soaring beauty we hope will always be there.

ALLAN R. KEITH

At Bolinas Lagoon, California, a group of cormorants await the falling tide to catch fish trapped in the shallows.

INTRODUCTION

I have many happy memories of childhood seaside holidays when those early experiences of sand, sea and 'seagulls' laid the foundation to my interest in birds, and seabirds in particular.

My first true seabird experience took place in 1951 when, at the age of 18, I joined my family to holiday at Scarborough in Yorkshire. I had recently been conscripted into the Royal Signals and had just finished basic training at Catterick. The weekend was memorable for the joy of being reunited with the family, for a civilian haircut and for a boat trip around Scarborough Bay. In early July the sea was alive with Gannets, Razorbills, Murres, Puffins and gulls. I had not been at such close quarters with seabirds before and found it enthralling and unforgettable, leaving me with the desire to see more of this group of birds.

But it was to be seven years later before I undertook anything similar. At Cley in Norfolk, with a group of friends, I spent an idyllic two weeks in early September 1958, looking at waders, gulls, skuas and terns. From the shore we watched the passing of seabird species, some quite close, but some way out or on the horizon: what were they? We decided to charter a boat to be amongst them and with the aid of Ted Eales, the warden then of Blakeney Point National Trust Reserve, Chas Brown, Bev Craddock, Mac Campbell, Ken Darlow, George Evans, Gordon Ireson, Mike Warren and Ron Johns and I hired the boat of a local skipper. At the agreed price of £1 each we chugged out of Blakeney Harbour in the MV *Morning Flight*. Since then I have avidly undertaken sea trips, whether they be North Sea Ferry crossings, visits to the Isles of Scilly, trips around the Farne Islands or full-blown pelagic trips off the Californian coast. The expectation, excitement and thrill of looking at seabirds has never diminished.

The names of birds used in this book generally follow those in common use in Britain and North America. The sequence in which the species appear is based on the List of Recent Holarctic Bird Species (Non-Passerines), by K. H. Voous which appeared in *The Ibis*, 1973, Volume 115, No. 4. There are two exceptions to this listing: in the appendix the Black-vented Shearwater, *Puffinus opisthomelas*, and Yellow-footed Gull, *Larus livens*, are accorded full species status.

The Voous order does show some variation to that normally used by North American ornithologists where the AOU Checklist prevails, but it is hoped this will not detract from any value this book may provide for readers in the Americas.

In the compilation of this book I have included species from the following family groups that breed mainly on either (or both) the Pacific or Atlantic coasts of North America and those that breed around the coasts of Britain and western Europe or occur as non-breeding visitors to all or some of these areas. They are:

ALBATROSSES	DIOMEDEIDAE
PETRELS AND SHEARWATERS	PROCELLARIIDAE
STORM-PETRELS	HYDROBATIDAE
TROPICBIRDS	PHAETHONTIDAE
GANNETS AND BOOBIES	SULIDAE
CORMORANTS	PHALACROCORACIDAE
PELICANS	PELECANIDAE
FRIGATE BIRDS	FREGATIDAE
SKUAS AND JAEGERS	STERCORARIIDAE
GULLS	LARIDAE
TERNS AND NODDIES	STERNIDAE
SKIMMERS	RYNCHOPIDAE
AUKS	ALCIDAE

The term 'seabird' obviously indicates a close relationship with the sea and indeed there are some other families of birds which also come into this category but in my treatment of the subject I have excluded them. They are the:

LOONS	GAVIIDAE
GREBES	PODICIPEDIDAE
DUCKS AND GEESE	ANATIDAE
PHALAROPES	PHALAROPODIDAE

The decision to leave out these family groups is based on the premise that they are not so gregarious or colonial in their nesting habits as those I have dealt with. The Phalaropes were included in my earlier book, *Shorebirds* (Gallery Books, 1988) while the Anatidae have been covered in *Ducks of North America* (Facts on File, 1986).

Fortunately, all seabirds have to come to land to breed at some time and it is then possible to more readily watch them and enjoy their varied behaviour and displays. Some remain enigmatic and little known, especially the petrels and shearwaters, and some of the Pacific alcids. Even today not all seabirds have been photographed and some of them, in all their various plumages, have still to be captured on film. In this book I have attempted to bring together the finest selection of seabird photographs possible to illustrate the species to their best advantage. This cannot of course ever match the thrill and splendour of watching seabirds in their own environment – on or by the sea.

NORTHERN FULMAR

FULMARUS GLACIALIS

Perhaps now the most common seabird in the North Atlantic, the increase and spread of the Northern Fulmar is one of the major avian success stories of recent times. In the last 200 years, and particularly the last 100, it has enlarged its breeding range considerably. The whole of Britain has been colonized and breeding was proved for the first time in Norway in 1924, northern France in 1960 and West Germany in 1972.

Globally the species inhabits both the north Pacific and Atlantic oceans, there being three sub-species.

The nominate race breeds in the high Arctic regions of the North Atlantic, including Baffin Island, north east Greenland, Spitsbergen, Bear Island, Franz Josef Land and probably Novaya Zemlya. *F. g. auduboni* breeds mainly in the low Arctic and the North Atlantic region including north west Greenland, Newfoundland, Jan Mayan, Iceland, the Faeroes, the British Isles and France (Normandy). *F. g. rodgersii* breeds around Pacific coasts including the Kuril Islands, Commander Isles, Kamchatka, Wrangel, Pribilofs, St Lawrence Island, the Alaskan Peninsula and the coasts of Siberia.

Although the Northern Fulmar has been known in Iceland since at least the Middle Ages, it did not then breed in large numbers around the whole of the island. Its only other long established European breeding locale is St Kilda, where historical evidence indicates it formed a major part of a 'bird fowling' culture from Viking times.

By the end of the nineteenth century the Fulmar had spread around the whole of Iceland. In 1837 it started to nest in the Faeroes, the population there increasing dramatically. So rapid was its colonization that by the early 1930s up to 30,000 birds annually were being taken for food by the islanders. This cropping ceased in 1936 due to an outbreak of ornithosis which caused the deaths of some Faeroese.

The first Northern Fulmars to reach Shetland and breed nested on Foula in 1878. There followed a relatively rapid colonization of the whole of the British Isles and Ireland. By the middle of this century practically every suitable coastal site had breeding or prospecting birds. Even the low crumbling cliffs in north Norfolk have attracted them, though this is an isolated breeding site along an otherwise unsuitable part of the coast. In 1969–70,

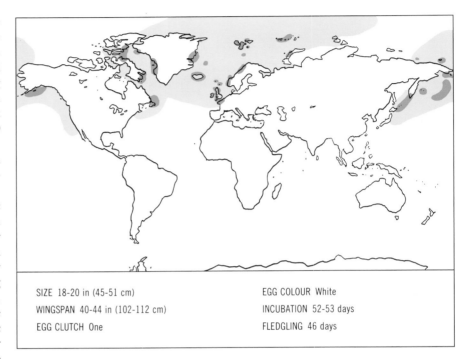

SIZE 18-20 in (45-51 cm)	EGG COLOUR White
WINGSPAN 40-44 in (102-112 cm)	INCUBATION 52-53 days
EGG CLUTCH One	FLEDGLING 46 days

ABOVE *A typical setting for breeding Northern Fulmars where several pairs can be seen as they sit on rock ledges amidst clumps of sea thrift.*

LEFT *The tube-like nostrils of the Northern Fulmar show well in this delightful picture of a pair at their nest site.*

Operation Seafarer estimated that there were around 300,000 occupied nest sites in Britain and Ireland, with nearly 90 per cent of these in Shetland, Orkney and the Outer Hebrides, St Kilda and north west Scotland.

Various reasons have been suggested to account for this population explosion. The most popular relates to the development of whaling, with its disposal of unwanted oily whale debris on which the Northern Fulmars eagerly fed. This source of food was no longer available after the mid-nineteenth century, when the whaling industry ceased to be a commercial proposition in the North Atlantic. However, steam trawling, which gutted fish catches at sea, in waters further to the south and nearer to the Faeroes, Britain and Ireland offered an alternative

food to satisfy an expanding Northern Fulmar population. Other hypotheses included the warming of the Atlantic and the development of a genetic mutation that could exist away from the dense colonies of the original Icelandic breeding sites.

Whatever the cause of the spread of this bird, it has provided many birdwatchers with more opportunities to watch this bird demonstrate its undoubted mastery over wind and sea.

A rather gull-like bird, the old Norse word for it is 'foulmaa', which means 'a gull'. It belongs to the order Procellariiformes, the group of seabirds which includes the albatrosses and shearwaters. They all have noticeable external tube-like nostrils which were once believed to be their only means of exuding salt from the body, but are now thought to

A Northern Fulmar demonstrates its mastery of the air as it sails past on stiff wings typical of its distinctive 'albatross-like' flight.

be a highly sensitive 'smell' mechanism which helps the birds to navigate, homing in on land and sea odours. In flight, the Northern Fulmar's shape and form does suggest a shearwater or small albatross, especially as it banks and glides on stiff wings just above the waves, though it flaps its wings more than any albatross species. At times its more leisurely wing beats are suddenly accelerated to a rapid rate during its aerial manoeuvres. The Northern Fulmar is best seen along a breeding site cliff face where it patrols in endless procession. On occasions it hangs in the wind just a few yards (metres) out from the cliff edge, perhaps at eye level to the observer, revealing its diagnostic features. The head and neck and underparts are ivory white and the back wings and tail (which is rounded) are bluish grey, which at close range shows the feathering to be tinged with an ashy brown. The bill is greenish brown, parts of which are tinged blue and pink, being brownish horn at the blunt hooked tip. The legs, which are frequently used as air brakes, are greenish grey. The dark eye is emphasized by a small patch of dark feathering in front of the socket, giving the bird a gentle expression. Young birds of the year have a pure white look to the plumage, with the upperparts more uniformly grey. The legs are usually a flesh colour at this early age.

Slow to mature, it is probably at least six years old before they start to breed, though nest sites are visited from around the third year.

Preferred nest sites are narrow ledges on precipitous sea cliffs, but competition has driven birds to accept low earth banks, mouths of deserted burrows, crevices in rocks, and unused stone buildings.

The most usual form of display at the nest comprises a great deal of head waving, accompanied by cackling noises, at which times the neck is distended and the beak widely opened. Considerable amounts of nibbling and billing also take place along with a series of low crooning notes. This is usually followed by copulation. The single oval white egg, which has a rough texture, is laid directly onto the bare rock, or shallow depression if on soft soil, when a few small stones might be added as a primitive lining.

Incubation lasts 52 to 53 days with both adults taking alternate spells of roughly 24 hours' duration. After hatching, one parent usually tends the chick continually during the first week, defending it against any intruder by the well-known means of spitting out evil-smelling stomach oil – accurate up to a yard (metre). When left by themselves, young birds are capable of this defence from an early age. The young chick is fed on regurgitated food, putting its head into the adult's mouth. After about 46 days it can fly and then makes for the sea, the adults having left a few days beforehand. Not really migratory, Northern Fulmars disperse over the sea, deserting inshore waters from August through to October, during their main period of moult.

Fulmars feed on fish, fish offal, crustaceans, cephalopods and any fish or mammalian carrion, mostly seized from the surface of the water. At times they dabble like a duck, but they rarely dive. When resting, Northern Fulmars sit on rocks and ice floes in the same manner as shearwaters, lying on the full length of the tarsii, for their legs are not designed for walking. They have great difficulty in launching themselves from other than an elevated position, and when on the sea, require a long running takeoff. At times Northern Fulmars will gather in large numbers at major food sources, such as a whale carcass or around fishing boats, when a thousand or more birds feed in a noisy, voracious manner, squabbling and fighting over scraps of fish. When feeding alone they are quite silent.

There are both light and dark morphs of the Northern Fulmar, the darkest phase being a uniform smoky grey. It is found predominantly within the Pacific range, where intermediates of all shades are known to occur. Light phase morphs predominate in the Atlantic range, where dark morphs are rare.

The species continues to increase and in North American waters particularly it is becoming more common.

MANX SHEARWATER

PUFFINUS PUFFINUS

This is the most common Western Palearctic shearwater. Its family classification is even now not fully agreed, with the 'splitters' and the 'lumpers' still battling it out! There are six forms of this bird, all of which are identifiable at sea. At present all are grouped into a single (allopatric) species. However, there is growing opinion, mainly based on breeding biology, in favour of separating two or more of them.

The nominate race around British coasts is possibly most frequently observed as it flies in typical 'shearwater' manner, skimming the waves, rising and falling to appear above the horizon and then to disappear again beneath it. At such times it presents sharply contrasting black upperparts and white underparts. A closer view will show the head is mainly black to just below eye level while the bill is slender. As well as the gleaming white underwing coverts, it will be noted the undertail coverts are also mostly white. Originally called the Common Shearwater, it owes its present name to the fact that the most easily accessible colonies of this bird were first discovered on the Calf of Man at the southern tip of the Isle of Man, in the Irish Sea. Sadly this colony was exterminated by the attentions of man and by rats. As a breeding site it remained unused for 150 years. In 1967 breeding was proved and happily there is a thriving colony once again.

Another previous name for this bird was the 'Manx Puffin', given to it in an earlier time when it

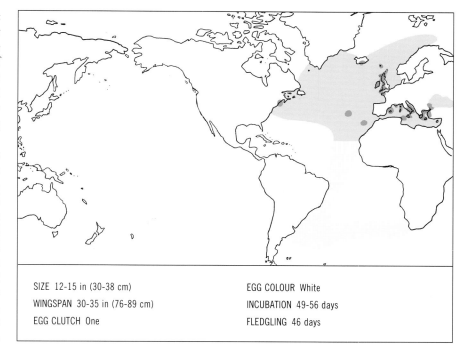

SIZE 12-15 in (30-38 cm)	EGG COLOUR White
WINGSPAN 30-35 in (76-89 cm)	INCUBATION 49-56 days
EGG CLUTCH One	FLEDGLING 46 days

A Manx Shearwater at its nest site caught in the photographer's flash. These birds return to underground breeding burrows at night to avoid predation by gulls.

was thought all web-footed birds were more directly related to each other. This may go some way to explaining the seemingly inappropriate Latin name, *Puffinus puffinus*.

Feeding out at sea, Manx Shearwater take mostly small fish, but also cephalopods, small crustaceans and various surface food. At times they will dive for fish when in full flight, whilst on other occasions they feed from the surface, or by fluttering or pattering just above the waves. Large flocks gather together to feed on anchovy or other small shoaling fish, at which times they are silent.

Manx Shearwaters begin to return to their breeding colonies from February to March when they gather together forming large 'rafts' sitting on the sea just offshore; there they wait until dark before going to their underground burrows. During these offshore gatherings, social activity would appear to be confined to periodic flights, when part, or at times the whole flock rises up and flies around in circles or a figure of eight.

At the chosen nesting location, which is usually on a turfy offshore island, the pair excavate a long underground burrow up to a yard (metre) in length. Due to their considerable subterranean existence, spending at least a quarter of the day underground,

little of their courtship behaviour is known. However pairing is usually for life. The female lays one white oval egg at the end of May which, at 2 inches (5 cm) in length, is extremely large in relation to the size of the bird. Incubation lasts from seven to eight weeks, with both parents taking turns and relieving each other after a period of several days. For a short time after hatching, the young chick is brooded by the parents and then fed only at night for about two months. During this period the adult bird may travel hundreds of miles from the breeding site in order to obtain food. Towards the end of the fledging period the chick will have grown quite fat and its original grey down will have been replaced by·the feathers of its first-year plumage.

Around this time the parents desert the young bird, which completes its development alone in the burrow, coming to the entrance at night to exercise its wings, until hunger drives it to make for the sea. In calm weather it may have a laborious and difficult scramble to the shore, but in windy conditions it will be able to launch itself into the air. By October the colony that was once alive with the comings and goings of many birds, whose raucous underground cooings, growls and croaks filled the night air, will be silent and empty for another year.

From July, some birds will move back to their winter quarters with non-breeding birds and failed breeders starting earlier than those with young to rear. Both young and mature birds move south and west to the main wintering area of eastern South America while small numbers make for the seas off the east South African coast.

Shearwater movements are most evident around Britain in late summer and autumn, when birders put their identification skills to the test in separating *P. p. puffinus* from the eastern Mediterranean race *P. p. yelkouan*, whose appearance is less sharply contrasted, and the western Mediterranean (Balearic) race *P. p. mauretanicus*, which appears browner and even less contrasted. Also there is the possibility that some individuals with dark underparts may be mistaken for Sooty Shearwater, while paler individuals might be mistaken for Cory's Shearwater. The Manx Shearwater, however, is much smaller and slimmer than these last two mentioned species (see Appendix).

In the North Atlantic the breeding range of the Manx Shearwater includes the Westmann Isles (Southern Iceland), Faeroes, Shetland, Orkney, Inner Hebrides, Skokholm, Skomer, the Blaskets, and Puffin Isle (Kerry), with smaller colonies at Anglesey, the Scilly Isles and off west and north east Ireland. The latest estimate of the breeding numbers in Britain was put at 300,000, but it could well be more. There are breeding colonies off the Brittany coast and in the Azores and Madeira.

In North America there is a recently discovered (1973) colony off Cape Cod. It is fairly common off the North Atlantic coast of North America from June to October, but less common farther south and rare in winter from Maryland southwards.

Manx Shearwaters are less frequently seen at rest on the sea. This photograph shows the race P. p. mauretanicus *or Balearic Shearwater.*

BRITISH STORM-PETREL

HYDROBATES PELAGICUS

In the normal course of a year's birding the watcher will only occasionally come across this species unless he takes a boat far out to sea. It is then most likely to be seen as it follows in the wake of a ship. More rarely it can be observed from the shore when autumn gales drive birds within viewing range. Sometimes after severe weather British Storm-petrels, or 'Mother Carey's Chickens' as they were called by sailors, are 'land wrecked'. At such times they may occur far inland, miles from their normal environment in the vastness of the ocean: hence they are 'storm birds' to mariners and land dwellers alike. Nevertheless, they are less prone to being storm driven than Leach's Storm-petrels.

The Storm-petrel has a fluttering almost bat-like flight interspersed with short glides just above the waves. At times, particularly when feeding, it patters its feet on the surface of the water. This habit of 'walking on water' undoubtedly has some connection with the name 'petrel' which links it with St Peter who walked on the Sea of Galilee. In appearance the Storm-petrel is not unlike a large

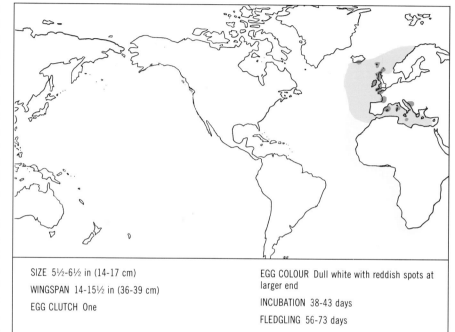

SIZE 5½-6½ in (14-17 cm)

WINGSPAN 14-15½ in (36-39 cm)

EGG CLUTCH One

EGG COLOUR Dull white with reddish spots at larger end

INCUBATION 38-43 days

FLEDGLING 56-73 days

An almost fully grown, young British Storm-petrel. At six to seven weeks old it is ready to leave its underground nesting burrow to spend its early life entirely at sea.

House Martin in that it has a striking white rump which contrasts with the rest of its plumage, which is dark apart from a diagnostic white stripe on the underwing. At close range a barely discernible, pale, diagonal bar can be seen on the upperwing. The black, squarish tail helps to separate it from the similar Leach's Petrel, but other characteristics and field marks need to be considered to rule out Wilson's Petrel and Band-rumped Storm-petrel (see Appendix). It is perhaps only when in the hand that the thin, black legs and tiny, webbed feet can be seen well, along with the slender, hook-tipped bill with its long, single, tubular nostril.

This smallest and darkest of the Atlantic Petrels has a relatively limited breeding range along the eastern coastline of the North Atlantic and the Western Mediterranean. The most northerly known breeding colony is situated in the Westmann Islands, Iceland. Further south they are found breeding in the Faeroe Islands, Shetland and Orkney Islands and certain parts of the western coasts of Britain and Ireland. Main colonies are located off south west Ireland, especially County Kerry where there are probably over 50,000 pairs, with an estimated 25,000 pairs on Inishtearaght alone. There are smaller colonies in the Channel Islands, Brittany and Biarritz. Some other colonies are located off Sardinia, Sicily, the Balearics, Malta and a few islets in the Adriatic. Most colonies in Britain and Ireland are on offshore islands, but some are on the mainland, though usually in inaccessible places making them difficult to locate. Some may still be unknown for this reason.

Birds return to their breeding colonies from April to May when a suitable nest site is located. Though British Storm-petrels can and do excavate their own burrows, many choose a natural rock crevice or fissure or opening under a boulder. As well as natural sites, man-made constructions such as dry stone walls, old buildings and sometimes even occupied dwellings are utilized. The most well-known example of this form of nest site preference is the large colony found in the great brach on Mousa (Shetland). The bird observatory on Skokholm is also used in this way.

British Storm-petrels are best detected by the musical creaking calls used in their nightly courtship chases, when they might briefly be glimpsed in torchlight beams. Nests can be located by examining likely sites for the characteristic 'musky' smell, or another indication of their presence is the quiet murmuring sound that is uttered by the sitting bird.

A British Storm-petrel shuffles into position on thin legs that are too weak to stand on, and settles down to incubate its one white egg in an underground nesting chamber.

A single dull-white egg often zoned with reddish-brown spots at the larger end, is laid usually in the latter half of June, but the laying period can extend from May through to mid-August. The incubation period varies from 38 to 43 days and is undertaken by both birds with a change over every several days. The off-duty birds feed away at sea and only return at night.

On hatching, the chick is covered in soft silver-grey down and its eyes are closed. Until they open after five to ten days, the chick will be brooded continually by one of the parents. After this period the chick is left on its own during the day, but the parents return each night to feed the youngster for around seven weeks. Feeding then becomes less frequent and gaps of four to five days are quite usual.

British Storm-petrels feed mainly on zoo-plankton, small fish no more than 2 inches (5 cm) in length, or small pieces of fish waste. Such a mixture is fed to the young bird by partial regurgitation.

By the end of the eighth week of the fledging period, the chick's down has been almost totally replaced by its first feathers. Departure from the nesting burrow by the fledgling bird can vary from 56 to 73 days. The period between the last feed and departure is quite short, no longer than a couple of days, but before leaving the youngster comes to the nest entrance at night and exercises its wings before launching itself into its oceanic world. General dispersal of the adult and young birds to their winter quarters begins in September. By the end of October most will have left, though stragglers are frequently noted into November and sometimes December. Birds are known to move past north west Africa from mid-November as they head southward to sea areas around the Namibian and South African coast. The Mediterranean population, though, may remain in adjacent waters throughout the winter.

The British Storm-petrel is rarely recorded off the North American coast.

A British Storm-petrel, frozen in the light of the photographer's flash, is seen flying to its nesting burrow under cover of darkness, avoiding being taken by any of the larger gulls which prey on these birds.

LEACH'S STORM-PETREL

OCEANODROMA LEUCORHOA

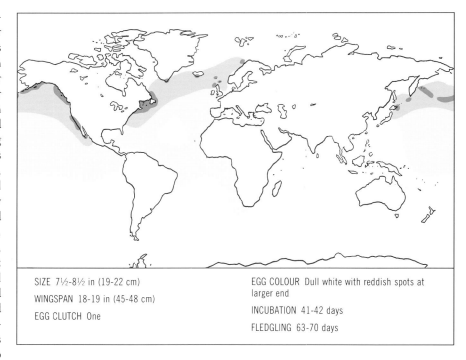

SIZE 7½-8½ in (19-22 cm)

WINGSPAN 18-19 in (45-48 cm)

EGG CLUTCH One

EGG COLOUR Dull white with reddish spots at larger end

INCUBATION 41-42 days

FLEDGLING 63-70 days

Like the British Storm-petrel, this bird is sometimes wind blown, providing the British birder with an infrequent sighting along the coast or, less often, miles inland from the sea. For me, one such an occasion happened at Chasewater, a canal feeder reservoir in Staffordshire, England, in September 1957. Walking the reservoir edge that day an unfamiliar bird flew past me at not more than head height and settled on a shingle bank in a crouching position less than a dozen or so yards away. I was able to approach to within a few feet of a small, sooty plumaged bird with a distinctively forked tail and short, tube-like nostrils. It took wing and flew out over the water to reveal a white rump and noticeably pale diagonal bars across the upper wing. There were sailing dinghies out on the water, zipping about in the strong north west wind, and it dodged between these in a buoyant, graceful manner with a mixture of deep wing beats and shearwater-like glides. Occasionally it settled momentarily on the water (something it is supposed rarely to do), with wings held parallel. It was apparently feeding, for each time it appeared to pick something from the surface.

I later learned that the previous day good numbers of Leach's Petrels had been seen on the Dee estuary, which is approximately 70 miles in a direct line to the north west of Chasewater. The Dee is probably one of the best places in Britain to see this species during periods of strong north-westerly winds, which often occur in September when birds are migrating to winter quarters. I was to visit the Dee many times in later years to witness such events and to see many other seabirds for which the area is so renowned.

This still little-known bird, formerly called Leach's Fork-tailed Petrel, was named by Dr William Elford Leach, who bought a specimen of this then undescribed species at an auction in 1819. It had been taken on St Kilda the year before. Today the St Kilda group of islands is known to be one of the four principal breeding locations of the species in Britain, with colonies on Hirta, Dun and Boreray and smaller ones on Stac Levenish and Soay.

On the Flannan Islands the major colony is on Eilean Mor, but breeding has also been established on Eilean Tigne, Roareim, Eilean a Ghobha Soray and Sgeir Toman. The other two principal breeding sites are on North Rona and Sula Sgeir, of which the latter probably has the fewest breeding birds. Some may well nest at locations in western Ireland from where there have been past records. Such is the difficulty of determining this bird's breeding status that the concentrated efforts of Operation Seafarer in 1969–70 were unable to come up with any

A fully grown young Leach's Storm-petrel in its underground burrow just prior to departure for oceanic life.

meaningful figures to indicate sizes and trends for any of the Scottish breeding populations, let alone those in Ireland. However, today's total breeding population is thought to be around 10,000 pairs.

Elsewhere in Europe there are colonies on the Westmann Islands, the Faeroes and the Lofoten Islands, and far more numerous across the Atlantic and on the east coast of North America where there are major colonies at Nova Scotia, Massachusetts, Maine and Newfoundland, with numbers estimated in their millions! Smaller colonies are to be found in southern Greenland.

The same form of Leach's Petrel also breeds from Hokkaido, Japan, north east to the Aleutian

LEFT *This small, downy covered chick is a young Leach's Storm-petrel probably no more than moments old.*

BELOW *Strong onshore winds occasionally bring Leach's Storm-petrels to land and here a storm-driven bird flutters along the beach of the Dee estuary, Cheshire, England.*

Only at their nesting sites can such nocturnal breeding species as Leach's Storm-petrel be photographed. Here the photographer has captured a bird on film before it enters its underground burrow.

Islands and Alaska and southwards on various offshore islands of western North America to Islas San Bantos, Mexico. There are two subspecies: *O. I. socorrensis*, which breeds only on Guadalupe Island off Mexico, May to September; the other *O. I. cheimonestes*, which breeds at the same location but during the period October to April.

After a winter at sea, birds return to their various, usually bleak, windswept colonies in late April to early May where they excavate nesting chambers two feet or more into the soft peaty soil. This is lined with grass or other locally obtained dry vegetation, but often none at all. Other sites might be under boulders or in deserted stone buildings. In North America some colonies have been found in dense woodland and situated among tree roots.

Little is known of the courtship rituals, most of which goes on underground, though there is considerable night time aerial display which is equally difficult to observe.

Ringing, however, has shown the species to be monogamous, pairing for life with the pair bond being re-established on return to the nest site. The male entices the female to the burrow by its 'crooning' and 'chattering' calls, along with other occasional higher pitched notes. These sounds reach a crescendo sometime after midnight. It is certainly a noisier bird than the British Storm-petrel, which aids detection, though the nest site

gives off an equally musty odour as a means of determining the bird's presence.

There is one dull-white egg, similar to the British Storm-petrel's but slightly larger and often zoned with fine reddish spots at the larger end. This is usually laid at the beginning of June, though the egg laying period can last through until August.

Incubation lasts for 41 to 42 days with both sexes taking turns of approximately three days' duration. After hatching, the chicks are brooded continuously for the first five days, then fed nightly by partial regurgitation. Their food comprises various planktonic crustaceans, molluscs and small fish, which is this bird's usual diet, though it also takes any oily or fatty substances, especially fish offal thrown from fishing vessels.

Fledging takes place after 63 to 70 days by which time the young bird is completely independent, leaving its nesting burrow for a life at sea and probably not breeding until its fourth or fifth year.

After their nesting period, Leach's Storm-petrels generally disperse southwards. Unlike the British Storm-petrels, they do not follow ships. Atlantic breeding birds are believed to winter in the Gulf of Guinea and off Brazil, but some move south to Namibia, South Africa and even beyond, to the east of Cape of Good Hope. Pacific breeding birds winter south of the Equator, possibly reaching waters off the coast of Peru.

NORTHERN GANNET

SULA BASSANA

A colony of Gannets in full swing is an awe-inspiring sight, wherever this might be, and for me especially it was Bass Rock. Though perhaps not the most spectacular of the world's gannetries, the Rock, with its 18,000 or so breeding pairs, cannot fail to impress. Pleasantly situated in the outer reaches of the Firth of Forth, just three miles off North Berwick, it is from this small West Lothian coastal town, weather permitting, that boats will take you to this seabird city. Fine views can also be had from the mainland, especially from nearby Tantallon Castle, from where the toings and froings of thousands of these magnificent birds in endless procession is a joy to behold.

To watch them plunge dive for food, often from a height of 30 feet (10 m) or more, sending up a shower of spray, is a thrilling sight especially when many birds, attracted by a shoal of fish, are seen hitting the water one after another.

The adult Gannet is unmistakable; a large, dazzling white bird, its long, narrow wings, spanning 6 feet (2 m) and tipped with black, identify it even

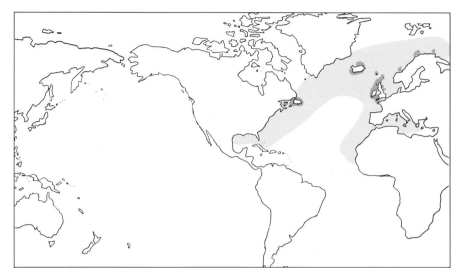

SIZE 34-39 in (87-100 cm)	EGG COLOUR Pale blue to white with chalky deposit which stains yellow and brown
WINGSPAN 65-71 in (165-180 cm)	INCUBATION 44 days
EGG CLUTCH One-two	FLEDGLING 90 days

LEFT *A fully grown young Gannet just before it leaves the nest is quite unlike its wholly white parent being covered in blackish feathering speckled with white, a plumage phase it will keep for the first year of its life.*

RIGHT *During the course of its early life the Gannet undergoes plumage changes annually until by the fifth year it assumes the all-white, black wing-tipped, appearance of the adult. This bird is only in its third-year plumage.*

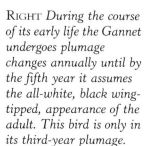

at the longest range (immatures might be more difficult to identify on occasions).

In breeding plumage the head and neck are tinged a yellowish buff colour, while the spear-shaped bill is slate blue with a horn-coloured tip. The piercing eye, which is usually described as creamy white, is ringed with blue skin. The legs are slate blue and closer inspection will show the toes and the front of the tarsus are lined with green.

This splendid creature is probably the world's most studied seabird. All the world's gannetries (34 at present) are known and the birds are regularly counted, sometimes by aerial photography. As with any colonial species though, neither this means nor direct counting from the ground can be wholly accurate. Nevertheless it is currently reckoned there are some 275,000 breeding pairs in the world. Twenty-eight of the world's colonies are located in the eastern Atlantic, mainly in Britain, but with some in Ireland, Iceland, the Faeroes and Norway and one in France. Together these comprise three-quarters of the total population. The remainder are on the Canadian eastern seaboard, in the Gulf of St Lawrence.

The total world population of Gannets is around three-quarters of a million birds, of which about one-third are non-breeding, immature birds.

Numbers are presently increasing at an estimated three per cent a year. This is a far different story to that of the last century, when Gannet numbers were decreasing on both sides of the Atlantic, with predation by man a major factor in its decline.

Birds were being shot for sport and thousands died in this manner wherever the more accessible colonies could be reached. The Bird Rocks colony in the Gulf of St Lawrence, formerly the world's largest, was ruthlessly persecuted and in a few short years was reduced from an estimated 125,000 pairs in 1833 to possibly under 1000 pairs by the end of the century! Even now Bird Rock has not recovered to its former strength, with a population of only 5000 pairs today. Bonaventure Island, Quebec, is now Canada's largest gannetry with currently 20,000 pairs breeding. Britain's major gannetries are St Kilda with 60,000+ pairs, Ailsa Craig and Grassholm with around 20,000 pairs each, and the Bass Rock, with about 18,000 pairs. Little Skellig is Ireland's largest colony at 20,000+ pairs, with all others at 5000 pairs or under. The only British mainland site is Bempton, Yorkshire, where one or two pairs were first noted nesting in the 1920s. Even by the 1950s there were still less than ten occupied sites. Since the 1960s and 1970s this has increased markedly and there are now approximately 200 pairs. Established as an RSPB reserve in 1974, Bempton provides its many visitors with excellent views of these and other nesting seabirds from strategically placed viewing platforms.

Iceland has the other major European breeding sites, with over 16,000 pairs at Eldey, 5000+ pairs on the Westmann Islands and smaller numbers at other locations. The Faeroes has under 5000 breeding birds, with Norway supporting around 3000. The only French gannetry is at Rouzic in Brittany. This has increased its numbers from 30 pairs in 1939 to around 5000 pairs at the present time.

From early January adult birds begin to assemble at their more southerly breeding stations, though it can be February or early March before they return to their more northerly sites. With Gannets life-long monogamy is the rule, with the pair-bond renewed each breeding season. Birds return to the same nest site, where they re-establish relationship with various head shaking and bowing rituals. Prolonged bill fencing forms part of the greeting ceremony and this is often followed by mutual preening. Copulation takes place after vigorous bouts of bill fencing. The nest is constructed from seaweed, grass and feathers to form a pile usually 1 to 2 feet (30–60 cm) high. A firm cup is formed by the bird turning and pushing with its breast and belly to compress the fine grasses and feathers into shape. During incubation further material is often added. The site might be on a cliff face or on flat or sloping ground where, over the years, nests become enlarged, measuring up to 6 to 7 feet (2 m) in height, and compacted with the birds' droppings. At some sites, however, the nest may be no more than a depression in the ground.

One or two eggs are laid from April onwards. These are elongated, elliptical to oval and pale translucent blue, turning white. They are covered with a chalky deposit which gradually becomes stained yellow and brown. If eggs are lost in the early stages they are quite often replaced, even twice or more. Incubation is carried out under the bird's web feet, both birds taking turns.

After hatching, the young birds are cared for by both parents. They are brooded continually for the first fourteen days and, as during incubation, this is carried out under the parents' feet or between them as the bird gets larger. Feeding is by partial regurgitation, the young putting their heads into the parent's gape.

The fledging period is about 90 days, during which time the young bird loses its original white fluffy down to become an all-dark looking bird closely speckled with white. Though the plumage is not a bit like its parents, it is easily identified when in flight by its distinctive cigar-shaped body and characteristic actions. During the next three years the plumage of the juvenile bird becomes progres-

PREVIOUS PAGE Here a group of nesting Gannets have chosen a broken sheer cliff face for breeding. The guano-splashed rocks indicate this has been a favoured site for many years.

RIGHT An adult Gannet on its nest, against a backdrop of the breeding cliff-top site and the sea beyond, makes an imposing picture. Note the very young chick in the nest: what an ugly, reptilian looking creature it is at this early age.

sively whiter, starting with the head, rump and underparts. By the end of the second year most show broad white tops to the mantle, scapulars and back. The upperwing has by then blackish primaries and primary coverts, the remainder being mostly white with blackish streaks. By the end of the third year, apart from some irregular blackish streaks along the secondaries and dark black central feathers, it is as the adult bird.

Non-breeding birds are first to desert the colony and general dispersal southwards can be seen along British coasts from July onwards. Through August and September the passage of juvenile and adult bird is continuous, with fewer birds in October. At such times they may be seen moving with steady, purposeful flight in a series of shallow flaps and glides, sometimes almost on the horizon, at other times close to the shore. In strong winds they will swoop and plane like a large shearwater. At times they will dive to feed, taking any locally obtainable prey within accessible depths of usually less than 70 to 80 feet (20–25 m). This might be cod, pollack, whiting, haddock, sprats, pilchards, mackerel, or sand eels. During these migratory flights they have to suffer the attentions of the occasional Great Skua which will particularly single out the less experienced youngsters to attack.

Winter distribution is quite wide, but mostly to adjacent continental shelf waters, for Gannets are not truly pelagic. Many reach equatorial waters off the West African coast, where some first-year birds remain until their third year before making their first return visit to natal waters. Gannets are also found quite regularly in small numbers along the North African coast where formerly not known.

After breeding, North American birds move south to winter off the coast from New England to Florida, with smaller numbers moving towards the Gulf of Mexico, where they are regular off Alabama, but more rarely off west Texas coast.

LEFT The adult Gannet in its all-white plumage with its black-tipped, six-foot long wings is surely one of the world's most impressive sea birds and a joy to behold.

BELOW A small part of the huge Bass Rock gannetry with its thousands of nesting birds each only a few feet from the other. Out at sea there is a constant traffic of birds coming and going as they leave and return to the respective sites.

GREAT CORMORANT

PHALACROCORAX CARBO

The Great Cormorant is a widespread species occurring in many parts of the world. It is to be found particularly in Europe, most of Africa, the Middle and Far East, southern Siberia, Australasia and in eastern North America. It is especially common around the North Atlantic coasts of Europe, but is equally at home many miles from the sea as long as there are suitable large stretches of water with a high population of fish.

In Europe there are two recognizable subspecies, *P. c. carbo* and *P. c. sinensis*, generally referred to as Northern Cormorant and Southern Cormorant respectively. The Southern Cormorant in breeding plumage shows an almost totally white head which readily separates it from *P. c. carbo*. The Great Cormorant is basically a dark, long-necked bird, well-known for perching on buoys, rocks or posts, where it will stand in an heraldic pose drying its wings, for these very soon become waterlogged after underwater activity in its search for food. In summer plumage the bronze, brown or black feathering on the upperparts appears well-defined at close quarters, whilst the bluish black underparts are offset by a white cheek and white thigh patch – the latter visible at long range especially in flight. The similar-looking Shag does not have either of these features. Additionally, the Great Cormorant's larger build and stouter bill, with its yellow gular area, should help prevent confusion with Shag. The immature birds of both these species are also similar, but the Great Cormorant has much more extensive white on its underparts and this should help identify the species at that stage in its life.

The Great Cormorant flies low over the water at most times (but at much greater height over land), often in small parties, line astern, the strong, regular beats and outstretched neck reminiscent of geese. On the water it often swims with back awash and inclined upwards, and in this pose it may be mistaken for a Loon (*Gavia* spp.). However the Great Cormorant is a much more lively bird, looking this way and that, while the much heavier bill with its obvious downcurved tip should be discernible with a good telescope even at a distance.

A voracious fish eater, this 'crow of the sea', as it is sometimes called, dives for its prey, but invariably brings its catch to the surface before swallowing it. Dives are irregular in duration and quite short compared to some fish-hunting birds, often

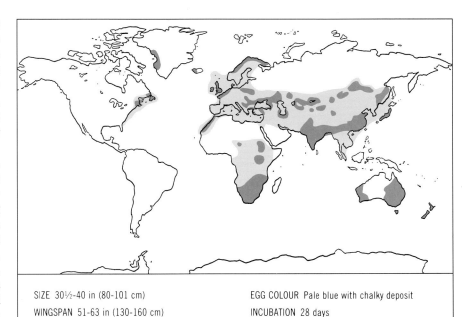

SIZE 30½-40 in (80-101 cm)	EGG COLOUR Pale blue with chalky deposit
WINGSPAN 51-63 in (130-160 cm)	INCUBATION 28 days
EGG CLUTCH Three to four	FLEDGLING 84 days

A Great Cormorant on its large, untidy nest of seaweed, pants in the heat. Its prominent gular pouch can be seen clearly in this picture.

lasting less than 30 seconds. At times, however, it may spend up to a minute under water. Essentially an inshore feeder, it finds its food on the sea-bed in less than 30 feet (10 m) of water, where flat fish are the most usual prey. It will, however, given the opportunity, take more typically deep sea fish, such as herring, when they are available. The Great Cormorant, though a great fish eater, surely offers no threat to commercial fish stocks in its coastal environment, but at some inland reservoirs where angling for trout is a commercial enterprise the presence of large numbers of Great Cormorants has led to a conflict of interests between man and bird.

In the North Atlantic the Great Cormorant is to be found breeding in southern Greenland, Iceland, Labrador, Nova Scotia, Newfoundland, Gulf of St Lawrence, the Faeroes, Norway, the British Isles and Ireland.

Great Cormorants do not generally undertake any extensive migratory journeys and rarely stray far from their breeding areas. In North America, however, birds undertake regular movements extending south to New Jersey, and occasionally reaching Florida in winter. Small coastal movements also occur southwards of the north eastern Atlantic states from August to October and then northwards during March to April.

The subspecies, *P. c. sinensis*, breeds in Holland, and from southern and central Europe east to central Asia, India and China. More migratory than the nominate race, some move south to Egypt and the Persian Gulf, though these movements apparently depend on the severity of the European winter.

Rocky coasts are favoured for nesting, with a preference for cliff ledges and rocky islets at just above the high water mark, upwards to 300 feet (100 m) or more. Tree sites are also used at inland locations, as are reed beds. Very occasionally nests are constructed on bare, flat ground.

Great Cormorants nest in colonies which range from no more than half a dozen birds to several hundreds of pairs. Such large concentrations are very noisy and smelly and an approach from downwind on a hot summer's day is to be avoided if possible! The nest itself is an untidy affair of seaweed lined with grass, in which the three to four eggs are laid. These are oval, usually pale blue covered with a chalky white deposit, and are laid in April or May. There is only one brood.

Prior to nesting, display mainly comprises a lot of neck writhing and entwining, with a great deal of threatening postures directed towards any other bird that intrudes into the pair's immediate nesting territory. Both birds share incubation and after approximately 28 days the young hatch out. The chicks are blind, black and ugly. They very quickly develop a covering of thick, black, downy plumage during the six to seven weeks they are in the nest. During this time they are fed twice daily on regurgitated fish. By the tenth week they are almost independent and, usually by the twelfth week, they leave the family unit and move to the estuaries and shallow coastal waters, where they associate with other newly fledged birds.

In Britain there are estimated to be around 8000 to 9000 pairs, which form a major part of the European population.

BELOW LEFT *Whereas Great Cormorants quite frequently prefer sea coasts, some are equally at home on marshes and lake sides. Here is such a colony at Naardermeer in Holland.*

BELOW RIGHT *After fishing, Cormorants need to dry their plumage, and can be seen with their wings held out. This heraldic pose is more often to be seen as the bird perches on a post or buoy.*

RIGHT *A Great Cormorant in full breeding plumage. This is the subspecies* P. c. sinensis *or Southern Cormorant. The white thigh patch of summer dress shows well but the almost white head is the most distinctive feature of this race.*

PELAGIC CORMORANT

PHALACROCORAX PELAGICUS

This small cormorant is distributed around the shores of the North Pacific Ocean, ranging as far south as Hokkaido in Japan on the Asian side and on the American shore through Alaska, Canada and the West Coast to Baja California, in Mexico. It is found almost exclusively in salt-water environments, feeding beneath its breeding cliffs and off other rocky shores; sometimes well out to sea, but at others in kelp beds and along the edge of the surf. Like other species of cormorant, it feeds almost exclusively on fish. When swimming, most of the body is submerged, with only the head and upper back projecting above the waterline. When not fishing, it rests up on cliffs, rocky islands, sandbars, piling, buoys and other man-made structures. It tends to be rather less gregarious than other West Coast cormorants.

The smallest of the North Pacific cormorants, its breeding plumage is assumed for a relatively brief period from around February to July, when it appears largely black at a distance, with a neat white patch on the rear flanks. Closer to, however, the head can be seen to be glossed violet and the body glossed deep bottle-green. The head has two crests, one on the forehead and one on the nape, and there are fine, hair-like white filoplumes on the neck. The eye is green, the bill dark horn-yellow and the bare skin around the eye and the base of the bill dull red (this is often difficult to see at any distance). In non-breeding plumage, the adult is simply black (with a faint greenish gloss), becoming browner with wear. The crests and white flank patch are lost and the facial skin and gular pouch are dull ochre. The sexes are similar, though on average males are slightly larger. Juveniles are duller still, sooty brown with slightly paler underparts and a brownish bill and legs.

Three other species of cormorant occur on the Pacific coast of North America, Red-faced Cormorant, Double-crested Cormorant and Brandt's Cormorant. Compared to the noticeably larger Brandt's Cormorant and Double-crested Cormorant, the Pelagic Cormorant has a more slender bill and is usually more uniformly dark, lacking a yellow or yellow-bordered gular pouch. In breeding plumage it is further distinguished by its double crests and white flank patch, and in juvenile plumage it lacks the contrastingly paler underparts of the two larger species, especially Double-crested Cormorant.

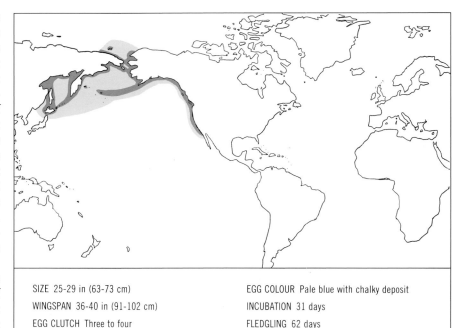

SIZE 25-29 in (63-73 cm)	EGG COLOUR Pale blue with chalky deposit
WINGSPAN 36-40 in (91-102 cm)	INCUBATION 31 days
EGG CLUTCH Three to four	FLEDGLING 62 days

ABOVE *A juvenile Pelagic Cormorant in its mostly uniform brown plumage, is smaller and has a much finer bill than either Double-crested Cormorant or Brandt's Cormorant.*

LEFT *An adult Pelagic Cormorant at its Alaskan nest site with two well-grown young. The reddish facial skin of its breeding dress is not readily apparent in this picture but its rich, greenish lustre is clearly seen.*

Separation from Red-faced Cormorant is more difficult, though this species is confined to the far north and does not occur south of Alaska. However, at close range it may be possible to see that Pelagic Cormorant lacks yellow in the bill and that its red facial skin does not join above the base of the bill. In non-breeding plumage separation from Red-faced Cormorant depends on subtle differences in the proportions of head, neck and bill, and the patterning of the red facial skin, which is as in breeding plumage, though less extensive. The juvenile closely resembles juvenile Red-faced Cormorant, but has a darker bill and the facial skin does not join over the base of the bill. In all plumages, but especially non-breeding and juvenile, separation from Red-faced Cormorant is probably impossible at any distance.

In flight, the Pelagic Cormorant looks small as cormorants go, with a proportionally small head on a slender neck, which is held straight out. The shape is very simliar to Red-faced Cormorant, but unlike that species, there is no contrast between the colour of the wings and body.

A colonial breeder, the nest tends to be placed on narrow ledges on steep, precipitous cliffs, often amongst those of other seabird species. Occasionally, however, man-made structures, such as a lighthouse, may be used. The birds build an untidy pile of seaweed, grass and sticks, on which they lay their three or four eggs in May or June. These are pale blue with a chalky deposit. Both sexes incubate for an average of 31 days. The young fledge from August onwards.

The species is largely resident over most of its range, undertaking only local movements. It does not normally move further south than the breeding range, though young birds may wander further afield. Not surprisingly, those in the far north are forced to move south for the winter, leaving their breeding grounds from October to May. These more migratory populations may be responsible for the records of vagrants from Hawaii.

BRANDT'S CORMORANT

PHALACROCORAX PENICILLATUS

Brandt's Cormorant is the most common species of cormorant on the Pacific coast of North America, breeding from southern Alaska south to Baja California. It is rather erratic in the northern part of the range however, perhaps breeding only occasionally in Alaska. Certainly the bulk of the population is found from Washington southwards. It is more or less resident, most remaining within the breeding range the whole year round, but there is some dispersal, perhaps mainly by young birds. It is regular in the Gulf of California (where it has bred in the past) and there are records south to the coast of Sinaloa in Mexico. The species is primarily marine, usually being found at sea off rocky coasts, but it also occurs inshore in sheltered bays and estuaries. It is very unlikely to be seen inland.

In breeding plumage it is entirely black, with an oily purple-green gloss. There are hair-like white filoplumes on the head, neck, scapulars and rump. The eye is blue and the bill and facial skin are dull greyish. The gular pouch is bright sky blue – though this is often surprisingly difficult to see. The

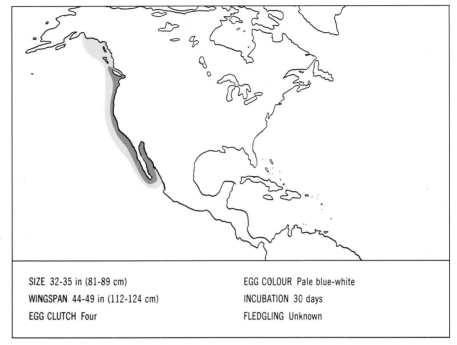

SIZE 32-35 in (81-89 cm)	EGG COLOUR Pale blue-white
WINGSPAN 44-49 in (112-124 cm)	INCUBATION 30 days
EGG CLUTCH Four	FLEDGLING Unknown

The pale buffy feathers bordering the throat of this Brandt's Cormorant identify the species at all ages. As with all Cormorants, it spends a great deal of time preening and attending to its plumage.

non-breeding plumage is rather similar, but the body is duller (sometimes slatey-grey) and less glossy, with a faint sheen confined to the head and rump. The gular pouch area is also duller. The juvenile is sooty-brown above, faintly scaled and with some fine pale spotting. The underparts are slightly paler, with a conspicuous pale border to the gular pouch and a pale 'V' at the border of the breast and neck. In all plumages, the bill, feet and facial skin are dark and there is a diagnostic band of pale (usually buffy) feathers on the border of the bare skin of the gular pouch. The sexes are similar, though the male is slightly larger.

The main confusion species is Double-crested Cormorant, which is also common on the West Coast. Brandt's Cormorant is slightly smaller and tends to adopt a more upright pose, thus its tail, despite being relatively shorter, almost touches the ground when the bird is perched on a sandbar. In flight its neck is held straight, not distinctly kinked as in Double-crested Cormorant. In breeding plumage its dark lores, sky-blue gular pouch with a pale border, and white filoplumes distinguish it from Double-crested Cormorant which has yellowish facial skin and gular pouch and is almost entirely dark-bodied. In non-breeding plumage the two species are more similar, but Brandt's Cormorant's gular pouch is dark with a pale border, while the Double-crested Cormorant's gular pouch remains entirely yellowish. Brandt's Cormorant also has a darker bill, lacks yellowish skin on the lores, and has less scaly upperparts. Juvenile Brandt's Cormorant are darker below than Double-crested Cormorant, and have a pale greyish-brown border to the dark (not yellow) gular pouch.

Compared to Pelagic Cormorant, the other Pacific coast species with which it overlaps, Brandt's Cormorant is larger, with a proportionally stockier head, neck and bill. This is often particularly obvious in flight. Pelagic Cormorants have dull reddish skin on the lores, but this is difficult to see at the best of times. Of more use as an aid in identification is Brandt's Cormorant's pale border to the gular pouch, which Pelagic Cormorants never show. In the breeding season, Pelagic Cormorants are conspicuously crested, and show a white patch

In full breeding plumage the Brandt's Cormorant throat pouch becomes bright blue and a hint of this coloration can be seen on this bird, though this individual lacks the fine white plumes that appear on the head and neck when in full breeding attire.

on the rear flanks, which is most conspicuous in flight. Neither crest nor thigh patch are ever shown by Brandt's Cormorants. Juvenile Brandt's Cormorants can be distinguished from juvenile Pelagic Cormorants by the pale 'V' on the breast, as well as by their conspicuous pale border to the gular pouch.

The species breeds colonially on rocky islands and cliffs, building a nest of seaweed, moss and grass on open ground in rocky areas. Usually four pale blue-white eggs are laid, in the period from March to July. The fledging period is apparently unknown.

A gregarious species, Brandt's Cormorant usually occurs in flocks, fishing together. In the evening, they can often be seen, flying in long, goose-like lines, to roost on rocky islands. Like other cormorants, Brandt's feeds almost exclusively on fish. It tends to swim rather low in the water, with only the head and upper mantle above the surface.

DOUBLE-CRESTED CORMORANT
PHALACROCORAX AURITUS

The Double-crested Cormorant is the most common and widespread North American cormorant, breeding all around the coast from southern Alaska and the Aleutian Islands south to the Gulf of California, the Gulf Coast, and in the east, north to Newfoundland. It is also found in the interior, where it is increasing, breeding north to northern Alberta. It is also found on Cuba, the Bahamas and the Isle of Pines. Northern and inland populations are migratory, wintering south to Honduras and the Caribbean, and in the fall there are often impressive movements during September and October.

In breeding plumage the species is basically black, with a green gloss to the head and body. At close range, or in good light, the mantle and wing coverts are deep bronzey-brown, with blackish borders to the feathers forming a neat scaled pattern. There may be a few white hair-like filoplumes around the eye and on the neck. The eye is green, the bill is greyish-horn, and the facial skin and gular pouch are a conspicuous orange-yellow.

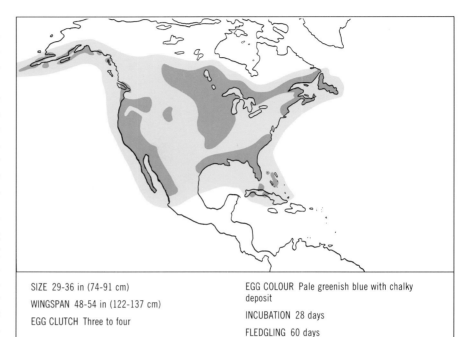

SIZE 29-36 in (74-91 cm)

WINGSPAN 48-54 in (122-137 cm)

EGG CLUTCH Three to four

EGG COLOUR Pale greenish blue with chalky deposit

INCUBATION 28 days

FLEDGLING 60 days

Despite its name, Double-crested Cormorant is not marked by a conspicuous crest. For a short time during the courtship season there are short, curly crests on the sides of the crown, just behind the eyes. These are white in the West and black in the East. However, they are quickly lost and have usually disappeared by late May. Both Red-faced and Pelagic Cormorants are much more conspicuously crested – yet another example of the vagaries of the English language!

In non-breeding plumage the bird is basically similar, though less glossy green, and as the year goes on the plumage becomes browner with wear. The juvenile is a dull brown or brownish/black with a scaled appearance to the mantle and coverts. The head is similar, with a paler, slightly mottled throat and breast. The bill is pinkish or yellowish with a darker culmen, and the facial skin and gular pouch are yellowish.

This is the only species of cormorant likely to be seen in interior North America, or in freshwater habitats. On the Atlantic coast, though, Great Cormorant is also present. The Double-crested Cormorant is smaller (size intermediate between Great Cormorant and Shag), and is somewhat stockier, especially about the neck, though its bill is proportionally slimmer. In flight, the neck is usually distinctly kinked, giving it a short-necked appearance, with the head held slightly above the line of the body. Breeding birds differ from Great Cormorant in their yellow facial skin and gular pouch and their lack of conspicuous white thighs. The bright yellow bill of juveniles, together with their orange-yellow facial skin (especially on the lores, between the eye and the bill) and scaled upper breast, provide a good distinction from juvenile Great Cormorants. Sub-adult birds have darker underparts than Great Cormorants, with a slightly paler breast than belly, whereas the reverse is true for Great Cormorants. In all plumages, as well as the differences in size and proportions outlined above, Double-crested Cormorant has a straight, not pointed, border between the feathering of the throat and the bare skin of the gular pouch and, like Shag, twelve rather than fourteen tail feathers.

On the Pacific coast, the Double-crested Cormorant must be distinguished from Pelagic, Red-faced and Brandt's Cormorant. It differs from all three in flight in its stocky head and bill and kinked neck, with the head held above the line of the body. Double-crested Cormorants are rather larger than Pelagic or Red-faced Cormorants, have a yellow gular pouch and lack their reddish facial skin. Compared to Brandt's Cormorant, the Double-crested Cormorant is relatively larger and long-tailed, the upperparts appearing generally paler with orange-yellow facial skin and gular pouch. The juvenile lacks juvenile Brandt's Cormorant's

LEFT *Two Double-crested Cormorants, one adult (left) and one immature bird (right), hang their wings out to dry in a pose typical of this group of birds.*

RIGHT *A Double-crested Cormorant, one of the largest of the Cormorants, takes flight to reveal its 52 in (132 cm) wing length.*

An adult Double-crested Cormorant at the nest with its downy chick. Both birds are panting to keep cool in the heat of the day.

pale border to the gular pouch. A fine distinction, which may be useful at close range, is that, in all plumages, the back and scapular feathers are blunter and more prominently scaled than Brandt's Cormorant.

The Double-crested Cormorant is a gregarious species, and is often found in groups, resting on piers, sandbars, buoys and rocks, with its wings spread out to dry. At favoured migration stop-overs, concentrations of up to 10,000 have been logged. It is catholic in its choice of habitats, choosing rocky coasts, beaches, inland lakes and rivers. On the coast, it seldom strays far out to sea. It feeds almost entirely on fish, diving for 20 or 30 seconds, propelling itself underwater with its feet.

Double-crested Cormorants nest colonially, both on the coast and inland. Colonies are found on cliffs, islands and trees near water, sometimes in association with gulls or other seabirds. The nest is a bulky structure of sticks, weeds, seaweed. Laying usually takes place in the period from April to July, when three or four pale, greenish blue eggs are laid; like other species, these are covered with a chalky deposit. Incubation averages 28 days, and is performed by both male and female. The young are on the wing from July onwards. Like all cormorants, the Double-crested Cormorant is rather silent, but in courtship gives a series of 'oak oak oak' calls and a loud 'r-r-r-o-o-o-o-p', as well as a variety of croaks and squeaks.

The Double-crested Cormorant has been recorded once in Europe, an immature bird which spent December 1988 to April 1989 on a small suburban pond in Billingham, north east England.

A group of Double-crested Cormorants, one of which hangs out its wings to dry, sit around possibly digesting their recent meal. The wildfowl present include Blue-winged Teal.

SHAG

Slightly smaller than the Great Cormorant, this bird is sometimes referred to as the Green Cormorant, for it is very similar in appearance to the larger bird and behaves very much like its namesake in most ways. It is essentially more of a marine species than the Great Cormorant, but at times strays into estuaries and even turns up at inland waters during winter months. In its summer plumage the Shag sports a distinctive recurved crest for a short period, while the dark plumage will be seen to have a greenish gloss, hence its alternative name.

At close quarters it will be noted that the black gular pouch is spotted with yellow, with the skin at the base of the slender, hooked bill, a chrome yellow. The large, web-footed legs are black, with the eye an emerald green. Immature birds are dark brown, showing little or no white on the breast (see *P. a. desmarestii*), while the slender appearance and even slimmer bill than that of the parent, should prevent confusion with the immature Great Cormorant. However, the Shag has twelve tail

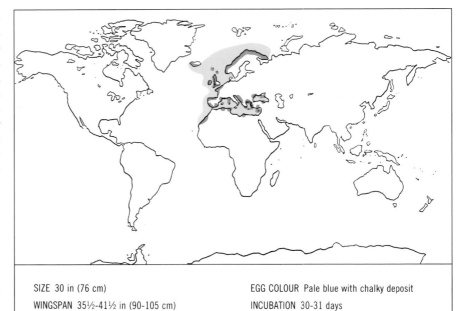

SIZE 30 in (76 cm)	EGG COLOUR Pale blue with chalky deposit
WINGSPAN 35½-41½ in (90-105 cm)	INCUBATION 30-31 days
EGG CLUTCH Three, occasionally up to six	FLEDGLING 53 days

feathers and the Great Cormorant has fourteen, which is the safest way of putting a name to it!

In their marine environment Shags perch on wave-drenched rocks, standing in a graceful, but less upright stance than the Great Cormorant, with the body inclined at an angle, and the neck curved almost swan-like. It is also common to see them in typical heraldic pose drying their wings, though they are less inclined to perch on posts or buoys than the Great Cormorant. When swimming, the Shag sits low on the water with the bill tilted slightly upwards. It is possibly more of an expert diver than the Great Cormorant and usually remains under water for about a minute. However, dives of twice that duration have frequently been recorded. The dive commences with a little leap by the swimming bird. Deep water is preferred and it has been found to reach depths of up to 60 feet (18 m). It feeds entirely on fish caught between the mandibles when under water. If fairly large, these are usually brought to the surface for swallowing. Sprats and sand eels form a major part of the diet.

The Shag takes flight with some difficulty, splashing along with its wings and threshing the water with its feet for some distance before becoming airborne. Once on the wing its flight is steady, usually close to the water's surface. Its wingbeats are quicker than the Great Cormorant and the head is held lower, below the line of the body.

In Britain and Ireland the distribution of this bird reflects the presence of rocky cliffs and islands, which are a prerequisite for nesting. They frequently share the same nesting locations as the Great Cormorant, but tend to occupy narrower ledges and frequently favour concealed sites inside sea caves and in crevices among boulders. Also in mixed colonies the Shag generally chooses sites at lower levels, nearer to the surface of the sea.

A monogamous pair bond is normal within the species and quite frequently the same pair will come together in successive seasons. Ritualized aggression and greeting displays which include gaping, and the uttering of a sharp guttural note, various head movements such as throwing back the head over the back of the body, bowing and tail cocking, are all indulged in before copulation and egg laying.

The nest is a flattish heap of vegetation which can include bracken or heather for its base, but normally consists mostly of seaweed. As it rots and becomes covered with birds' droppings it creates an overpowering aroma noticeable at considerable distances downwind. Building is carried out by both birds and the same site may be used in successive years by the same pair. The Shag is quite an early nester and some birds can be on eggs in March, or more usually April. Late starters, though, may not lay until July and sometimes even August.

RIGHT *This dramatic shot beautifully portrays an adult Shag, or Green Cormorant as they are sometimes called, with its family of three.*

LEFT *In breeding dress the Shag has a green gloss to its plumage while the hook-tipped bill is much slimmer than that of the Great Cormorant. However it builds an equally untidy nest of seaweed and other debris.*

LEFT *An immature Shag perches on a sea-splashed rock. Usually showing more white on the throat and underparts than the Great Cormorant, the slimmer bill is also a useful pointer to its identification.*

RIGHT *A pair of Shags in full breeding plumage sit in regal splendour at their cliff nest site. One of possibly two or three young, which comprise the usual brood, can just be seen at the rear of the two parents.*

The usual clutch is three eggs with occasionally as many as six. They are pale blue and covered with a white, chalky deposit.

Incubation is by both parents and lasts for 30 to 31 days with changeover taking place twice a day. At hatching the chick is an ugly, naked, brown creature, but within a few days a brown covering of down develops. Both adults feed the chicks by partial regurgitation, the young putting their bills into the parents' gape. By the time the young fledge at around 53 days, their down is replaced by dark brown feathers, with a pale patch around the throat. The parents feed their offspring for a further 20 days at least, but sometimes for much longer.

After the nesting season is finished, adults and young move to the open sea though some adults stay relatively close to the breeding area. For example, whereas Lundy Isle is completely deserted, those that nest on the Farne Islands stay in the area thoughout the winter. This variable dispersal is probably related to the availability of food.

Most young British birds in their first year tend to move further afield, some occasionally reaching the waters off the coast of Spain and even into the Mediterranean. In Britain the species has shown an increase in numbers since the 1920s, especially in north east England and south east Scotland with the current population now estimated to be between 35,000 and 40,000 pairs.

Britain is one of the species' stronghold with other main breeding areas located in Western Iceland, the Faeroes, Ireland, the Channel Islands and from the Kola Peninsula in the USSR to Stavanger, Norway with other nesting off the coasts of Brittany, France, and Spain.

There are two subspecies: *P. a. riggenbachi* breeds on the Moroccan coast from Casablanca south to Tarfaya and *P. a. demarestii*, which breeds in the Mediterranean basin from the Balearics eastward to the Aegean Sea, Cyprus and the Crimea, with scattered sites along the North African coast. This latter subspecies has legs that are brown with yellow webs whilst the juvenile tends to show a lot more white on the underparts. Otherwise differences between this bird, *P. a. riggenbachi* and the nominate race are based on size.

The species is unknown on the Atlantic coast of North America.

AMERICAN WHITE PELICAN

PELECANUS ERYTHRORHYNCHOS

Whereas the Brown Pelican is totally marine in its life-style, the White Pelican is largely the opposite, for it prefers freshwater and nests in colonies which are mostly located on the islands of inland lakes, now mainly in the North American prairie provinces. There are other scattered breeding centres in east Washington, south and north California, west Nevada, south Idaho, north Utah, Montana, Wyoming and the Dakotas, Minnesota and coastal Texas. It was however formerly more widespread, ranging from British Columbia and the prairie heartland of Canada south to Texas.

More distinctively marked than the Brown Pelican, this species is the only black and white pelican of the region. Larger than *P. occidentalis*, the adult White Pelican in breeding plumage is all white, with a small, pale yellow crest and bright orange bill. This usually has a fibrous plate on the upper mandible, which is shed during the nesting period. The eye is orange-yellow with an orange orbital ring, while the face skin is yellow and the legs and huge webbed feet are orange-red.

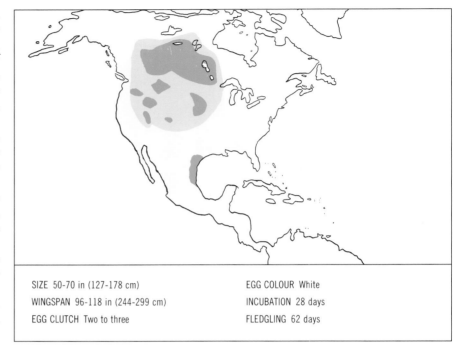

SIZE 50-70 in (127-178 cm)	EGG COLOUR White
WINGSPAN 96-118 in (244-299 cm)	INCUBATION 28 days
EGG CLUTCH Two to three	FLEDGLING 62 days

LEFT *A group of White Pelicans on a typical island nest site. Double-crested Cormorants can be seen to the rear.*

RIGHT *A well-grown White Pelican chick thrusts its head into the huge distensible pouch of the parent bird to obtain its food of regurgitated fish.*

It is in flight that the White Pelican is most impressive, making regal progress across the sky, with neck hunched back to the body and slow, deliberate flaps followed by long glides. It is then that the distinctive black primaries and secondaries can be seen, contrasting with the all white body. This colour combination is similar to Wood Stork (*Mycteria americana*), the Whooping Crane (*Grus americana*) and Snow Goose (*Anser caerulescens*); when viewed at a distance the American White Pelican might be mistaken for any of these species, though of course all three fly with necks stretched out and not hunched up.

Feeding behaviour is also quite different to that of the Brown Pelican. It does not dive for food, but fishes in small swimming groups, often in line, threshing the water with its wings to herd fish into suitable shallow water, where it scoops up its prey with its highly distensible bill. Birds quite frequently fly considerable distances to feed and 100 to 150 miles (160–240 km) from the breeding colony to its favoured feeding area is not unusual. For example, those that breed around the fishless Great Salt Lake in Utah have to travel up to a hundred miles a day to obtain food for their young.

The White Pelican's breeding display is simplistic, as is that of most pelicans, with all rituals strangely silent. The nest is usually located on the ground and comprises no more than a shallow depression lined with a few small sticks, some grass and perhaps the odd feather or two for good measure. Two to three white eggs are laid during the period April to June, when a nesting colony can contain a range of young from very small birds to some that are almost fully fledged. Incubation lasts about four weeks and is shared by both parents.

On hatching, the tiny chick is naked and blind. It seems incredible that the adult Pelican can feed this 3 inch (7.5 cm) long creature with such a huge ungainly bill, but it does manage to dribble a mush of regurgitated fish into the tiny gape. The young chick grows rapidly and by the end of the first week it has the strength and ability to push its head into the parent's mouth. It is soon covered with white down that is gradually shed as the first feathers show. In a couple of months it is fully fledged and able to fly.

After nesting, White Pelicans gather together in large flocks, particularly in the area of the southern Great Plains, where thousands congregate prior to their southwards migration. Their wintering area is mainly in the Gulf of Mexico, Florida and the coasts of Central America south to the West Indies and Guatemala. In western USA flocks of hundreds of birds winter along the coast of central California southward to the Gulf of California,

whilst stragglers have reached as far north as eastern Alaska. On the eastern North American coast it is scarce north to Nova Scotia. Migrating birds almost exclusively fly overland, usually at a considerable height, when they might be seen in extended skeins or V-formation in the manner of geese.

The immature American White Pelican looks like the parent, but the gular pouch and facial skin are grey, while the crown, nape and hind neck are brownish. The primaries and secondaries are also brown. Young pelicans take three years before they attain their adult feathering and it may be their fourth summer before they breed. A long-lived bird, some are known to have reached an age of at least 30 years.

The American White Pelican is not known in Europe, where the similar White Pelican (*P. onocrotalus*) occurs. Formerly more numerous and widely spread, persecution and loss of habitat have drastically reduced its numbers to possibly only several thousand. Its European breeding distribution is confined to Romania, Yugoslavia, Albania, Turkey and scattered locations in the USSR.

The Pink-backed Pelican (*P. rufescens*) which breeds in much of Africa south of the Sahara, has occasionally strayed into the Western Palaearctic, with records from Egypt and Israel.

In majestic flight, a pair of White Pelicans plane across the waves revealing their distinctive black and white wing pattern.

BROWN PELICAN

PELECANUS OCCIDENTALIS

The adult Brown Pelican is easily identified by its large body, long neck, short legs and, in flight, long broad wings. However, the single most noticeable feature is the large bill and distensible pouch, which is most obvious when the bird is carrying food. This pouch can vary in colour from red to blackish white, while the upperpart of the bill is grey or yellowish, with a scarlet cast on the distal portion, and a red tip. In breeding plumage it looks a darkish bird overall at a distance, but a close view will reveal that the forehead, crown and ear coverts are white with a tinge of yellow. The nape and hind neck are also white, and the base of the foreneck yellow. The upperparts are silver-grey, but have a warm, brownish look. The underparts are blackish brown. Even closer inspection will reveal a pale yellow eye, with a pink orbital ring, blue-grey facial skin, and blue grey to black legs and feet.

The Brown Pelican becomes even more impressive in flight as it glides across the water on its 6½ feet (2 m) wing span or flies with slow, methodical flaps of its huge wings in loose formation at greater heights.

Entirely coastal, it is rarely noted any distance from the sea. Its feeding behaviour is as spectacular as a gannet's or booby's, as it dives into the water from 30 feet (10 m) or more above the waves. When prey is spotted the head and bill are thrust downwards and the wings are slightly angled as it goes into a corkscrewing, vertical dive, pushing the wings right back to enter the water with a splash. When successful, the bird returns to the surface and throws back its head to swallow its catch.

At the turn of this century birds were nesting in Florida in November and December each year. Since then it has laid eggs later and later until, by 1935, eggs were being laid in May. When birds arrive back at their breeding sites a short silent display ritual takes place. At first the female sits on the ground, while the male moves slowly round her. During this process the female raises her wings and tilts back her head. She then flies to the water, followed by the male, where mating takes place.

The Brown Pelican is a colonial species, choosing a variety of nest sites including trees, bushes, mangroves and, at times, dry flat ground. In trees and mangroves a bulky nest of twigs is constructed, but on flat, dry ground little material is employed and the nest may comprise just a few twigs and

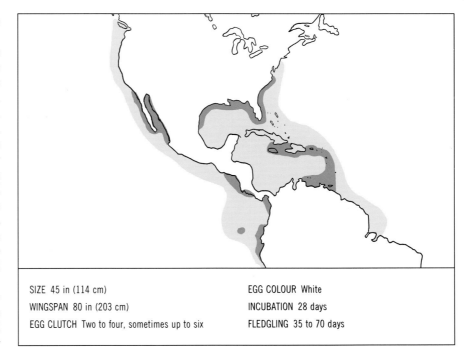

SIZE 45 in (114 cm)	EGG COLOUR White
WINGSPAN 80 in (203 cm)	INCUBATION 28 days
EGG CLUTCH Two to four, sometimes up to six	FLEDGLING 35 to 70 days

sticks and maybe a few feathers. Within the colony, nest spacing is determined by the reach of the sitting bird, with territories closely guarded.

Two to four white eggs are usually laid, though sometimes up to six. These are incubated by both parents for around four weeks. On hatching, the young bird is blind and naked, presenting a most

In its drab plumage, an immature Brown Pelican sits on the rocky seashore. It will be three to four years before it attains the grandeur of the adult bird.

pitiful sight with seemingly insufficient strength to lift its top-heavy head. Development, however, is rapid and within a couple of weeks the young bird is covered in downy feathers. It becomes increasingly active and its parents have their work cut out to satisfy its insatiable appetite. The young are fed, by both parents, with a mixture of semi-digested fish which is obtained by plunging the whole head into the gullet of the adult bird.

After about five weeks those in ground nests begin to move about in the colony. Tree nesting birds, however, though capable of clambering about at the same age, cannot safely leave their lofty nurseries for at least another two weeks and it is nearer nine to ten weeks before they are capable of any extended flight. During this pre-flight stage there is considerable mortality amongst tree-nesters. Some lose their balance and fall to the ground in their exuberance to be fed, whilst others inadvertently hang themselves amongst the branches as they attempt to climb to the ground. Ground-nesters are also at some risk, for should they beg food from the wrong parent they might be eaten or trampled underfoot.

Brown Pelicans are otherwise sociable birds, feeding and roosting together in most circumstances. Although a partial migrant in its more northerly range, its movements are erratic and depend very much on local conditions as to whether

they stay or leave. It is confined to North and South America, with the nominate race breeding in the West Indies. There are six subspecies within its range which are mainly determined by size alone. However, within these different races there is also considerable size variance between the sexes, with the male larger than the female in all cases. By far the largest is *P. o. thagus*, which is usually referred to as the Chilean or Peruvian Pelican. This race is also darker than the nominate race, with the adult showing a much pinker bill, a more developed straw-coloured crest and generally greyer underparts with white streaks on the belly. It is actually considered to be a separate species by some authorities. It breeds from central Peru south to Chile where, though not so numerous as formerly, it is still economically important as a guano-producing species.

Of the other races, *P. o. carolinensis* breeds along the coasts of tropical America from southern Carolina south to the Orinoco, while on the Pacific coast *P. o. californicus* is found from California south to Mexico. The race *P. o. murphy* breeds along the Columbian coast to northern Peru, whilst *P. o. urinator* is confined to the Galapagos Islands.

In recent years the number of Brown Pelicans in the USA has declined. It is considered that pesticides have been responsible, causing egg-shell thinning and greater chick mortality.

POMARINE JAEGER

STERCORARIUS POMARINUS

One of the most fearsome predatory birds of the ocean, the Pomarine Jaeger, or Skua, is powerfully built and perfectly adapted to its piratical lifestyle. Quite at home in the middle of the ocean, or inshore, this species is the largest of the three 'long-tailed' jaegers and is also closely related to the larger *Catharacta* genus.

The Pomarine Jaeger, like the Parasitic Jaeger, has a circumpolar breeding range, but is more restricted and generally breeds further to the north. Birds nest from Alaska, north central Canada and Greenland, to Spitsbergen in Norway and across Siberia. They favour tundra areas near the coast but sometimes occupy similar habitat further inland besides rivers and lakes.

As with the Parasitic Jaeger, the Pomarine Jaeger has two colour phases – either light or dark – with intermediates occasionally being seen. In breeding plumage the adults are distinguished by their elongated central tail feathers, which extend beyond the rest of the tail and are broadly twisted into a spoon shape at the tip. Slightly smaller than the Great

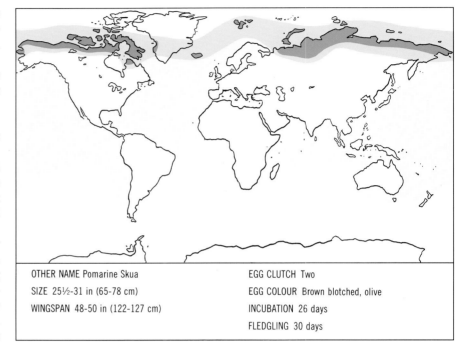

OTHER NAME Pomarine Skua	EGG CLUTCH Two
SIZE 25½-31 in (65-78 cm)	EGG COLOUR Brown blotched, olive
WINGSPAN 48-50 in (122-127 cm)	INCUBATION 26 days
	FLEDGLING 30 days

ABOVE *Looking much more powerful and deep chested than other skuas, this immature Pomarine Jaeger flies with direct predatory intent as it seeks out a seabird victim it can force to disgorge or drop any fish it has caught.*

LEFT *An adult Pomarine Jaeger on its nest in the Canadian tundra. The twisted, blunt-ended tail, which is a major identifying feature of this bird, can be clearly seen.*

Skua, the Pomarine is always larger and more heavily built than the Parasitic Jaeger, while its deep-chested and broad-winged appearance give a greater impression of power. Light phase birds usually show a dark, blackish brown crown and whitish underparts, the latter often crossed by a broad, dark brown breast band. The ventral area is also usually darker, and there is often a yellowish tinge to the sides of the neck. The upperparts are generally a plain dark brown, with a white flash ·at the base of the outer primaries. The bill and legs are usually fairly dull greyish, with the former often showing a black tip. Dark phase birds are blackish brown, with the crown looking darker at close range, and the white wing flashes contrasting strongly with the rest of the upperwing in flight. This colour phase usually comprises less than twenty per cent of any particular population and in some areas less than five per cent.

Younger birds and non-breeding adults are more difficult to identify and are best separated from Parasitic Jaeger on their general size and behaviour. With no direct comparison between the two species, the Pomarine Jaeger's more leisurely and seemingly more effortless flight, together with its habit of flying at slightly higher levels above the sea, are

useful pointers to its identification.

This species is a highly accomplished predator and obtains much of its food by scavenging from other seabirds. It feeds mainly on fish, obtained either by forcing gannets, terns, gulls and other seabirds to disgorge, or by dipping below the surface for direct catches. It will also scavenge offal from fishing boats and on occasions kill other birds for food. On the breeding grounds, lemmings and other small rodents are a major food source and their relative abundance will often dictate the number of jaegers breeding and their rearing success in any one season.

Adults begin their return to the breeding grounds during April and continue through May, with the northernmost nesting sites not being re-occupied until mid-June. Initially they gather in groups, but pairs then claim a territory of up to 0.5 square miles (1.5 sq km). The territory size depends upon the continuity of the tundra habitat and also the abundance of food in that year. When food is plentiful, nest sites may only be 300 to 600 feet (90–180 m) apart.

Aerial displays are performed over the territory, involving a slow flight and frequent calling by both birds. This serves to strengthen the pair bond and at the same time warn off any intruders. The nest is built in an area of open ground, often on a slight hummock. It is normally just a shallow depression with a minimal lining of finer vegetation. The two brown-blotched, olive-coloured eggs are laid in June and incubated by both parents for about 26 days. On hatching, the young remain close to the nest and are fed totally on regurgitated food until they are able to fly about 30 days later. They remain dependent upon the adults for food for about another two weeks before they are left to fend for themselves.

At this stage the juveniles are mainly dark brown, with paler edges to their upperpart feathers, giving them a finely barred effect. On pale phase juveniles the underparts are a pale brownish white, with a darkish breast band and with the head showing a slightly darker cap. Barring is at its heaviest on the upper and undertail coverts and on the axillaries, whilst the outer primaries show a white flash at their bases. Even at this age the tail will normally show a couple of blunt extensions to the central feathers.

In years of poor food supply, the adults soon disperse, moving south fairly quickly if they fail to breed successfully. Otherwise, those birds that do raise young will head southwards from the end of August with the juveniles following in late September and October. In the Atlantic many birds winter north of the equator off West Africa and around the Caribbean. Some birds also visit the Indian Ocean, perhaps having migrated part of the distance overland, whilst in the Pacific many individuals winter as far south as south east Australia and off the coasts of South America.

In winter, Pomarine Jaegers are found singly or in small groups. Larger concentrations occur in good feeding areas, but are specifically noted on the northward spring migration. This occurs on a broad front, with evidence that some Pomarine Jaegers follow migrating groups of shearwaters and terns, and are to be seen moving along the English Channel and off the Scottish coast. First-year birds will often remain to the south during their first summer, foraging widely across the oceans for food. They may migrate further north in their second year, but they probably will not attempt to breed until they are at least three years old.

Adult, light phase Pomarine Jaegers rest along the shores of the Arabian coast, where some are to be found during the northern hemisphere winter.

PARASITIC JAEGER
STERCORARIUS PARASITICUS

The Parasitic Jaeger, or Arctic Skua as it is known in Europe, is perhaps the most familiar species in its group, being more frequently encountered inshore and even inland than any of its congeners. Renowned for its piratical habits, this species is the most falcon-like of seabirds and to an extent fills an equivalent niche over the oceans.

With a breeding range extending virtually unbroken around the higher latitudes of the northern hemisphere, this species is more widely distributed than either the Pomarine or Long-tailed Jaeger. It can be found nesting from the high arctic to the cool temperate climatic zone, in a variety of habitats from Alaska across the northern Canadian coast through Greenland, Iceland, northern Britain, Scandinavia and right across Northern Siberia.

The Parasitic Jaeger has two distinct colour phases, with a range of intermediates also appearing. The dark phase is predominant in the south of the breeding range, while a greater proportion of pale phase birds occur in the north. Some recent research has suggested that the pale phase is slowly

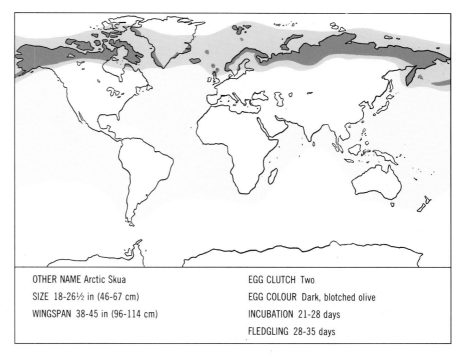

OTHER NAME Arctic Skua	EGG CLUTCH Two
SIZE 18-26½ in (46-67 cm)	EGG COLOUR Dark, blotched olive
WINGSPAN 38-45 in (96-114 cm)	INCUBATION 21-28 days
	FLEDGLING 28-35 days

A pair of Parasitic Jaegers, at their nest with one small chick and an unhatched egg. The bird in the foreground is a dark phase, or dark morph, bird, at the rear is a light phase bird.

becoming the more numerous and widespread, even in the south of the range, and that eventually it will more or less completely replace dark phase birds.

About the size of a Mew Gull, the adults are dark blackish brown above, with a small white flash at the base of the outer primaries which can be conspicuous even at quite long range. Pale phase birds are creamy white below with a dark brown underwing, ventral area and undertail. They also show a contrasting black crown, separated from the mantle by a pale nape, while the sides of the neck show a yellowish wash and on some birds there may be a darker breast band. The dark phase is essentially dark blackish brown all over, although the crown does appear blacker at close range. In fresh plumage, all adults have long pointed extensions to their two central tail feathers, but these are often damaged or broken by the end of the breeding season. They are never as long as those of the Long-tailed Jaeger, but usually extend up to 5 inches (12 cm) beyond the rest of the tail.

Parasitic Jaegers obtain much of their food by harrying other seabirds and forcing them to disgorge their last meal – a method of feeding known as kleptoparasitism. Their main victims tend to be kittiwakes, terns and auks, although they do pursue other species. They are very agile and relentless in pursuit and will chase their target over a fair distance. Despite this, their success rate is not high. Occasionally two or more birds will 'team up', and this normally results in the victim surrendering rather more quickly. Once food has been disgorged, the jaeger will attempt to catch it acrobatically in mid-air, but may ignore it if it misses first time.

Birds also feed on fish caught directly from the sea and they will scavenge fish offal behind trawlers when the opportunity arises. During the breeding season small birds, eggs and mammals become prey, and if food is scarce, insects and vegetable matter, such as seeds and berries, are eaten.

The adults begin moving north to their breeding grounds during April and will start claiming a territory as soon as they arrive later in the month or in May. Mixed light and dark phase pairings frequently occur, with many birds remaining faithful to the same partner from year to year. Territories are generally staked out over areas of tundra or moorland, with the size being determined by both the available habitat and the food supply. When food is plentiful, pairs may nest in loose colonies and it is then that they are most vigorous in their display behaviour and defence of the nest site. Any intruder, whether a human being or an Arctic Fox, will be driven away by the birds continually dive-bombing their target, striking out with bills and feet

once they are within range. It is at this stage that they are at their most vocal, giving hoarse kittiwake-like calls and various buzzard-like mews.

The nest is generally sited on a dry patch amongst more marshy ground. There will often be a raised area or boulder within 32 to 65 feet (10–20 m), which the adults use as a sentinel post. Two dark, blotched, olive-coloured eggs are laid in late May or early June and then incubated by both birds for 21 to 28 days.

Soon after the young hatch they will leave the nest and separate, although remaining within their parents' territory. They stay some distance apart until they can fly about four weeks later. The adults will then continue to feed them for another two to five weeks before they become fully independent.

Juveniles are mainly dark above, with many showing paler underparts. The chest and belly usually have darker bars, and these become more extensive on the undertail and underwing coverts. Most birds are paler on the nape and are generally warmer brown in colour than either Pomarine

An adult, dark phase Parasitic Jaeger, on its Canadian tundra nest site.

A light phase Parasitic Jaeger, stands alert and ready to defend its nest site at its Canadian tundra summer home.

Jaegers or Long-tailed Jaegers of a similar age. Even these young birds will normally show a short extension to their two central tail feathers, although at this age this is normally only visible at close range.

A leisurely southward migration commences from early August and continues well into October. Birds move on a broad front over the Atlantic and it has been noted that there is a general correlation with the southerly movement of Arctic Terns. The Parasitic Jaeger is more frequently encountered along European and North American coastlines,

and even inland, than Pomarine Jaegers and Long-tailed Jaegers, although they generally pass through singly or in small groups.

In the Pacific region, the Parasitic Jaeger is known to winter in quite large numbers around the coasts of south east Australia and the coasts of South America whilst the majority of Atlantic birds will cross the Equator where they winter off Argentina and southern Africa. Odd individuals may, however, wander the oceans and these birds have been recorded in the North Atlantic during December and January.

LONG-TAILED JAEGER

STERCORARIUS LONGICAUDUS

Once named 'Buffons Skua' after the wealthy French naturalist Georges-Louis-Leclerc, Compte de Buffon (1707–1788), it is now known by its more descriptive English name of Long-tailed Jaeger or, as British ornithologists call it, Long-tailed Skua. In Britain it is a highly prized sighting by birders, for it is the least frequently noted skua. Indeed, it was an official rarity during the period 1976–1979.

A recent discovery is the May passage of Long-tailed Skuas past the Outer Hebrides, which can be witnessed best at Balranald, North Uist. Otherwise it is only infrequently noted around the rest of Britain during spring. In autumn it is seen slightly more often, especially down the east coast of England from Northumberland to Norfolk, where on occasions I have thrilled to the sight of these birds myself.

Its breeding is circumpolar, occurring in both the high and low arctic regions. It nests on islands and along the coasts of the Arctic Ocean, south to the tundra regions of North America and Eurasia, but generally north of the Arctic Circle. The numbers of birds breeding vary from year to year and fluctuate markedly with changes in food supply. In Europe it is generally fairly numerous in Finland, and an estimated 10,000 pairs are to be found in Sweden.

In its breeding plumage there is little likelihood of misidentification. It is the smallest of the jaegers, although the extremely long central tail feathers make it approximately the same length as the other two bulkier jaegers. These central feathers extend 5 to 10 inches (12–25 cm) beyond the rest of the tail and, in a full-plumaged adult, are the most distinguishing feature. However, it should be noted that some Parasitic Jaegers do have quite long tails and occasionally Long-tailed Jaegers with broken tail streamers may cause confusion.

The Long-tailed Jaeger has a much 'cleaner' appearance than either the Parasitic or Pomarine Jaegers, showing completely whitish underparts with no sign of the breast band that is usually to be found on the pale morphs of the other two. Whereas dark morphs are quite common within the Parasitic and Pomarine populations, they are virtually unknown in the Long-tailed Jaeger. The Long-tailed Jaeger also shows a more clear-cut black cap which contrasts with a broad white collar and a pale

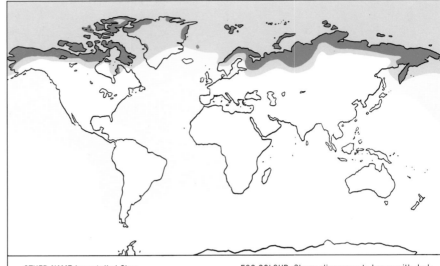

OTHER NAME Long-tailed Skua	EGG COLOUR Glossy olive green to brown with dark brown, grey spots at front end
SIZE 19½-23 in (50-58 cm)	
WINGSPAN 30-33 in (76-84 cm)	INCUBATION 23 days
EGG CLUTCH Two, exceptionally three	FLEDGLING 21 days

ABOVE *The Long-tailed Jaeger, in flight shows its five long, wispy tail streamers that give the bird its name and distinctive appearance.*

LEFT *The distinctive, capped appearance and the extremely long tail streamers easily identify a Long-tailed Jaeger, on its tundra nest site.*

back, while the cheeks are a clean yellow. It should be noted that the bill is black, not brown, and the legs are grey, not black as in Parasitic and Pomarine Jaegers.

The flight is light and airy, the wing beats much shallower, and there is less white in the wings than either Parasitic or Pomarine Jaeger. At sea, it will occasionally catch fish by 'dipping' to the surface, but more usually it obtains them by its piratical behaviour, stealing from other seabirds. When at its inland breeding sites, the Long-tailed Jaeger feeds on small birds, taken in flight or picked up from the ground. Mammals, especially lemmings, also form a major part of its diet, and it also eats insects, berries and at times the eggs of other birds. It is the lemming population which determines the

occupancy of particular areas of the Long-tailed Jaeger's range, with the cyclical nature of this animal's abundance determining the success or otherwise of the Long-tailed Jaeger's breeding activity.

The more lemmings, the more successful the breeding rate of the Jaeger. In years when lemmings are few, Long-tailed Jaegers do not bother to breed at all, whilst in good lemming years they will lay more eggs than usual. Since laying occurs before the lemming 'plague' begins, this phenomenon still requires a satisfactory explanation.

European birds arrive back at their breeding grounds in late May or early June to take up their territories. These range from flat coastal tundra and stony plateaux to vegetated uplands. Birds will return to the same site even if a non-breeding year

An adult Long-tailed Jaeger, stands over its nest and eggs, showing its clear-cut pattern of dark cap and white face, neck and breast.

intervenes. There they indulge in aerial displays to establish and strengthen their pair bonds.

The nest site is on open ground, usually a dry spot, such as a slightly raised hummock, where a shallow depression is created. This is often unlined to start, but small pieces of lichen are added during incubation.

The eggs are smooth, slightly glossy and coloured olive green to brown, with dark brown and grey spots and blotches which are often concentrated at the front end. The usual clutch size is two, exceptionally three. Both parents share the incubation which lasts about 23 days. Because the food supply is variable, incubation begins with the laying of the first egg. Thus the chicks hatch at different times, giving rise to young of varying ages. When there are plenty of lemmings about there is sufficient food for two or even three young, but when food is scarce it is given to the oldest chick, which never-

theless may fail to survive.

The young jaegers move away from the nest even before they are fully fledged, and become totally independent at around three weeks.

The immature bird, though often indistinguishable from the young Parasitic Jaeger, is greyer and has little or no white in the wing. At close range it usually shows a pale hind collar and bolder barring on the tail coverts.

The Long-tailed Jaeger is generally a silent bird, except on the breeding grounds when it utters various shrill cries.

In normal nesting years birds leave their breeding territories from late August onwards, moving southwards overland and far out to sea. The precise wintering areas are still not known, but the present extent of knowledge indicates a wide dispersal throughout the Pacific and Atlantic Oceans to about 50° South.

GREAT SKUA

CATHARACTA SKUA

The cry 'Bonxie', which is the Norse name for Great Skua, perhaps trips more easily off the tongue whenever this bird is sighted. But whatever the term used for this large powerful bird, its appearance seems to stir the blood of most British birders, more than many other sea-haunting species. My first Bonxie sighting was many years ago on the east coast of Britain, where these predatory birds can be seen as they follow the terns and the gannets southwards, especially from September through to November.

About the size of a Herring Gull, it is larger and bulkier than the other skuas of North Atlantic waters.

The plumage is fairly uniform dark brown, but at very close quarters pale streakings are visible on the neck and upperparts. It is no doubt the broad rounded wings, which almost suggest the form of a buzzard (*Buteo*), that most readily separate it from the other slender-winged skua species. The piratical behaviour of the Bonxie (and other skuas) is generally sufficient to identify it 'family-wise', for they relentlessly chase terns, gulls, or sometimes even

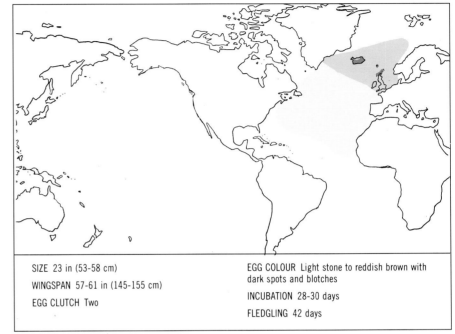

SIZE 23 in (53-58 cm)

WINGSPAN 57-61 in (145-155 cm)

EGG CLUTCH Two

EGG COLOUR Light stone to reddish brown with dark spots and blotches

INCUBATION 28-30 days

FLEDGLING 42 days

The Great Skua is perhaps the most powerful and predatory of all the skuas. Its powerful and fearsome bill can intimidate even birds the size of a Gannet.

gannets! Some gulls, notably the Mew Gull, pursue other gulls to divest them of their food. They quickly give up the chase however, whereas skuas will persist, matching every twist and turn until the poor victim releases or regurgitates its last meal. The Bonxie (or other skua species) will invariably catch its meal in mid-air, usually long before it reaches the water below.

When in flight, the overall dark appearance of the Great Skua might render it unidentifiable at long distance were it not for the prominent white wing patches, formed by the white base of the primaries, which signal its presence far out at sea. This distinctive field mark should also preclude misidentification with immature gannets, which less experienced watchers may do.

The nesting areas of this bird are limited to the north Atlantic, where breeding takes place only in Iceland, the Faeroes, Shetland and the Orkney Islands. There are, however, a few localities on the mainland of northern Scotland where birds now nest and there have been some more recent records of birds breeding in Spitsbergen and Finmark.

The headquarters of the Bonxie in Britain is undoubtedly the Shetlands where, thanks to protection during this century, numbers have increased from a dangerously low point. In 1850 only two small groups of breeding birds existed: on Foula there were around 100 pairs, but on Hermaness there were only nine pairs. Today Foula has more than 2000 pairs, almost half the total Scottish breeding population.

From late March to April birds return to their respective colonies which are situated on flat or sloping grassy areas or heather moorland near to the sea. The proximity of a freshwater pool, where they drink and indulge in communal bathing, is also a necessary ingredient of its preferred nesting areas. Here they will display to one another in a most aggressive manner, frequently with wings raised above the back to show the white base of the primaries, and with their necks extended and enlarged. This is invariably accompanied by a repeated '-ek-ek-ek-ek' at which time the head is raised. Great Skuas, like large gulls, take up to four years to reach maturity and it is usually not until the fifth year onwards that birds will pair off. Their territories are quite large, but many nest close together in particularly favoured areas. There they make a scrape, often lined with grassy material obtained nearby. The two eggs are laid in May or June and are variable in colour, ranging from light stone to reddish brown, usually with dark spots and blotches. It is at this time that the Great Skua is most aggressive, dive-bombing anything that invades its domain. Sheep, dogs and humans all receive the same quite frightening treatment. At such times it will press home its attacks with considerable vigour, the pair sometimes working in unison and coming in from different directions.

Incubation lasts for 28 to 30 days, with both parents taking turns. Shortly after hatching, the two young leave the nest, but remain separately within the territory guarded by the female. Both parents feed their offspring by regurgitation, with the male bringing most of the food. The young fledge after around six weeks and become totally independent around three weeks later. Birds then leave the breeding area and become totally pelagic, wandering the north Atlantic before returning to their natal home the following year. British waters are generally deserted throughout the winter, though one or two roam the Bay of Biscay or the North Sea and I have seen them from the ferry on crossings from the Hook of Holland to Harwich in February.

The Great Skua is omnivorous, but fish is a major ingredient of its diet, either caught, scavenged or pirated from other birds. It will also kill and eat other birds.

Sightings from the USA's eastern coast are infrequent but when seen are usually well offshore, during the months November to April.

The taxonomy of the *Catharacta* genus is not fully agreed upon with one authority, Devillers (1977), proposing three species, and Brooke (1978) four species. In line with Harrison (1983) who followed Brooke's treatment, we refer to all four species, but make just passing reference to the three which breed only in the southern hemisphere. Of these three, the Chilean Skua is apparently confined to the coasts of Chile and southern Argentina, with the extent of its northwards migrations unknown. Slightly smaller than the Great Skua, it has a weaker bill, but is generally similar to Great Skua.

The South Polar Skua, sometimes referred to as McCormick's Skua, breeds in the Antarctic. These are dark, light and intermediate morphs. The light morphs are particularly distinctive, showing uniform blackish upperparts that contrast strongly with the pale head and underparts. On average it is smaller than the Great Skua, but otherwise its habits and flight are similar. South Polar Skuas occur off both the Pacific and Atlantic coasts of North America, but generally stay well offshore. They are most numerous in the spring and autumn off the west coast and in the spring off the east coast. Elsewhere they are rare on the south coast of Alaska and occasional in the Gulf of Mexico, but has yet to be identified in European waters!

The Antarctic Skua (*C. antarctica*) has three races. *C. a. antarctica* breeds in the Falkland Islands and the coasts of southern Argentina; *C. a. hamiltoni* breeds on Gough and Tristan da Cuhna; and *C. a. longbergi* is the most widespread, breeding right round the polar region and sub-Antarctic islands. It is not known in either North American or north European waters.

ABOVE *Great Skuas are scavengers and will take any carrion they come across whether it is along the shore or on land. Here a juvenile bird feeds on a dead rabbit.*

MEDITERRANEAN GULL

LARUS MELANOCEPHALUS

For the gull enthusiast anywhere, there are certain 'quarry species'. These are scarce enough to be worth spending hours of searching, often in cold and uncomfortable conditions, but not so rare as to be a once in a lifetime event. Over much of Britain the Mediterranean Gull falls exactly into this category. It is most frequent on the south coast at certain favoured sites, such as Folkestone in Kent or Radipole Lake in Dorset, and at Blackpill in West Glamorgan it is regularly found, sometimes in small flocks. Elsewhere it is rather scarce, with many inland counties recording just one or two birds a year.

In addition to its scarcity value, the Mediterranean Gull offers an identification challenge in all but adult plumage. It is most often found among flocks of Black-headed or Mew Gulls, where it can be seen to be slightly bigger and bulkier than a Black-headed Gull, with longer legs, a deeper and heavier bill and slightly more rounded, paddle-shaped wings. In breeding plumage the hood is black, with a conspicuous broken white eye-ring. The upper-

SIZE 15-17 in (38-43 cm)

WINGSPAN 36 in (91 cm)

EGG CLUTCH Three

EGG COLOUR Creamy to buff, speckled with dark brown

INCUBATION 23-25 days

FLEDGLING 35-40 days

RIGHT *A Mediterranean Gull, in non-breeding plumage, shows a dark eye crescent and dusky ear coverts. The red and black, yellow-tipped bill is also evident. Note the thick-set body, the broader, less angled and more rounded tipped wings than the Black-headed Gull.*

parts are pale grey (paler than Black-headed) and the wingtips are white. The bill and legs are bright red. The white wingtips, bright red bill, black (not brown) hood and white eye-ring easily separate the adult Mediterranean Gull from a Black-headed Gull; indeed, the white wingtips recall a Little Gull, but the latter is much smaller, has a dusky grey underwing and no eye-ring. The non-breeding adult has a white head with a variable dark shadow behind the eye. The white wingtips are still an excellent distinction from the Black-headed Gull on both perched and flying birds.

In its immature plumage the Mediterranean Gull is rather more difficult to pick out. The first-winter bird has a pale grey mantle, blackish outer primaries and secondaries and a dark tail band. At rest, whether on the water or the ground, it is very similar to a first-winter Black-headed Gull, and can be picked out only by such subtle features as its greater bulk, heavier bill and blacker primary tips and head markings. Conversely, in flight it recalls a young Mew Gull, differing from that species in its blacker outer primaries and secondaries, which contrast more with the pale mid-wing panel and pale grey mantle. The mantle is much paler than the somewhat dusky grey mantle of a Mew Gull. The head, body and underwings are also much whiter than a first-winter Mew. In its second winter, the Mediterranean Gull is much more distinctive, resembling the adult but with black fingers on the outer primaries, which produce a distinctive pattern both in flight and at rest.

With the bulk of the world population breeding on the Black Sea coast of the USSR, and just a few hundred pairs breeding on Mediterranean shores (in Greece, Italy and France), it is easy to wonder how the species got its name. A map of the total distribution, summer, and winter combined, shows that it is centred around the Mediterranean, where the bulk of the population winter. Elsewhere small numbers winter around the shores of the North Sea, English Channel and southern Baltic.

The main breeding colonies are in the southern USSR, with over 170,000 pairs at the Tendra Bay reserve. A marked increase there in recent years has been matched by the increasingly regular records of occasional birds breeding in north west Europe. Breeding was first proved in Britain in 1968, and reached a maximum of four pairs in 1984. As often happens when isolated colonists try to breed well away from a species' main range, many of the attempts have involved Mediterranean Gulls paired with Black-headed Gulls.

Mediterranean Gulls breed colonially, sometimes in vast numbers. They arrive on their breeding grounds where, from April onwards, they are very pugnacious, constantly bickering and pecking. Display involves the male, with his head thrown back and wings slightly drooped towards the ground, giving the 'long-call', a 'whaa-whaa-whaa-whaa-whaa--oo-ah' (that recalls a Lesser Black-backed Gull in quality, rather than Black-headed). The nest is placed on bare sandy ground or in low vegetation, and is a shallow scrape lined with grass and sometimes a few feathers. Laying takes place from mid-May to the end of June, and the normal clutch comprises three eggs, creamy to buff, speckled and spotted with dark brown. Both sexes take

RIGHT *An immature Mediterranean Gull which, in this plumage, might be confused with a young Mew Gull. However, note the dusky sides to face, the very contrasting upperwing pattern, and the more robust, slightly drooping bill.*

part in incubation, which lasts from 23 to 25 days. The young are brooded on the nest while they are small, but after a few days they become more adventurous, leaving the nest and hiding in the surrounding vegetation.

Post-breeding dispersal takes place from late June onwards, and the gingery young spread out in all directions, with the major exodus of birds from the Black Sea occurring in September. In winter they can be found on the Atlantic coast of Morocco, Portugal and Spain. As already noted, increasing numbers are also found on the coasts of the English Channel and North Sea. Vagrants have occurred north to Sweden and Norway, west to the Azores and south to Kuwait and Kenya.

Although primarily a salt-water species, occasional birds winter inland, especially in north west Europe. The species occurs in all situations that attract gulls: around fish quays, following trawlers, on rubbish dumps and around sewage outfalls. Their food consists of small fish and marine snails, as well as earthworms and a variety of insects for those wintering inland.

RIGHT *A first-winter Mediterranean Gull showing blackish eye crescent and ear coverts which give the impression of a distinct face patch. The back is a pale grey whilst the outer primaries are conspicuously black.*

BELOW *In summer plumage the Mediterranean Gull with its black head, broken white eye ring, scarlet bill with yellow tip and scarlet legs is relatively easy to identify. In this picture it is flanked by a Mew Gull both left and right.*

LAUGHING GULL

LARUS ATRICILLA

A rather distinctive species, the Laughing Gull is characterized at all ages by its rather heavy, dark, 'drooping' bill which, together with a long sloping forehead, give its head a rather snout-like profile. A little larger than Franklin's Gull, the Laughing Gull is about the size of a Mew Gull. It has proportionally rather longer legs and longer, slender and more pointed wings than either of these species, which give it a rather rakish appearance, both on the ground and in the air.

The adult is dark grey above, about the same shade as a Franklin's Gull, and has the same neat, contrastingly white trailing edge to the wing. However, the wingtips are solidly black, with no white 'mirrors' or primary tips, but unlike Franklin's Gull the tail is all white. In summer plumage, the Laughing Gull has a black hood with a broken white eye-ring, which is slightly narrower than Franklin's. The bill and legs are dull red. In winter plumage the head is white, with a variably streaked greyish-brown wash on the ear-coverts and rear-crown compared with the rather solid 'half-hood' of

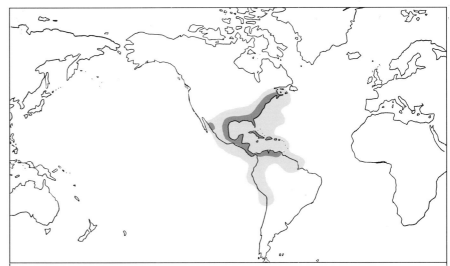

SIZE 15-17 in (38-43 cm)	EGG COLOUR Buffy to olive, spotted with brown over grey or purple
WINGSPAN 39-42 in (99-107 cm)	INCUBATION 20-23 days
EGG CLUTCH Three	FLEDGLING 24 days

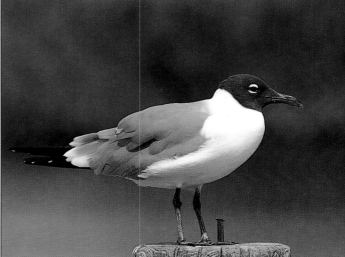

LEFT *A Laughing Gull in winter plumage. Note the mostly grey underwing, white trailing edge to the secondaries and the all-white tail.*

ABOVE *An adult Laughing Gull in full breeding plumage is most likely to be confused with Franklin's Gull but this latter species is noticeably smaller.*

a winter Franklin's Gull. The bill and legs are blackish.

A juvenile Laughing Gull is very dark. The feathers of the mantle and wing-coverts are greyish-brown with neat pale fringes that produce a scalloped pattern. The flight feathers are blackish, while the rump is white and the tail has a wide blackish terminal band. The head, neck, breast and flanks are washed dull brown, with a paler, whitish forehead and throat, and the same white 'spectacles' as the adult. The bill and legs are blackish. All in all, it is rather similar to a Franklin's Gull, but differs not only in size and shape, but also in a darker, more heavily marked underwing.

Like all gulls, the Laughing Gull assumes its first-winter plumage by moulting its head and body feathers only. Thus the first-winter has the same pattern on the wing-coverts, flight feathers and tail as a juvenile. However the scaly mantle feathers are replaced by uniform dark grey ones, and the brownish wash on the head and body by a greyish wash. At rest it appears largely grey with a whitish forehead, chin and belly, while in flight it appears largely sooty-brown. I well remember the early difficulty I had in reconciling the dull brown gull that I had seen wheeling in the distance around a fishing fleet, with the steely grey bird that then spent the afternoon loafing on a tourist beach. The extensive grey breast band, rear-crown and nape, and wide tail-band (extending onto the outer feathers) separate first-winters from Franklin's Gulls. Second-year birds resemble adults, but still show traces of a dark bar on the tail and secondaries, with more extensive black tips to the wings. The best distinction from sub-adult Franklin's Gulls, which lack the diagnostic white markings at the wingtips, is the very different shape.

The Laughing Gull breeds on the east coast of North America, from Nova Scotia south to Florida, around the Gulf Coast to Mexico, on the Caribbean Islands and south to Venezuela. On the Pacific Coast it breeds in Mexico, from Sonora to Sinaloa. Northern populations are migratory, with the southward passage beginning in August. It can be found in the winter from North Carolina south along the coasts of South America to northern Brazil and northern Chile, also occasionally as far north as California. The species has also been recorded from Hawaii, Greenland, Morocco and Western Europe, with records from Sweden and Austria. Over 45 have been seen in the British Isles, all but two since 1966. They have been well scattered around the country, and recorded throughout the year.

Mainly a coastal species, the Laughing Gull is found on sea coasts, bays and estuaries, and may

follow ships well out to sea. Though generally found on rivers only in tidal reaches, birds will often visit fresh water near the coast to bathe and preen. They also visit coastal farming areas to follow the plough or feed on earthworms. Otherwise, they are rare inland, though fairly regular on the Great Lakes, especially Erie and Michigan, and in summer and early autumn on the Salton Sea in southern California. They feed on small fish, which they may catch themselves or steal from Brown Pelicans. To do this they will even sit on the pelican's head to get their food. They will sometimes steal eggs, and also scavenge like other gulls, but perhaps not so persistently as some species.

The Laughing Gull breeds colonially, each pair building a nest of grass, weeds and other vegetation on the ground. The nest is usually on sandy areas with plenty of low vegetation, but also sometimes on salt-marshes or even, in warmer latitudes, under mangroves. The normal clutch is three, laid by North American birds from April to July. The eggs are buffy to olive, spotted and blotched with brown over grey or purple. The birds incubate for 20 to 23 days, and the young fledge from July onwards. The species gets its name from its call, which is a strident, laughing 'ha-ha-ha'.

A winter-plumaged Laughing Gull showing the long, narrow wings tapering to thin points and projecting well beyond the tail.

FRANKLIN'S GULL

LARUS PIPIXCAN

This small, hooded gull breeds in interior North America on prairie sloughs, lakes and marshes from northern Alberta, south to north west Utah and north west Iowa. Though numbers are reported to be decreasing, it remains a common bird.

Rather larger than a Little Gull, Franklin's Gull is distinctly smaller than Laughing Gull or Black-headed Gull, though at times this may be difficult to appreciate. Compared to Laughing Gull, it is much more compact, with a higher and more rounded crown, relatively shorter bill, shorter legs, and broader, more paddle-shaped wings. In flight its shape may recall a Little Gull.

In adult plumage, the upperparts are mid- to dark grey, neatly set-off by a white trailing edge to the wing. However, the most distinctive feature is the wingtips. The outer primaries are tipped white, backed by a blackish band and, most importantly, a further narrow white band which separates the tips from the grey of the wings. This pattern immediately distinguishes it from Laughing Gull, on which the grey of the wing grades into solidly black wingtips with no white at all. Another diagnostic feature (though usually difficult to see) is that the centre of the tail is pale grey.

In summer plumage the hood is black with a broken white eye-ring, the bill is red with a narrow black subterminal band, the feet are red, and the underparts may show a delicate rosy flush. In winter plumage there is a blackish 'half-hood' on the back of the head, while the bill and feet have faded to dull red or blackish. The sexes are similar.

Juveniles are brown scaled with white above, with blackish outer primaries and a white trailing edge to the wing. The forehead and underparts are whitish, and the tail shows a blackish terminal band. The bill and legs are blackish. Even at this early age, it shows the broken white eye-ring and grey centre to the tail. Franklin's Gull reaches maturity in its third calendar year. Immatures do not show the diagnostic wingtip pattern of the adult and, like winter adults, only show a half-hood and have blackish bills and legs. They also generally have whitish underparts and a narrow, dark tail band which, importantly, does not extend right across the tail. They can be distinguished from Laughing Gulls by their size, shape and grey centres to their tails and half-hoods.

Franklin's Gull is easily separated from Bona-

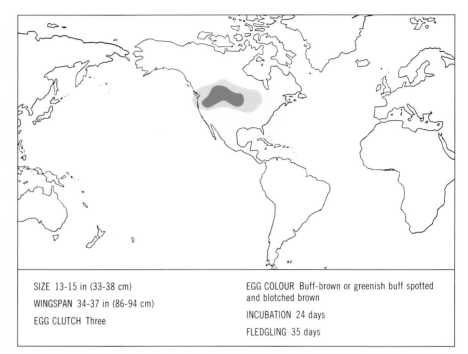

SIZE 13-15 in (33-38 cm)

WINGSPAN 34-37 in (86-94 cm)

EGG CLUTCH Three

EGG COLOUR Buff-brown or greenish buff spotted and blotched brown

INCUBATION 24 days

FLEDGLING 35 days

parte's Gull by the rather darker upperparts, stouter bill and distinctive wingtip pattern. Bonaparte's lacks the thick white broken eye-ring shown by Franklin's at all ages, and in winter or immature plumage it has a white head, with just a small dark spot on the ear-coverts.

The species breeds colonially, the birds returning to the breeding grounds in April. On arrival, they can often be seen in large flocks following the plough across the prairie fields or feeding on areas of short grass. Extremely agile, they may hawk insects or dip down to the surface of the water to pick up morsels of food.

Once settled, each pair builds a floating nest from scraps of vegetation, anchored to the bottom of a lake or marsh. The usual clutch is three eggs, which are buffy to olive-brown, irregularly spotted and blotched with darker brown. Laying takes place in May and June. Both male and female incubate, the eggs hatching after 24 days and the young fledging in early August. Although generally rather silent, breeding birds may give a soft 'krruk'.

Franklin's Gull winters in South America, on sea coasts and in estuaries, as well as around lakes, rivers and marshes. From the breeding grounds, they move south across the Great Plains and the

Rockies and then down the west coast of the Americas as far south as the Straits of Magellan at the tip of Chile. The bulk of the population winters from Guatemala southwards, but a few are recorded in winter as far north as southern California and the Gulf Coast. At all times of the year it is a gregarious species, but most especially on migration.

On passage, it is a rare migrant on both the east and west coasts, which perhaps makes its occurrences in Europe rather surprising. Since the first report in 1970 however, there have been eleven widely scattered records in Britain. There are also records of vagrants from Hawaii, South Africa and Tristan da Cunha in the South Atlantic.

A Franklin's Gull in summer plumage shows a rather squat appearance while the rounded head and stoutish bill help separate it from the similar Laughing Gull.

LITTLE GULL

LARUS MINUTUS

The world's smallest gull, this bird really lives up to both its scientific and vernacular names for it is indeed minute. It is probably more tern-like in its actions and behaviour than any gull. Certainly its airy, buoyant flight and its habit of picking food from the surface of the water when on the wing suggest a tern, or more especially marsh tern rather than a gull.

At sea mainly small fish are taken, while in other situations a whole variety of invertebrates are its prey. A large number of insects also feature in its diet, including dragonflies, mayflies, and stoneflies.

In summer plumage there is a superficial resemblance to the Black-headed Gull, but whereas the latter has a brown hood, the Little Gull has a completely black head. The underparts are white, and when in full breeding condition shows a suffusion of pink on the breast, while the back and upperwing are pale blue grey. The short legs are red and the small, pointed bill is reddish brown. However at all seasons it is the dark underwing that quickly identifies the adult of the species, even at long distances over the sea. At such times the light upper surface and the dark under surface appear to flicker, an effect further heightened when viewed against a lowering sun. It will also be noted that the wingtips have a slightly rounded look and the tail is square-ended, unlike any tern.

In May birds start to arrive back at their breeding grounds, which are lakesides or the lowland fresh-water wetlands of river basins, where there is plenty of lush vegetation and emergent plant-life. Some also favour the coast. The monogamous pair bond is established by a series of display flights, when the male circles, calling with a shrill, rapid, rhythmic 'ke-ko ke-ko'. At other times it is a silent bird. It will often attack nearby birds, with the prospective mate joining in to repulse encroachment by neighbours into the pair's airspace.

The chosen nest site is usually in wet vegetation close to, or in, shallow water, but occasionally it might be on a bare sand bank. Dependent upon the habitat type, the nest may be no more than a scrape lined with a few pieces of grass in a drier situation, or a much more substantial structure that may be semi-floating in a watery situation. Both birds take part in the next building. The usual clutch comprises two to three eggs which are smooth, olive green, marked with blotches of grey, brown or black.

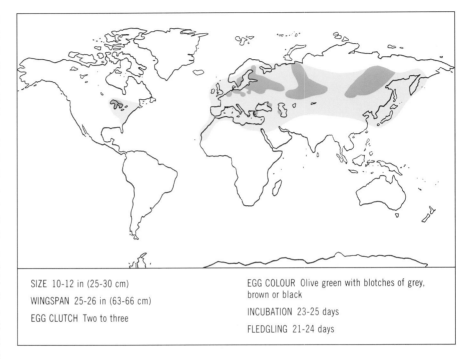

SIZE 10-12 in (25-30 cm)

WINGSPAN 25-26 in (63-66 cm)

EGG CLUTCH Two to three

EGG COLOUR Olive green with blotches of grey, brown or black

INCUBATION 23-25 days

FLEDGLING 21-24 days

Incubation takes 23 to 25 days and is undertaken by both parents.

A few days after hatching the young chicks will wander away from the actual nest, but they are fed and cared for by the parents for around 21 to 24 days, by which time they are virtually free flying.

The parents and juvenile birds leave the colony together towards the end of July, but the family groups soon split up to disperse throughout the main wintering areas of the Black Sea, the Mediterranean and beyond. Many reach the North Sea via the Baltic, and off the Dutch coast daily totals of over a thousand birds are noted in autumn. Lesser numbers are recorded in British waters, with some often penetrating inland to occur singly or in small groups at the large reservoirs. In the main such occurrences are sporadic. At Radipole Lake, Weymouth, on the south coast of Britain, they are quite frequent and this location is considered to be one of the best places in Britain to see the species. There is also some overland passage in Europe along principal river systems.

Throughout the winter Little Gulls can be found from the English Channel south to north west Africa. The Siberian population moves to winter in the Japan Sea.

LEFT *An adult Little Gull in breeding plumage displays its characteristic black underwing and head and red legs.*

ABOVE *A Little Gull in winter plumage is distinguished from the Black-headed Gull by its dull red legs, black bill, dusky grey crown, dark ear spot, and minute size.*

The small American population, where nesting was first recorded near Toronto in 1962 and in the USA in 1975, disperses through the Great Lakes to spend the winter along the coasts of the Atlantic states, south to Long Island. It is occasionally noted in Florida and more rarely inland, but is most infrequent on the west coast of the USA.

The juvenile Little Gull is quite distinctive and in its first-year plumage shows black outer primaries which contrast sharply with the grey, white-tipped, inner primaries. This pattern of black continues from the carpal joint across the secondary coverts to form an 'M' pattern along the whole of the wing. However the juvenile kittiwake shows a similar field mark and care is required in separating the two species. The major difference is their size and if seen side by side they present no problem. Otherwise, the young kittiwake has a blackish collar, which shows quite well in flight. The Little Gull does not normally show this neck mark, though there are blackish brown patches on the side of the breast at this age. It also has a white head with a blackish crown and blackish brown ear spots. The upperparts, mantle and scapulars are blackish brown, edged with white, which gives the wing a scaly look. The rump and tail are white, the latter showing a black sub-terminal band. The bill is black and the legs a pale flesh colour. By the first summer it begins to develop the black hood, but it is a further two years before it is fully mature.

In winter plumage the adult has a white head with a noticeable black ear spot and the bill is black.

Little Gulls breed mainly in eastern and western Siberia, locally in the Baltic basin and in isolated colonies in the Netherlands, Denmark and Sweden. They also nest in south east Europe, mainly Poland and the Black Sea area. Its numbers have fluctuated markedly in many areas of its range and there have been scattered attempts to extend the western parts of its range which have brought about attempts to breed in Britain. If successful, it would be a welcome addition to the British breeding birds list.

SABINE'S GULL

LARUS SABINI

This species was first encountered by the 1818 Ross expedition which was searching for the North West Passage. A number of specimens were collected and described by one of its members, Edward Sabine. Examples of this 'new' gull were returned to England and shown to the Linnaean Society. As was the custom, the bird was named after the original discoverer. In later years Sabine's Gulls were to be discovered and identified well away from their original remote Arctic breeding grounds and subsequently proved to be regular visitors to European waters, with increasing numbers noted in Britain as the years went by. Even so, until almost the mid-twentieth-century, its status was still that of a scarce autumn and winter visitor. Indeed, the infrequency of occurrences in British waters required that all records be adjudged by the British Birds Rarities Committee. However, in 1963, it was decided to remove this species from the rarities list as over the previous five years more than ten acceptable records a year were being submitted by various observers. Some of these records were made in the month of September. In 1957 a small passage of Sabine's Gulls was noted off St Ives (Cornwall) and it was suggested at the time that this could very well be a regular event, and so it subsequently proved to be. On 29 September 1969 I saw two for myself, one being chased by a Great Skua! This paled into insignificance when over a hundred, almost all adults, were noted there after an exceptional storm on 3 September 1983. In more recent years records have also come from some inland waters, one such place being Draycote Water (Warwickshire), where I was fortunate enough to find one on 30 September 1985. As the number of competent observers increases, so the regularity with which the species is now annually recorded will undoubtedly continue around Britain.

A circumpolar breeding bird, the Sabine's Gull nests in West Alaska, Greenland, the Canadian Arctic and eastern Siberia. A small number have on occasions bred in Spitsbergen, but the few proved cases have only been single pairs.

In its summer plumage this is one of the most handsome of the gulls, with its grey head separated from the white neck and body by a narrow black collar. The upper parts are bluish grey and when at rest the black primaries show prominent white patches. The bill is black with a yellow tip and, if it

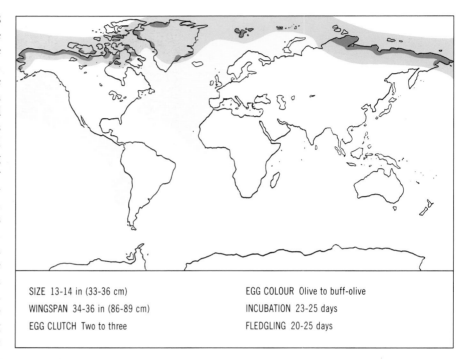

SIZE 13-14 in (33-36 cm)

WINGSPAN 34-36 in (86-89 cm)

EGG CLUTCH Two to three

EGG COLOUR Olive to buff-olive

INCUBATION 23-25 days

FLEDGLING 20-25 days

can be seen, it will be noted that the gape is red. The legs are black.

It is in flight however that this bird shows its most distinctive field mark, a striking arrangement of black, grey and white triangles in the wing. Grey in the middle (greyish brown in the immature bird), with black on the outer primaries and white on the secondaries and inner primaries. The tail is slightly forked with a black subterminal band in the immature bird.

When feeding over water, this graceful little gull (it is the third smallest of the Laridae in the Western Palaearctic), hovers and swoops like a tern to pick food from the surface. Occasionally it will dive, rather clumsily, for fish. It also takes food in other ways, such as scavenging the tideline, pecking at insects or crustacea in wader-like fashion, or spinning on the water like a phalarope. It has also been known to take the eggs of nearby nesting Arctic Terns and even those of its own kind.

The calls of the Sabine's Gull are hard and grating (not dissimilar to those of an Arctic Tern). The species is most vociferous on its breeding grounds.

The nesting season lasts from May to August, with birds arriving at the breeding site already

RIGHT *A group of Sabine's Gulls returning to their still snow-scattered breeding areas, reveal their distinctive flight pattern of black, white and grey, a feature which identifies them in winter or summer.*

BONAPARTE'S GULL

LARUS PHILADELPHIA

In the first days of spring a small roadside pond may be graced by a flock of Bonaparte's Gulls, on their way north to their taiga breeding grounds. As they dip and hawk over the water, the leading edge of their wings flashes white and they constantly give their distinctive chattering calls, a Coot-like (*Fulica americana*) cackling. Moving on, they may stop to hawk insects over cultivated fields, or rest for a while against the dark of the plough before continuing northwards.

The adult is pale grey above, with whitish outer primaries tipped black that serve to distinguish it from all the other common North American gulls. In summer plumage, it has a slate-black hood with white crescents above and below the eye, the bill is black with a reddish base and the legs are reddish-orange. For a brief period, in very fresh plumage, there is a lovely rosy flush to the underparts. In winter it loses its black hood, having instead just two small blackish spots – one just in front of the eye and the other on the ear-coverts. The juvenile has a white head with two blackish spots, like a winter adult's, as well as a blackish crown. It has brown upperparts, mottled with buff, and a white rump and tail, with a blackish terminal band across the latter. The wing-coverts are a mixture of pale grey and blackish feathers, the darker feathers forming a 'carpal bar' across the wing. The flight feathers are pale grey-white, with a black trailing edge to the primaries and secondaries, as well as blackish outer primaries. The bill is black and the legs fleshy. The first-winter is similar, but the brown of the mantle is replaced with pale grey and the black crown is lost. By its second winter, it resembles the adult.

Bonaparte's Gull is very similar to the Black-headed Gull, but Bonaparte's Gull is slightly smaller, and rather more dainty and acrobatic, often picking food off the surface of the water like a tern, trailing its legs as it does so. At all ages the best distinction, apart from size and shape, is the all-white underwing, especially the underside of the primaries. These are slightly translucent when viewed against the light, and they show a neat, clear-cut black trailing edge. The upperwing pattern is almost identical to that of a Black-headed Gull. The bill is slightly more slender than a Black-headed Gull's and is usually rather darker (often blackish). The upperparts are a shade darker grey,

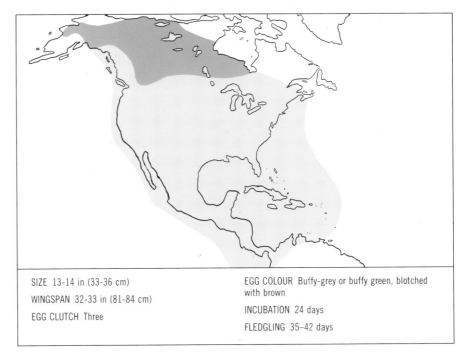

SIZE 13-14 in (33-36 cm)	EGG COLOUR Buffy-grey or buffy green, blotched with brown
WINGSPAN 32-33 in (81-84 cm)	INCUBATION 24 days
EGG CLUTCH Three	FLEDGLING 35–42 days

and this, colour characteristically extends onto the hind-neck and sides of the breast in winter and immature plumages. First-year birds are also distinguished by fine details of the wing pattern, especially the black outer primary coverts (these are pale grey in Black-headed Gull, with dark *inner* primary coverts), and the more uniformly dark trailing edge.

The breeding range is Alaska and Canada east to northern Manitoba, extending south to southern British Columbia and central Ontario. The species favours the muskeg – open, coniferous woodland – usually near ponds and lakes in lowland areas. The birds arrive on the breeding grounds from April onwards, before the snow has fully melted. Very unusually for a gull, the nest is seldom on the ground. Rather it is placed in a tree, usually a spruce, and is composed of twigs, grass, moss and lichen. The clutch normally comprises three eggs, laid in June or July, which are coloured buffy-grey or buffy-green, and blotched and spotted with brown. They are incubated for 24 days.

Bonaparte's Gull feeds on crustacea and insects, which are picked from the surface of the water either in flight, or while swimming. Flocks are quite 'talkative', but the cry is rather feeble.

Outside the breeding season Bonaparte's Gull is primarily coastal, being found in bays and harbours, and on sand and mudflats. However it also occurs inland on rivers and marshes, especially around the Great Lakes, and often feeds in flooded fields. Birds begin departing for the breeding grounds in August, and may form large flocks, sometimes comprising tens of thousands of individuals. In the winter they can be found on the American west coast from Washington south to Sinaloa in Mexico, where, for example, I have seen the first birds of the winter at Abbots Lagoon Point Reyes National Seashore, California in the first weeks of October; they also occur from the Great Lakes south along the major rivers, especially the Mississippi, to the Gulf Coast (south to the Yucatan peninsula), and around the Caribbean islands. On the east coast they can be found from Massachusetts southwards.

The species has occurred as a vagrant in Hawaii, the Azores and in Western Europe, with as many as 50 records in Britain and Ireland where, unlike several other American gulls, occurrences are clearly concentrated in the south and west.

ABOVE *A small, dainty bird, this winter-plumaged Bonaparte's Gull resembles a miniature Black-headed Gull. On both sides of the Atlantic birders scrutinize the indigenous species in the hope of discovering it to be the other!*

RIGHT *A Bonaparte's Gull in summer plumage at its nest which, unlike most other species of its genus, is placed in a tree.*

COMMON BLACK-HEADED GULL

LARUS RIDIBUNDUS

The shape, form and generally white plumage of most of the gull family is familiar to everyone. This species is as widely known as any in Europe, for it is widespread and common throughout its range. A Palaearctic species, it can be found breeding in Iceland, the Faroes, the British Isles, then eastward through central and northern Europe to Asia including the shores of the Black and Caspian Seas, and onwards to the Sea of Okhotsk and the Kamchatka Peninsula. To Europeans, it is probably second only to the Herring Gull in its long association with man. It frequents not only seaside towns, but in some cases the very heart of big cities far from the coast where it will fearlessly take food from the hand.

One of the smaller gulls, it can look deceptively large on the wing as it drifts by in effortless flight. As well as frequenting all manner of coastal and freshwater habitats, Black-headed Gulls are regularly seen scavenging on rubbish dumps, squabbling over bread thrown to them in public parks and feeding on agricultural land where they follow

SIZE 15-17 in (38-43 cm)	EGG COLOUR Pale blue to greenish, to deep brown, blotched dark brown
WINGSPAN 36-37 in (91-94 cm)	INCUBATION 22-24 days
EGG CLUTCH Two to three	FLEDGLING 35-42 days

A Black-headed Gull in first-winter plumage side-swoops above the water, calling as it goes. It has no doubt sighted a possible food source that it intends to investigate.

the plough. As its behaviour suggests, it will eat all manner of food. In coastal settings any marine life that it can swallow will be taken. It frequently plunge-dives over water and occasionally tramples wet mud or sand in order to bring worms to the surface. On newly ploughed fields or on grassy pastures it will wait for Lapwings to find a morsel which it promptly steals from them. In warm sunny weather it can at times be observed spiralling upwards feeding on flying insects carried aloft on thermals.

In breeding plumage the adult Black-headed Gull has pale grey upperparts with blackish wing-tips. The underparts are white and the head and face is a dark chocolate brown, giving a hooded effect: at a distance this looks black, hence the bird's name. There is an incomplete white ring round the eye, while the bill and legs are red. The sexes are similar. In winter, the dark coloured hood is repla-ced by just a dark smudge behind the eye. The time at which birds moult into this plumage varies enormously and individuals can be seen with com-pletely dark brown hoods early in the year, whilst others are still in nuptial dress well after breeding has been completed.

Juvenile birds have dull orange, flesh-coloured legs and bill, the latter tipped with black. The head of the young bird generally shows a partial ginger-buff hood, while ginger-brown feathering edged with white gives the back a somewhat scaly appear-ance. In its first winter the head becomes whiter, with a pronounced blackish ear spot, and the back by then is mostly pale grey.

By the end of its second winter it is more or less as the adult bird, with some individuals attaining a full brown hood by the turn of the year. In all plumages the leading edge of the wing is white, and this is the surest means of immediate identification, except in areas where the Slender-billed Gull might commonly be found.

In winter, birds scatter far and wide; inland as well as around coasts. In March they drift back to their breeding areas, where they make a great deal of noise fighting and squabbling and consolidating the pair bond, for many arrive at the chosen nesting site already paired. Black-headed Gulls are noisy birds and their raucous calls fill the air, with the most distinguishable note, a harsh 'kwarp' or 'kawup'. By mid-April breeding is usually well under way. Nests are quickly constructed in a few days, both sexes contributing to the effort.

The type and size of nest varies considerably depending on the location. In tussocky, marshy situations, typical of many upland colonies in Wales that I know, the nest will be a sizeable construction of reeds and grasses. In a flat, drier

setting the nest can comprise but a few strands of grass, straw or other handy materials. The eggs are generally laid from mid-April into May, or some-times in June as well if the first clutch is lost.

Two or three in number, they vary considerably in colour from pale blue to greenish to deep brown, blotched dark brown: sometimes a clutch will contain one blue, unmarked egg. Incubation from the first egg is 22 to 24 days. Five to six weeks after hatching the young are fully fledged. Colonies vary considerably from a few pairs to hundreds.

In Britain the Black-headed Gull has the widest breeding distribution of all the gulls. Like others of the Laridae, its numbers have increased consider-ably in recent times, as it has benefited from man's activities in exploiting food sources such as rubbish tips and sewage outfalls. Sand and gravel workings and reservoirs are used for roosting and in winter months many large roosts form in inland reservoirs. All this is a marked change from the situation no further back than the early 1930s, when in the British Midlands, for example, a concentration of 150 at a reservoir was considered notable. By the 1960s and 1970s estimated numbers of roosting Black-headed Gulls throughout the West Midlands region had risen from 10,000 to 15,000 (pre-1955) to between 150,000 and 250,000. One reservoir alone (Draycote Water in Warwickshire) was attracting between 80,000 to 100,000 during that period. In more recent years there has been some slight contraction from these very high numbers.

In North America it is a rare visitor and all Bonaparte's Gulls are scrutinized by birders in the hope one might be *L. ridibundus*. Small numbers have occurred in Newfoundland, Nova Scotia and New Brunswick in recent times.

ABOVE *A Black-headed Gull in full summer plumage stands over its eggs. The nest is a fairly substantial construction, typical of an inland, waterside, breeding location.*

PREVIOUS PAGE *A flock of foraging Black-headed Gulls in winter. Most birds show the dark smudge of their non-breeding dress behind the eye. However, even though it is February, at least two birds are already showing signs of the dark hood of breeding plumage.*

SLENDER-BILLED GULL

LARUS GENEI

The fragmented breeding range of this species suggests it is possibly in decline globally. However, though its numbers have gone down at some locations in recent times, particularly in Romania, it has increased in others.

The two main strongholds for the Slender-billed Gull are the Black Sea and Caspian Sea. In the Black Sea area alone it is estimated that well over 100,000 pairs nest in some years. It also breeds at Sea of Azov, in Egypt, Iraq, Sardinia, Turkey, the Persian Gulf and the Makran coast east to Karachi.

Breeding has also occurred irregularly and with variable success in Algeria, the Canary Islands, France, Greece, Morocco, and Tunisia. In 1959 a colony was discovered in the Banc D'Arguin in Mauritania and there may well be other undiscovered West African sites.

It is mainly a bird of sheltered lowland coasts around seas that are more or less landlocked. Here it breeds in a variety of sites, including islands, beaches of shallow tidal water, meadows and moist grassland close to marine inlets, and brackish or

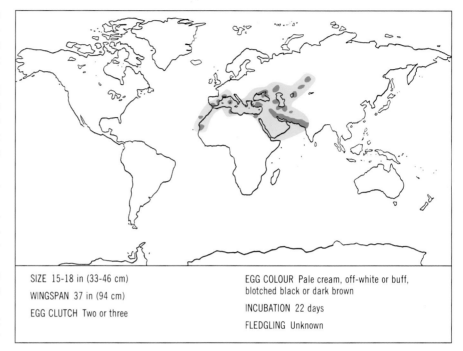

SIZE 15-18 in (33-46 cm)

WINGSPAN 37 in (94 cm)

EGG CLUTCH Two or three

EGG COLOUR Pale cream, off-white or buff, blotched black or dark brown

INCUBATION 22 days

FLEDGLING Unknown

An adult Slender-billed Gull beginning to moult out of its breeding plumage. The white leading forewing is reminiscent of the Black-headed Gull but the more prominent bill shape is an obvious distinguishing feature of the Slender-billed Gull.

A Slender-billed Gull in first-winter plumage but showing the pale straw iris of an adult. There is only a faint ear spot while the more substantial orange-coloured bill should help to identify the species.

freshwater lagoons in deltas or broad river valleys. In these settings it frequently associates with the terns. In some areas of the USSR, it breeds around inland seas as well as on more elevated mountain lakes. Often it chooses rocky islets where it will nest in quite large numbers.

The Slender-billed Gull can generally be compared to the slightly smaller Black-headed Gull, which it closely resembles at all ages, though it never has a dark hood. However, the neck and tail are longer, while the head looks smaller. This long-necked feature is most noticeable when it is standing. It then appears to be stretching its neck to see what is going on around it. Despite its name, the bill is not slender but is longer, more pointed and heavier than a Black-headed Gull's. At a distance it appears black though it is actually dark red. The Slender-billed and Black-headed Gulls also share a similar wing pattern, both having a white forewing; it is this feature that possibly leads to misidentification of immature birds, especially where both species are found together. In flight the neck has a 'drooped' look, with the head and bill tilted downwards.

In breeding plumage the Slender-billed Gull shows a strong pink flush on the white underparts. At close range it will be seen that the white iris is surrounded by a red orbital ring. The bill, feet and legs are also red.

It is also similar to the Black-headed Gull in its feeding actions, picking food from the surface of the water, surface plunging, up-ending, foot paddling or generally scavenging to secure whatever fish, crustaceans or insects are available.

The voice is also much like a Black-headed Gull,

but its calls are deeper, mellower and more nasal.

Nesting commences April or May, when birds gather to form colonies that range from a dozen pairs to several hundred. Display and breeding rituals are much as the Black-headed Gull, but it is less aggressive and there are fewer quarrels despite their high nest densities.

The nest is a scrape or shallow depression lined with some feathers or various plant materials including seaweed. The rim becomes built up with droppings as nesting progresses.

A full clutch comprises two to three pale cream, off-white, or buff eggs, variably marked with blotches and spots of black or dark brown. These are laid May or June.

Incubation is carried out by both parents and lasts around 22 days. At a site in Bahrain the ornithologist Colonel Meinertzhagen observed that some birds sprinkled their eggs with sea water, to cool them he suggests.

The downy young show great variation of colour and can range from striped grey brown to pure buff and pure grey. Even within a single brood, chicks of a different colour can be found together. The young are fed and cared for by both parents, though the full fledging period is not yet known.

From July or August, after breeding, birds move away from their colonies, mostly to winter in the Mediterranean basin, Egypt and the Persian Gulf. However, it is resident in many parts of its range. Slender-billed Gulls wander but rarely to Britain, where the first was recorded in 1960. There have been only four other occurrences, with the most recent noted at Cley, Norfolk, where a pair was present from 12 to 15 May 1987.

HEERMANN'S GULL

LARUS HEERMANNI

The world's gulls fall into two categories, those with widespread distributions spanning continents and oceans, and those that are extremely localized and confined to just a few hundred miles of coastline. Heermann's Gull falls into the latter group, being endemic to the West Coast of America. The bulk of the population breeds on Raza Island in the Gulf of California, where there are over 600,000 pairs. Smaller colonies can be found in Baja California and off the coasts of Sinaloa and Nayarit in Mexico. There are also occasional breeding records from southern California, with one record of nesting as far north as the infamous island of Alcatraz (a suitable subject for study by the famous birdman!). Outside the breeding season, from June onwards, birds disperse both north and south, as far as Vancouver Island in British Columbia and Guatemala. Non-breeding birds can be found year-round in these areas. It is a very rare visitor to the Salton Sea in California, and vagrants have been recorded east to Texas, Michigan and Ohio.

Heermann's Gull is a very distinctive species, easily separated from other West Coast gulls. It is a dark, medium-sized, long-legged bird, about the size of a Ring-billed Gull. In all plumages the uniform greyish or dusky-brownish body plumage is distinctive, and in all but juvenile plumage it lacks the prominent pale scalloping and fringes that are present on other gulls in their dark immature plumage. However, in flight its long wings are usually held angled, and in the distance it is easy to mistake for a skua.

Breeding plumage is assumed from January onwards, the birds being white-headed, shading to a soft grey on the underparts and dark grey on the upperparts. The rump and upper tail-coverts are pale grey, contrasting with the blackish tail, which is narrowly rimmed white. The wing-coverts are dark grey like the upperparts, with blackish flight feathers and a narrow white trailing edge. The dark iris and red orbital ring combine to give it a dark, staring eye; the bill is red with a black subterminal band and tiny yellowish tip, and the legs are slate-grey. Non-breeding adults are similar, except that the head is heavily mottled with grey-brown and the bill is a duller red.

Juvenile Heermann's Gulls are entirely sooty-brown, with slightly paler fringes to the upperparts,

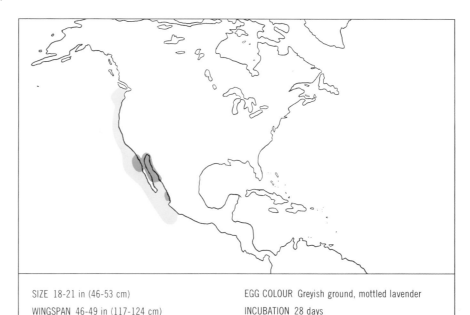

SIZE 18-21 in (46-53 cm)	EGG COLOUR Greyish ground, mottled lavender
WINGSPAN 46-49 in (117-124 cm)	INCUBATION 28 days
EGG CLUTCH Two or three	FLEDGLING Not known

Heerman's Gulls spend much of the day just loafing around and, typically, here is a first-winter bird standing along the rocky shore of Monterey Bay, California, wondering where the next meal is coming from.

Gulls tend to spend less time loafing around on the beach than other species of gull, rather they are more often seen flying buoyantly over the sea or foraging around kelp beds where they feed on fish, shrimps and other crustaceans. They also feed around flocks of Brown Pelicans, cormorants, seals, or even sea otters, from which they may pilfer food. They even steal fish from the bills of pelicans. Indeed, witnesses claim to have seen fish stolen from the throat of a pelican in the act of swallowing! Less often, they scavenge along the shore like other gulls. For example, they are readily noted at Monterey, California.

The usual breeding habitat is flat, rocky islets, usually with scattered clumps of grass. In some remote areas however, they will breed on the mainland. The birds return to their colonies in April. In the courtship display the male flutters over the female as she sits on the ground, while she responds by squatting down in an invitation to the male. The pair also engage in a kind of dance, holding each other's bills before backing off, calling all the while. The nest varies from a simple, unlined depression in gravel to a well-made construction of twigs, weeds and grass. The two or three eggs are laid in April or May. They are variable, with a generally greyish ground colour, mottled with lavender that in turn is spotted and blotched with brown or dark grey. The calls include an 'aow aow' and a laughing 'ah-ah-ah-ah-ah'.

ABOVE *In its breeding plumage the Heerman's Gull is unmistakable. It is the only gull found along the Californian coast (to where it is restricted), and has a white head, dusky underparts and a red bill with a black tip.*

and wing-coverts that form a scaly pattern, with a lighter area on the inner forewing. With wear, the plumage becomes browner. The bill and legs are blackish. First-winter birds are very similar, though a slightly greyer brown, differing most noticeably in the yellowish or fleshy base to their bill. Second-winter birds more closely resemble the adult, but have a much browner tone to their plumage. Their bill is reddish at the base and their legs are blackish. By the third-winter, they are like winter adults.

Rarely found away from the coast, Heermann's

LEFT *A second-winter Heerman's Gull shows some white in the secondary coverts while the orange-red, black-tipped bill and dark, sooty upperparts and paler grey underparts readily identify it.*

AUDOUIN'S GULL

LARUS AUDOUINII

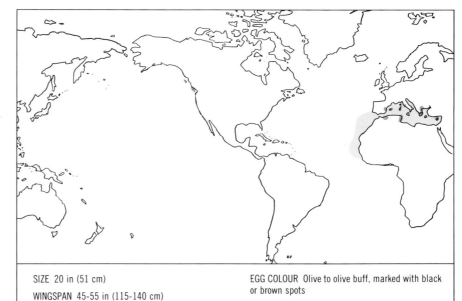

SIZE 20 in (51 cm)	EGG COLOUR Olive to olive buff, marked with black or brown spots
WINGSPAN 45-55 in (115-140 cm)	INCUBATION 28 days
EGG CLUTCH Two to three	FLEDGLING 30-40 days

With an estimated population of only 3500 or so pairs, this is considered to be the world's rarest gull.

As a breeding species, it is confined to the Mediterranean Basin, though within this region its complete distribution is still not known. Nesting is mainly centred on the islands of Cyprus, Sardinia, Corsica and the Balearics, plus a number of islets of western Italy. Other known locations include Libya, Morocco and Tunisia.

It was in 1826 that the French naturalist B. C. Payraudeau, after having recently returned from travels in Sardinia and Corsica, published the first description of Audouin's Gull. Payraudeau named the newly described gull after his friend, Jean Victor Audouin, who was actually better known for his entomological studies than for his ornithological pursuits. Any connection between the gull and Jean Victor Audouin must therefore be tenuous: a case of one scientist paying compliment to another.

Audouin's Gull falls between Herring Gull and Mew Gull in size and may well be confused with Herring Gull, especially the race *L. a. mictiahellis*, which also nests in the same Mediterranean region. However, Audouin's Gull is distinctly more slender and tapered looking when at rest. The head (which looks quite small) and underparts appear white at a distance, but the nape, sides of the breast, flanks, belly and upper rump are actually pale grey. This accentuates the white-headed and white-tailed appearance of this bird at certain angles. The longish legs look black at a distance, but are in fact olive green. Its main feature however is the bill. This is heavy, angular and bright red, with a yellow tip separated by a black band. At a distance the yellow tip is often invisible and the bill appears blackish and blunt-ended. When at rest the adult bird shows a row of white spots on the black primaries of the folded wing, and when alert the neck looks long and slender, emphasizing the smallness of the head. In flight it is a graceful bird, with slimmer wings than Herring Gull, on which it planes for long distances across the sea. At such times the black primaries are most apparent, forming a wedge-shaped patch in marked contrast to the pale grey inner wing. At long distance the white primary tips are hardly discernible. In second- and third-year birds the black wedge extends to the carpal joint which, coupled with a pale grey crown, dark mask behind the eye and brown upperparts, helps distinguish it from Herring Gull at these ages.

Audouin's Gull feeds almost exclusively on small fish, which it deftly picks from the surface with a lunge of its bill; at times it will briefly settle, without folding its wings, and plunge its head into the water to secure its prey. It is not a scavenger like most other Laridae and this feeding behaviour may

The Audouin's Gull favours well-vegetated, rocky coasts of islands for breeding and here an adult bird incubates its eggs at its Tuscany nest site.

An adult Audouin's Gull in flight might be confused with Herring Gull unless, as in this case, the bill can be clearly seen, though the lack of prominent white tips to the primaries is a feature of note.

most other Laridae and this feeding behaviour may well be a restrictive factor to its distribution.

Like other larger gulls, Audouin's Gull is not fully mature until it is five years of age. When they reach breeding condition, birds assemble at their chosen nest sites in early April. Favoured locations are stony, rocky slopes of islands, especially where bushes provide good ground cover, and it is here that small colonies are established. Nest building is carried out by both birds and the structure is typical of the Laridae, comprising a platform of grass and twigs with a shallow cup formed by the bird's body. A monogamous pair bond is established by various display rituals similar to those of the Common Gull. By the end of April or even into May, two to three eggs are laid. These are smooth and slightly glossy, coloured olive to olive buff, and variably marked with black or dark brown spots and blotches. Incubation is undertaken by both parents and lasts approximately 28 days. The downy young are very much like other gull chicks. After a day or two, they

leave the nest area to hide in the surrounding vegetation, from where they call to their parents with shrill, cheeping cries. They are fed by regurgitation. The length of the fledging period is not accurately known, but is probably between 30 to 40 days, though it is perhaps three to four months before the young are fully independent.

Outside the breeding season Audouin's Gull is not a very vocal species, but occasionally it utters a weak but harsh 'gi-erk'. When nesting, however, it becomes quite noisy with various braying calls and goose-like sounds. After nesting most birds disperse, mainly in a westerly direction which takes them beyond Gibraltar where they will winter off the Atlantic coasts of Morocco and the Spanish Sahara. Some birds do tend to remain in the area of the Mediterranean.

I have seen Audouin's Gulls passing Europa Point, Gibraltar in spring and like many other birders have been delighted to view them on the island of Majorca.

RING-BILLED GULL

LARUS DELAWARENSIS

A medium-sized species, the Ring-billed Gull is a familiar bird across North America and an increasingly familiar one in Europe. The subtle features which separate a Ring-billed from a Mew or Herring Gull provide a challenge for the birdwatcher interested in identification on both sides of the Atlantic.

At all times, one of the best clues to its identity is its size and shape. Compared with the Mew Gulls of the European race, it is slightly larger and heavier, with longer legs and a distinctly thicker bill. All in all, the jizz somewhat recalls the much larger Herring Gull and indeed, when size is difficult to judge, or with an especially large individual, Herring Gull is the frequently forgotten pitfall.

Adult Ring-billed Gulls are pale grey above (a shade or two paler than a Mew Gull) with extensive black wingtips marked by two white 'mirrors' on the outer primaries. The head is pure white in summer, but, together with the nape and sides of the neck, is marked with diffuse pale brown blotches

SIZE 18-21 in (45-53 cm)

WINGSPAN 47½-50 in (121-127 cm)

EGG CLUTCH Three

EGG COLOUR Buffy, spotted brown and purplish grey

INCUBATION 26 days

FLEDGLING 35 days

A young Ring-billed Gull, in its first-winter plumage, feeds on the remnants of a dead fish washed up on a Florida shoreline.

in winter plumage. They have a yellow bill with a broad, clear-cut subterminal band, hence the name. However, many Mew Gulls also show a dark subterminal band on the bill, so this is not such a good feature as it sounds. The legs are yellowish, and an important difference from the Mew Gull is that the iris is a pale yellow. This feature combined with the more angled crown, enhances the 'mean' expression.

First-year Ring-billed Gulls are similar to young Mew Gulls, but show more contrast in the upper-wing between the pale and dark areas. They lack the dark saddle of a Mew Gull, their mantle being the same pale grey as the adult, but they can be conclusively identified only by those minor details of the pattern of the dark centres to the tertials and wing-coverts. Indeed picking out a first-year Ring-billed Gull from a flock of Mew Gulls is one of the severest challenges facing the British gull enthu-siast. Fortunately the Mew Gull, of the American race has a conveniently more distinctive first-year plumage. It differs from the Ring-billed Gull by its brownish underparts and an almost entirely brown tail.

In first-year plumage, Ring-billed Gulls resemble a second-year Herring Gull, from which they have to be carefully distinguished. They have neat dark centres to the tertials and wing-coverts, rather than the rather messy, barred centres shown by Herring Gulls. Second-year Ring-billed Gulls are rather like adults, but usually show traces of a dark bar on the secondaries and a dark tail band. They also have more black on the outer wing, with only one small 'mirror', if any. By this age though, they have the pale iris and clearly ringed bill of the adult, and all these features are good ways of separating them from a second-year Mew Gull.

The Ring-billed Gull breeds widely across North America from Alberta to Labrador and Newfound-land, then southwards to northern California, South Dakota, Illinois and New York. A few also breed in south eastern British Columbia. In the summer some birds stray north to Alaska, Yukon and Mackenzie, as well as remaining throughout the wintering areas. Coastal-breeding populations have suffered a marked decline this century, but this has been surpassed by a dramatic increase in numbers in the eastern interior of North America.

For nesting, the species prefers rocky, grassy or sandy islands, but will also use isolated shorelines or occasionally marshes. Birds return to the colonies in March and April. In the courtship display the males bow to the females with swollen throats, and circumnavigate them, pumping their heads up and down. Ring-billed Gulls breed colonially, each pair building a nest from grass, weeds and refuse, which

they sometimes decorate with feathers. Nests are usually on the ground but have very occasionally been found in low trees. The eggs are buffy, spotted and blotched with brown and purplish grey. The normal clutch is three and the incubation period is probably around 26 days. The usual call, given in flight, is a 'kow kow kow', but when excited a bird on the ground will bob its head rapidly up and down, then throw its head backwards and give a laughing series of notes, rather similar to a Herring Gull's.

In the winter, Ring-billed Gulls can be found from British Columbia, the Great Lakes and Nova Scotia south to southern Mexico, the Gulf Coast, Florida, the Bahamas and the Greater Antilles, with a few as far south as El Salvador. Harbours, rubbish tips and sewage outfalls attract them, and they also follow ships or forage along the tideline. In the breeding season, they feed extensively in fields, often following the plough. Their food includes insects, worms and grubs, as well as rodents and occasionally birds' eggs; most food is taken from the ground but they will feed on flying insects.

Vagrants have been reported from Hawaii, Costa Rica, the Lesser Antilles and Honduras, whilst there has been a dramatic increase in the number of reports from Europe, fuelling speculation that this species may yet colonize the Old World. The first was recorded in Britain in 1973, but by 1987 it was averaging over 80 records a year and was decreed to be no longer an official rarity. Records occur throughout the year, with many birds staying for long periods, though the peak period is from Christmas until April. Occurrences are concentrated in western England, Wales and Ireland.

ABOVE *An adult Ring-billed Gull in flight shows only small white mirrors in the wing, but in this picture the yellow legs are a feature which helps identify the species in this plumage.*

PREVIOUS PAGE *Raucous cries fill the air as a colony of Ring-billed Gulls on Long Point, Ontario, Canada, establish their nesting territories at the beginning of the breeding season.*

MEW GULL

LARUS CANUS

Why it is called the 'Common' gull is a puzzle to many British birders, for it is certainly not the most numerous of the gulls in Britain as a whole or in England and Wales in particular; nor is it one of the world's most plentiful Laridae species. The term Mew Gull, used by the Americans for the race that occurs mainly along the west coast of the United States, would seem to be more appropriate. Indeed recently mooted name changes may well officially alter the present English misnomer to one that equates at least with its mewing call and not a supposed status. Even the scientific (Latin) name *canus*, given to it by Linnaeus, meaning hoary or grey, would hardly seem to be a noteworthy or definitive appellation. We perhaps find the reason for its misnomer in early listings by English ornithologists such as Willoughby (1678), who called it the Common Sea-mall, and Pennant (1776), who did in fact call it the Common Gull. This term, however, does not relate to its frequency of occurrence, but is used in the Middle English sense of the bird not having any particular distin-

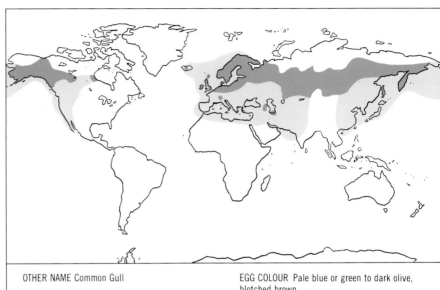

OTHER NAME Common Gull	EGG COLOUR Pale blue or green to dark olive, blotched brown
SIZE 16-18 in (40-46 cm)	
WINGSPAN 47-48 in (119-122 cm)	INCUBATION 22-28 days
EGG CLUTCH Two or three	FLEDGLING 35 days

The facial expression of the Mew Gull is gentler than most other gulls whilst the white, rounder headed appearance, smaller, all greenish-yellow bill and yellow legs readily identify it. Here an adult bird stands over its nest at a Shetland breeding location.

An adult Mew Gull incubates its eggs at a less conventional nest site, in this instance utilizing a derelict wooden pier.

guishing feature!

I am sure that today's birdwatcher would hardly describe the species as undistinguished, for certainly in breeding plumage it is a most attractive looking bird. Smaller than the similar looking Herring Gull, the noticeably rounder head, neck and body are pure white, with the mantle dark grey. When at rest the wings project further beyond the tail than the Herring Gull's, with the black primaries tipped with white. The bill is yellow and the legs greenish.

At close quarters it will be noted there is a red orbital ring around a dark eye. The flight is light and buoyant and the proportionately longer and thinner wings and more prominent 'mirrors' on the outer two primaries are usually obvious. Coupled with the smaller bill, these features should be sufficient to differentiate it from the heavier, more ponderous and thicker-billed Herring Gull.

During winter months the Mew Gull is possibly far more numerous in inland Britain, away from the coast, where it shows a distinct preference for grassland, with airfields and playing fields particularly attractive. At such locations earthworms appear to be a major part of its diet. Severe weather and long periods of frost will, however, drive some inland feeding and roosting birds to seek life support in tidal conditions, where all manner of invertebrates will be taken. It has also developed skua-like behaviour and will pursue other gulls, particularly Black-headed Gulls, in an attempt to make the victim drop or disgorge its prey. It has other feeding techniques, such as foot paddling and taking food from the surface of the water, either in flight or when swimming. It has also been recorded smashing shellfish by dropping them onto the sand. At sea it sometimes follows ships, while inland it joins other gulls and Lapwings (*Vanellus vanellus*) to follow the plough. Though less inclined than some other gulls to scavenge in urban situations, at times it frequents refuse tips, especially in hard weather.

Though many Mew Gulls feed inland, they prefer to roost on the coast, especially in Scotland and Wales where they will travel considerable distances to and from favoured sites. Large roosts are also to be found at some reservoirs well away from the sea, notably in the London area. Along with other gull species, increased feeding and roosting has been noted in Britain in relatively recent times. In the English Midlands in 1947, for example, it was considered exceptional when 150 were recorded roosting at Bartley Reservoir on the outskirts of Birmingham in February that year. Though numbers have not increased to the level of some other Laridae sp., one of the region's major waters, Draycote Water in Warwickshire, held an estimated 10,000 birds on 24 March 1979. However this would seem to have been an exceptional occurrence. It is believed the majority of the British and Irish wintering population of Mew Gulls come from Scandinavia, Denmark and Germany, with smaller numbers from Holland, the USSR and Iceland. Where British birds go to is not quite clear. However the British Trust for Ornithology's *Atlas of Wintering Birds in Britain and Northern Ireland* (BTO winter Atlas) estimates some 702,000 birds winter in Britain and Ireland, indicating that the area is a major wintering ground for the northwest European population.

As a breeding species the Mew Gull is almost circumpolar in the northern hemisphere with three subspecies. The nominate race, *L. c. canus*, breeds in Iceland and north west Europe south to Switzerland. The race *L. c. brachyrhynchus*, which is recognizably different from the nominate race in the field being generally darker and having a more uniform plumage, breeds from Alaska south along the coast to British Columbia and into north west Canada. The Siberian race, *L. c. kamtschatschensis*, breeds in eastern Siberia.

In spring, sometimes as early as March, but usually in April and May, birds arrive back at their breeding areas, some already paired. Nest site display is similar to that of the Herring Gull, with typical food begging, head tossing and long sessions of calling with head held upwards. On the coast the preferred nest site includes small rocky islets and islands, or grassy and rocky slopes. Inland it favours moorland with small pools or lochans but can also be found in other open areas, particularly on shingle bars or small islets on streams or rivers.

Mew Gulls nest in small colonies. Occasionally the nest site is well off the ground on stone walls, buildings (particularly so in Norway and Sweden) and even in specially provided nest boxes placed on poles. Tree nesting takes place in some areas. In Scotland they have been known to take over rooks' old nests, but in North America they are more inclined to utilize tree sites, located by tree-fringed lakes.

The nest varies from a lined scrape to a substantial platform of grass, seaweed or other vegetable matter, perhaps with the occasional feather or two included. The two to three eggs are pale blue or green to dark olive, with brown blotches, spots and streaks that are often concentrated at the larger end. These are laid in May or June, or sometimes as late as July, there being only one brood. Incubation lasts from 22 to 28 days and is undertaken by both parents, with a changeover every two to three hours. A day or so after hatching, the downy covered youngsters leave the nest of ground nesting sites but stay in the vicinity, being fed and cared for by both adult birds. The fledging period is around 35 days and they become totally independent very soon afterwards. The young, free-flying bird is generally brownish looking, being much darker than the adult on its underparts and showing pale edges to the feathering of the upperparts which give it a scaly look. By its first winter the head and

neck are whitish and the mantle, scapulars and back are clear grey. In flight the young bird shows a white rump and tail that has a sharply defined broad black terminal band. The primaries and most of the primary coverts are dark brown, the legs are flesh pink and the pink bill is tipped with black. It is at this age it may well be misidentified as a first winter Ring-billed Gull.

By its second year the head is whiter and less streaked, the upperparts are blue grey with the dark primaries showing 'white' mirrors on the two outer feathers and the tail is totally white. The bill is now yellowish or grey with a black tip. By its third year the bill has become yellowish, with a darker subterminal band, the mostly white head is streaked and mottled grey brown, and the grey wing area is more extensive with the black outer primaries showing a large white mirror. At this age the bird has reached maturity and, in this non-breeding plumage, care is again needed to avoid misidentification as Ring-billed Gull. Generally the smaller size, rounder head, thinner bill and large eyes of the Mew Gull should separate the two species.

However, the Siberian form, *L. c. kamtschatschensis*, is almost as large as the Ring-billed Gull. Although this race mainly winters south to Japan and Taiwan it has been recorded in the Aleutians. In the west the nominate race is to be found as far south as the Mediterranean Basin and the coast of North Africa, while in the east it reaches the northern end of the Red Sea, Egypt, Iraq and the Persian Gulf.

The race *L. c. brachyrhynchus* winters in the eastern Pacific, from south east Alaska to southern California, and rarely inland. Casual records of Mew Gull on the American east coast could well involve birds from Europe.

An adult Mew Gull in winter plumage shows a streaky head and an indistinct, dark subterminal band to the bill. The bird to the left is a first-winter Black-headed Gull which, apart from plumage differences, is much smaller.

LESSER BLACK-BACKED GULL

L A R U S   F U S C U S

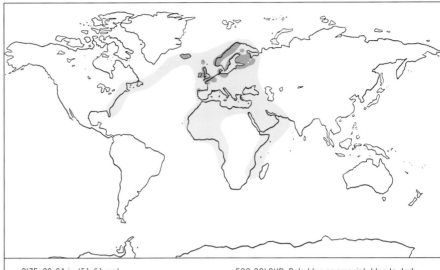

SIZE 20-24 in (51-61 cm)

WINGSPAN 49-50 in (124-127 cm)

EGG CLUTCH Two to three

EGG COLOUR Pale blue or greenish blue to dark brown, spotted blackish brown

INCUBATION 28 days

FLEDGLING 30-40 days

Brought up in the English Midlands, I recall that 40 years ago the sight of a 'seagull' inland used to evoke the knowing comment 'it must be rough weather on the coast'. Whereas that may well have been true and some weather displacement could have taken place (and still does for that matter), the sight of hundreds and even thousands of gulls, especially 'Lesser Black-backs' in Midland Britain today is quite a commonplace thing. The species now occurs not only in the winter months, but during the summer as well, when mostly non-breeding birds are present.

Formerly a scarce passage migrant to the area, it was in the 1950s that a few began to appear during the winter months. Even so, totals rarely reached double figures. Within a decade, numbers had increased dramatically to a regional total of some 10,000 birds. An even more dramatic increase was noted in the 1970s when as many as 35,000 were present at winter roosts. These increases may well be attributable to the construction of large new reservoirs which provide the areas of open water necessary for safe roosting sites. During the day birds fan out to feed either on arable or pasture land or on rubbish tips, a new major food source. This change in life-style by the Lesser Black-backed Gull in Britain is, of course, not only confined to the Midlands but extends to much of the country. It is especially concentrated in a broad band stretching from Yorkshire and Lancashire south eastwards to the London area. This is a most densely populated part of Britain, where many reservoirs and refuse tips have come into being in recent years. In winter there are now more Lesser Black-backed Gulls at inland sites than along the coast, with the exception of Merseyside, where a BTO survey in 1983 found 10,190 out of a total coastal count of 13,726.

The adult Lesser Black-backed Gull is usually compared to the Great Black-backed Gull, for this is the only other European gull with a dark saddle and upperwing and with which it might be mistaken. However, the Lesser Black-backed is much smaller, being closer to the Herring Gull in size but altogether slimmer and proportionately longer-winged.

The British sub-species, *L. f. graellsii*, has an immaculate slate-grey back, and slate-grey wings, with black and white tips, while the head and underparts are pure white. The yellow bill has a red

ABOVE *A Lesser Black-backed Gull of the paler backed race* L. f. graellsii *with its fairly well-grown youngster.*

LEFT *This immature Lesser Black-backed Gull, along with many other gulls, regularly scavenges rubbish tips in Britain, especially during the winter months when household refuse provides life support.*

spot on the gonys, while the yellow eye is ringed with red. It is the yellow legs which clinch the identification, though in winter these can look greyish or pinky, perhaps creating some confusion. However, confusion with the larger Great Black-backed Gull is most likely to occur with the Scandinavian race, *L. f. fuscus*, which has a mantle as black as that of the Great Black-backed Gull. Even so, size and the yellow legs should be sufficient to determine identification. In Britain the Scandinavian race is most frequent on passage during spring and autumn migration, when small parties are quite frequently seen inland, either in flight or perhaps resting awhile in the middle of a large field.

A colonial species, Lesser Black-backed Gulls favour undisturbed coastal nesting sites within sand dunes or on relatively flat, unbroken grassy slopes. Birds in breeding condition begin their movement back to nesting locations early in the year. During February and March thousands assemble at various points in south and south west England before they begin to drift back to their chosen colonies. Southern breeding sites are reached by April or May, though it may be June before they arrive back at their more northerly limits. Monogamous pair bonding can

last for several years, though there is no evidence that they stay together through the winter. At the chosen nest site the pair re-establish their relationship through a series of greeting ceremonies by the male, when the head is thrown forward accompanied by loud yelping calls from which the food soliciting develops. When the female begs for food the male may regurgitate and feed her. This leads to scrape forming and nest building. Head tossing by both sexes can continue and mating may then take place.

The nest is usually a substantial heap of grass, seaweed and other local materials, but rarely it might be no more than sparsely lined scrape. On inland sites nests are quite frequently well hidden in heather, bracken or other vegetation. Inland breeding, especially in the north and north west of Britain, is confined largely to high moorland and the margins of a few lakes, where some colonies are several thousand strong. However, the great proportion of the British breeding population is confined to a relatively few areas. The largest single colony, on Walney Island (Lancashire), comprises some 70,000 pairs, or about one-third the total breeding population of Great Britain and Ireland. It is still increasing, and some birds are now nesting along the shore, such is the demand for space.

they are already yellow at this age. At the end of its third year it looks very much like the adult, but vestiges of brown can still be present in the wings.

The British race *L. f. graellsii* breeds in southern Iceland, the Faeroes, the British Isles, the Netherlands and Brittany. *L. f. fuscus*, or the Scandinavian race, breeds in the Baltic and northern Norway. In winter it disperses on a broad southerly front, reaching south to Nigeria and throughout the Red Sea, south to Kenya. There is a third identifiable subspecies, *L. f. intermedius*, which resembles *L. f. graellsii* but is slightly darker on the mantle, back and upperwings. This race breeds in southern Norway, west Sweden and Denmark. Migration takes them in a similar direction to *L. f. fuscus*, but they are more inclined to move to the eastern end of the Mediterranean and the Red Sea.

In North America there is now a regular, but small, population passing through Newfoundland and wintering south to Florida. The origin of these birds is probably Iceland, from where southwards-migrating birds are drifted westwards. It is infrequently recorded in inland states and even more rarely found on the west coast of America.

LEFT *A Lesser Black-backed Gull's yellow legs readily identify it.*

BELOW *A Lesser Black-backed Gull at its nest.*

The two to three eggs, which are laid in May to June, vary from pale blue or greenish blue to dark brown. They are usually spotted and streaked with blackish brown and are indistinguishable from those of the Herring Gull. Incubation is carried out by both parents and lasts for about 28 days. On hatching the chicks are covered in pale grey down cryptically marked with black. This effectively camouflages them, for after only a couple of days they leave the nest to hide in the surrounding vegetation, emerging only to be fed. Their food can be virtually any edible matter the parents can scavenge, or obtain by plunge-diving for fish or searching the tideline for any invertebrates. After about 30 to 40 days the young can fly and they then move away from the nesting area to their winter quarters. These stretch from western Europe south to West Africa, but many move no further than south and south west England.

In its first-winter plumage the Lesser Black-backed Gull is very much like a juvenile Herring Gull, being a mottled brown and white bird. However, it has generally paler underparts, an entirely black bill and grey legs.

By the second year the dark grey back begins to develop and the pale bill has a blackish tip. The legs are usually still grey, though in some individuals

HERRING GULL

LARUS ARGENTATUS

This, the most widely distributed of northern hemisphere gulls, is to many people the most evocative bird of our coasts. There are few places around our shores that you visit today without seeing them hanging lazily in the wind, or hearing their raucous 'laughing' calls. This reflects the considerable success of the Herring Gull in adapting to a wide variety of man-made habitats during this century.

Circumpolar in its distribution, the Herring Gull can be found as far north as the Arctic circle during the breeding season, whilst in winter birds may move as far south as the equator. Breeding is generally concentrated around coasts, where there is no shortage of suitable nesting habitat.

This gull is an extremely variable species, with at least ten subspecies generally being recognized. They are:

L. a. argentatus: (the nominate race), it breeds southern Iceland, Faeroes, British Isles, north west France, Holland and Belgium. Winters within its breeding range south to northern Spain.

L. a. atlantis: Breeds Azores, Madeira and Canaries. Some of these birds possibly wander to north west African coast.

L. a. cachinnans: Breeds from Black Sea east through southern USSR, including southern Black Sea coast to Lake Balkash. Winters eastern Mediterranean, Red Sea, Persian Gulf and north west India.

L. a. heuglini: Breeds USSR from the White Sea east to the Kara Sea. Winters south through Black Sea to Aral Seas, north west India, and Gulf of Aden and perhaps to Kenya.

L. a. michahellis: Breeds in the Mediterranean basin north to Spain and more recently southern France. Some birds winter north to Holland but its dispersal after nesting is within its breeding range.

L. a. monogolicus: Breeds from Lake Balkash, southern USSR, east to Mongolia. Winter range not precisely known.

L. a. omissus: Breeds in Scandinavia east to the White Sea, USSR. Winters south to northern Spain.

L. a. smithsonianus: Confined to the North American continent, it breeds in south east Alaska, east to north west Greenland and south to North Carolina. Winters south to Mexico, Panama and Bermuda and Barbados. Has recently been recorded in Venezuela.

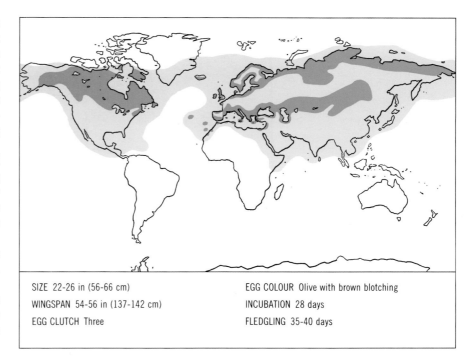

SIZE 22-26 in (56-66 cm)	EGG COLOUR Olive with brown blotching
WINGSPAN 54-56 in (137-142 cm)	INCUBATION 28 days
EGG CLUTCH Three	FLEDGLING 35-40 days

L. a. taimyrensis: Breeds Siberia, USSR. Its winter range not known but may reach Kenya.

L. a. vagae: Breeds along USSR coast of Laptev Sea east to Bering Strait. Winters south to Japan and China.

These subspecies fall into two reasonably distinct groups, with birds in the northern part of the range and across North America essentially pale-mantled with pink legs, whilst the southern races, across Europe and into Asia, generally show darker mantles and yellowish legs. This often causes confusion with the Lesser Black-backed Gull, though the Herring Gull is usually slightly the larger of the two, and lacks the Lesser Black-backed Gull's dark trailing edge to the underwing. It could also be confused with a Common Gull in Europe or a Ring-billed Gull and Mew Gull in North America. However, it is larger than both these species, broader-winged and with a shallower forehead that gives it a 'fiercer' expression. Adults show variably pale grey upperparts and black wingtips, with white 'mirrors' towards the primary tips. The head, underparts and tail are a clean white, except in winter when most birds become streaked on the head. This species takes four years to attain full adult plumage, during which period there is a

Wherever the location, birds pairing up will undergo a series of highly ritualized displays. These are continued throughout the breeding season and serve to reinforce the bond between two birds. Pairs may remain faithful to each other for life, although they do not usually stay together outside the breeding season. Younger birds may loosely associate with a colony and breeding has been observed amongst three-year-olds, though success rates at this age are much lower.

The nest is located in the centre of the small territory and is usually a mound of vegetation, hollowed out in the centre and lined with finer material. It is not unusual to see items of waste such as bits of plastic, strands of old rope or fish netting amongst the dried seaweed and grasses that make up the nest. Indeed, the gulls will incorporate any material that is readily available. The three eggs, which are olive coloured with brown blotching, are laid during April. Both parents will incubate these for about four weeks, although the slightly smaller female usually sits for longer periods than the male.

steady transition from a heavily streaked, dull, greyish-brown juvenile to the clean grey, white and black adult.

Herring Gulls are not conservative in either their choice of habitat or food. They are essentially omnivorous, but have become particularly adept at exploiting man's waste by scavenging for food on rubbish tips and in city centres, or by feeding on discarded fish offal in harbours and docks. Many are especially partial to discarded fish and chips. These have become very important sources of food at most times of the year, but especially during the winter months when a more 'natural' diet is harder to find. Birds will also follow the plough to pick up disturbed earthworms and insect larvae, whilst during the breeding season predation on other species' eggs and young can be an important food source. On the seashore, they may forage for small fish and crustacea, while at other times various vegetable matter may be consumed.

Generally a highly sociable species, large flocks gather at favoured localities in winter. Many adults then begin their dispersal back to their breeding colonies by March. Pairs will lay claim to a small territory, which is then vigorously defended from all surrounding pairs. This may be sited within a wide variety of habitats, with colonies often being found amongst sand dunes and on shingle ridges, rocky islets and sea cliffs. In more recent years birds have started nesting on flat rooftops in coastal towns and cities, and are now even spreading some way inland. In North America even tree nesting has been observed.

ABOVE *A group of young Herring Gulls show their patterned plumage.*

BELOW *A juvenile Herring Gull awaits its next feeding opportunity.*

RIGHT *The handsome adult Herring Gull in full breeding plumage.*

In recent years many Herring Gulls have taken to nesting on the roofs of seaside town buildings. Here one of the pair calls to its approaching mate prior to the change-over at its roof-top nest site.

The young chicks may leave the nest after two or three days, but will remain within their parents' territory until they can fly at 35 to 40 days of age. If they wander outside the territory during their first week or so of life, the juveniles are very vulnerable to predation by neighbouring adults, although their mottled, fawn-brown, downy feathering gives them a good camouflage against other ground or aerial intruders. The chicks grow quickly on a diet of fish, which is regurgitated for them by the adults in response to well aimed pecks at their red bill spots. They are able to fly four to five weeks after hatching, but are still fed by the adults for several weeks after that.

Juveniles are a rather indistinctive brownish grey colour, variably streaked darker, and have pinkish legs and a blackish bill. Until they start to develop the paler grey mantle feathering during their second year, they are best distinguished from a similar-aged Lesser Black-backed Gull in flight, when a paler area on their inner primaries contrasts with the darker wingtips and secondary bar.

The Herring Gull is more migratory within the more northerly populations, although Icelandic and North American birds appear to be mainly sedentary. Immature birds tend to wander further afield than the adults, although there is a general movement inland in winter by all age groups. The southern 'yellow-legged' group seems to be spreading its range northwards. Certainly there has been a definite upward trend in sightings in Britain, especially in late summer and autumn, with some birds found to be wintering near reliable food sources such as rubbish dumps.

CALIFORNIA GULL

LARUS CALIFORNICUS

A pale-mantled gull, which in many ways is intermediate to the 'middle-sized' gulls such as Ring-billed Gull and the 'large' gulls such as Herring Gull, the California Gull takes four years to reach maturity. It breeds abundantly in the interior of western North America, and winters on the Pacific coast south to Mexico.

The adult has a grey mantle, which is slightly, but clearly, darker in tone than a Herring or Ring-billed Gull. In breeding plumage the head is snowy white, but in winter it is heavily streaked and blotched with brown. The bill is yellow, with small red and black spots at the tip, though the black area may be reduced or even absent in the summer. The legs are yellow or greenish-yellow. Importantly, an adult California Gull has a dark eye. The combination of a pale grey mantle and yellow legs serves to distinguish it from all the other large North American gulls. Its larger size, relatively longer and slimmer body, rather upright stance with wings almost touching the ground, longer bill and relatively short legs, should separate it from Ring-billed and Mew Gulls. At close range the red spot on the bill should provide final confirmation.

The sequence of plumages from juvenile, through first, second and third years follows the usual complex pattern of all the larger gulls. The first-year bird has pink legs and a sharply two-toned bill, with a flesh-coloured base and blackish tip that recalls a young Glaucous Gull. These features, combined with the rather dark head and body, all-dark tail and barred mantle and wing-coverts, are the best means of separating a young California Gull from the other West Coast gulls. However, bare part colouration is notoriously variable, and some young Herring Gulls may show a similarly patterned bill. Then, the proportionally smaller and more rounded head, larger eye and longer and more slender bill of California Gull may be useful pointers. By the second winter the upperparts are grey, like the adult's, and the head and underparts are paler and more whitish. Otherwise the wings are just as the first year. Importantly, the bill and legs are now blue grey or grey green, the former with a neat dark tip. The third-year bird resembles the adult, but shows traces of a dark bar on the secondaries and the tail, and more black on the primaries. The bare parts may be as the adult, or may remain blue grey as in the second year.

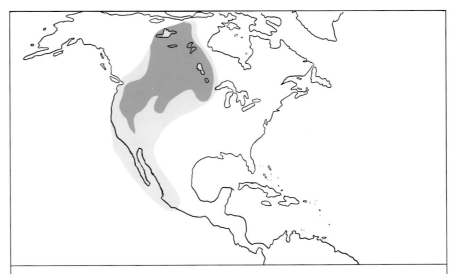

SIZE 20-23 in (51-58 cm)

WINGSPAN 48-55 in (122-140 cm)

EGG CLUTCH Three

EGG COLOUR Bluish white to buffy brown, blotched with brown and purplish grey

INCUBATION 26-28 days

FLEDGLING 35-40 days

A California Gull in winter plumage on the beach at Monterey Bay. This is just one area along the California coast of the USA where this species is found mainly in the non-breeding season.

California Gulls breed colonially, often in the company of other gulls and terns, especially Ring-billed Gulls. The colonies are found on open, sandy or gravelly areas around lakes, marshes and rivers, especially on islands. The nest is usually a simple affair consisting of a shallow scrape in the ground or a natural depression, with a lining of grass, weeds and refuse, but substantial structures, up to one foot (30 cm) high, have been observed. The normal clutch contains three eggs, which are laid in May or June. Their ground colour varies from bluish white to buffy brown and they are spotted and blotched with browns and purplish grey. The eggs are laid at daily intervals and both the sexes take part in incubation, starting from the day the first egg is laid. The chicks are quite precocial, and after a few days can run about and hide while their parents are absent. Even when small, they are good swimmers. The normal call is a soft 'kow-kow-kow',

The breeding range in interior North America extends from the southern Mackenzie southwards, through south east British Columbia, Alberta, southern Manitoba, the Dakotas and Washington to northern Colorado and northern California. Birds spread out from their waterside breeding areas to forage in fields, especially freshly ploughed ones. They feed on a wide variety of small animals and invertebrates, and their services as predators of agricultural pests are much valued.

A migratory species, the California Gull arrives on the breeding grounds from about April onwards. With the fledging of the young around August, post-breeding dispersal begins, with birds moving to the West Coast. They winter from British Columbia south to Colima in Mexico, in a variety of habitats from estuaries and mudflats to rockier coasts. They also occur inland locally in Mexico. Although a rare vagrant to eastern North America, California Gulls have been recorded east to New York, south to Florida and around the Gulf Coast. In the opposite direction, vagrants have occurred west to Hawaii and Japan.

A California Gull at its nest site typically located at a lakeside in the North American interior where these birds mostly breed.

WESTERN GULL

LARUS OCCIDENTALIS

The Western Gull is the most common and most ubiquitous gull along the coast of California, patrolling the beaches on foot or on the wing, and congregating in screaming hordes at rubbish dumps and sewer outfalls. Away from the coast however, it is really rather rare.

Taking four years to reach maturity, the Western Gull goes through the usual complex series of immature plumages. Adults have dark grey backs and wings, with a broad white trailing edge to the wing, and black wingtips with one or two 'mirrors', of which that on the outer primary is very large. The head, body and tail are white. The bill is yellow, with a paler, whitish tip and a red spot on the gonys. In winter, it fades and the red spot often becomes very faint. The iris is pale yellow and the legs are pink. The northern, nominate subspecies has a paler mantle than the southern race, or Yellow-footed Gull, whose upperparts may be only slightly paler than the blackish of the wingtips. Northern birds also tend to have darker eyes and to show faint darker mottling on the head in winter.

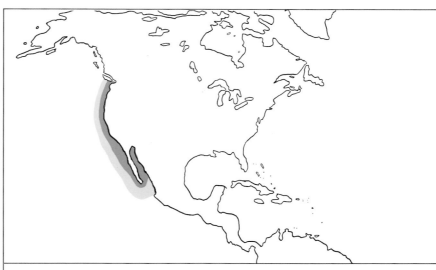

SIZE 24-27 in (61-68 cm)	EGG COLOUR Buffy or olive brown with darker blotches
WINGSPAN 52-56 in (132-142 cm)	INCUBATION 24 days
EGG CLUTCH Three	FLEDGLING 35-40 days

LEFT *An adult Western Gull in non-breeding plumage.*

ABOVE *Always ready to exploit a possible food source a first-winter Western Gull perches on* *a car at Drake's Bay, California to take discarded food fed by visitors.*

99

British Columbia. The resultant offspring, which occur all along the West Coast in winter, form a mighty challenge for the gull watcher. Notably, they often resemble a third species, Thayer's Gull. A careful check of şize, shape, especially the proportions of the bill, and of details of the wingtip pattern is necessary to be sure of their identification.

Like all large gulls, the Western begins to show adult colouration on the mantle from the second winter onwards, and such sub-adult birds are easily identified by their large size and grey mantles. First-years, though, are rather more difficult to identify as they resemble first-year Herring Gulls. However, their stocky build, short, broad wings and especially their stout, blunt-tipped bills give the impression of a much larger gull than they really are. This, coupled with their generally darker and more uniform colouration (the back contrasting with a pale rump) and all-black bill, should distinguish them from other young West Coast gulls in immature plumage.

The Western Gull is endemic to the Pacific Coast of North America, breeding from Washington south to central Baja California and Guadalupe Island in Mexico. The largest and most famous colony is on the Farallon Islands in California, where 32,000 pairs breed. In the winter, birds disperse slightly outside the breeding range, regularly moving north to Vancouver Island and Seymour Inlet in British Columbia and south to southern Baja California. More erratically, they travel further south to the coasts of Sonora, Sinaloa and Nayarit in western Mexico. Vagrants have occurred in Hawaii, Alaska, Arizona and Illinois.

This gull breeds colonially on rocky islands and coastal cliffs, building a nest of dried grasses, roots and weeds on ledges, in crannies, on grassy slopes and on rocks. The eggs are various shades of buffy-brown or olive-brown, with darker blotches, and the clutch of three is laid from May to mid-June. If the eggs are lost to a predator, a second clutch of two eggs is laid, but the species is otherwise single-brooded. Incubation lasts 24 days, and when hatched the young remain in the nest for a few days and are brooded by the adults, and fed on semi-digested food. Later they become more independent, and will freeze or hide at the first sign of danger.

Western Gulls have the usual catholic choice of food, scavenging anything they can and often joining the screaming masses of gulls at garbage tips. During the breeding season, they steal the eggs and young of other birds. Indeed, this large, powerful bird is frequently aggressive to other species. Its common call is a low, guttural 'quock kuck kuck kuck' in a rapid series.

A larger, fiercer, more powerful and thick-set bird than the California Gull, this adult Western Gull is almost exclusively found in a marine environment and occurs commonly along the coast from British Columbia southwards to northern California.

The adult Western Gull is the only common large West Coast gull with a dark grey mantle, and can be confused only with the Slaty-backed Gull in Alaska and with Yellow-footed Gull in the Gulf of California and Salton Sea. However, at both these northern and southern extremes, the Western Gull is very rare, so the problem seldom arises. The paler-mantled northern birds may approach Herring Gulls in appearance, but their heavy build, as well as a dusky band on the trailing edge of the underwing, help accurate identification. Another complication is that the Western Gulls and Glaucous-winged Gulls frequently hybridize where their breeding ranges meet in Washington and

GLAUCOUS-WINGED GULL

LARUS GLAUCESCENS

The most abundant and widespread gull on the north Pacific coast, the Glaucous-winged Gull breeds from the Commander Islands (USSR) and the Pribilof Islands eastwards along the Aleutian chain to southern Alaska, and then south to north west Oregon. In winter, some birds may be found in all but the northernmost part of the breeding range, and are frequently seen around the fringes of the sea-ice; others disperse southwards on either side of the Pacific Ocean, reaching Japan on the Asian shore and Baja California, the Gulf of California and, erratically, as far as Sonora (Mexico) on the American shore. Sub-adult birds frequently remain in the winter quarters during the summer, rather than migrating north with the adults.

The common pale-winged gull of the West Coast, Glaucous-winged Gull is intermediate between Herring and Glaucous in size and jizz. It is chunky and short-winged, and compared to a Herring Gull has a thick-set head and bill, and a slower, more laboured yet more powerful flight. A large gull, the Glaucous-winged Gull takes four years to reach

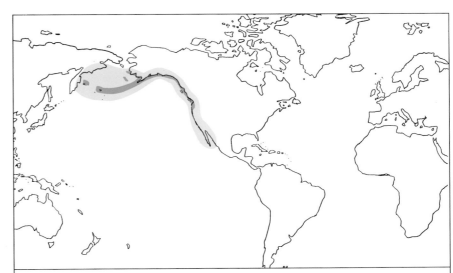

SIZE 24-27 in (61-68 cm)

WINGSPAN 52-54 in (132-137 cm)

EGG CLUTCH Two to three

EGG COLOUR Buff to olive, spotted with brown and lavender grey

INCUBATION 26-28 days

FLEDGLING 35-40 days

ABOVE *A first-winter Glaucous-winged Gull scavenges the shallows of the tideline.*

RIGHT *The Glaucous-winged Gull is more powerful and thick-set than similar-sized gulls.*

maturity, going through a complex series of immature plumages in the meantime. The adult is pale grey above with neat, white, trailing edge to the wing. Like the Herring Gull, it has fleshy legs, a yellow bill with a red spot near the tip, and a head which is white in summer and brown-streaked in winter. However, its primaries are pale grey, concolorous with the rest of the wing, and each feather has a white tip so that, at rest, the wingtip appears grey with a row of white spots. This pattern is rather similar to that of Glaucous Gull, but that species is much less common than Glaucous-winged south of its Arctic breeding grounds. Glaucous Gull also has uniformly pale outer primaries that are whitish in adults and pale fawn in immatures. Thus the species can be easily separated as long as a good view is obtained. At all ages, Thayer's Gull, a winter visitor to the West Coast, can be eliminated by its smaller size, relatively smaller bill, longer wings that project past its tail at rest, and dark markings on its wingtips (which are chocolate coloured in immatures and blackish in adults).

Juvenile and first-winter Glaucous-winged Gulls are a dirty pinkish-buff or fawn. Like other young gulls they are barred and mottled, the markings are so subtle that the bird appears rather uniform. Importantly, the primaries are no paler than the rest of the wing, and though the underwing is uniformly pale, the primaries are not translucent when viewed against the light (unlike Glaucous Gull), and the bill is all-black (not pink with a neat black tip as in a young Glaucous). The second-winter bird is similar, though a little paler, with a pale grey mantle and back. By the third winter it is much more like the adult, differing only in some buff mottling on the body, often traces of a darker tail band, and some dusky markings on the yellow bill.

The identification of the Glaucous-winged Gull is complicated by the fact that it frequently hybridizes with Western Gull where the ranges of the two species meet along the coast of Washington and British Columbia. It also hybridizes to a much lesser extent with Herring Gulls in southern Alaska and with Glaucous Gulls in western Alaska! Hybrids are extremely variable, showing every intermediate stage of plumage between the respective parents. Hybrids are most common near the breeding areas, and Glaucous-winged x Western are the only ones commonly found south of Alaska. In winter they can be quite common on the West Coast, but the proportion of hybrids to pure-bred birds gradually falls as you move south. Their identification is a complex subject, depending on careful observation of size, structure, bare part colouration and fine details of plumage. Needless to say, it is the realm of the real gull-maniac!

Glaucous-winged Gulls breed colonially on cliffs, rocky ledges and level areas such as grassy slopes and

flat islands – probably to evade predators such as foxes. The nest is an untidy heap of seaweed, herbs and grasses, sometimes decorated with feathers or fish bones. An interesting observation is that on Carroll Islet, off the coast of Washington, younger birds tend to build their nests in the open, whilst the better-constructed nests of full adults are built under the shelter of a bush. The two or three eggs are laid from late May to July, and are basically buff to olive in colouration, spotted and blotched with brown and lavender-grey. They are incubated for 26 to 28 days, with the young fledging from August onwards. The usual call is a deep 'kow kow'.

The Glaucous-winged Gull is first and foremost a coastal species, seldom being found far offshore, but frequenting bays, estuaries, beaches and mud-flats. It will readily scavenge from man, congregating around fish wharves, canning plants and rubbish dumps. On its breeding grounds, it is a fierce predator, freely taking both eggs and young of neighbouring seabirds. It will follow rivers inland, but usually not for any great distance, and is very rare away from the coast in Canada and the Pacific North-West. Further south, though, it does occur inland to Idaho and Arizona in the winter, and occasionally reaching as far east as Alberta on migration. Vagrants have been recorded in Manitoba, Oklahoma, and Hawaii.

A Glaucous-winged Gull in non-breeding plumage shows a heavily clouded or streaked head and nape. This bird is gorging on a dead sole it has discovered.

ICELAND GULL

LARUS GLAUCOIDES

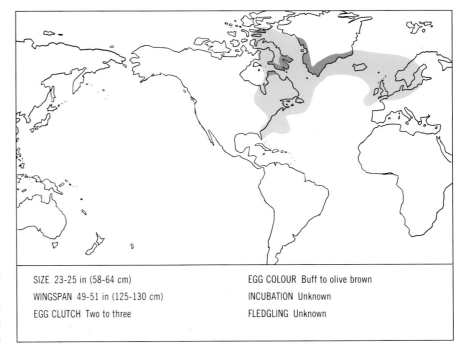

SIZE 23-25 in (58-64 cm)	EGG COLOUR Buff to olive brown
WINGSPAN 49-51 in (125-130 cm)	INCUBATION Unknown
EGG CLUTCH Two to three	FLEDGLING Unknown

The taxonomy of this bird has been the subject of much discussion by ornithologists. Even now there is divided thought as to its relationship with Thayer's Gull and Kumlien's Gull and is considered by some to be a subspecies! The problem is further compounded by occurrences of hybrid Iceland x Glaucous and Iceland x Lesser Black-backed Gulls.

Even the name Iceland Gull is somewhat misleading, for though it commonly occurs there during the winter, it rarely nests on the island. Rather, it breeds extensively in Greenland and also in North America, from Ellesmere Island south to Baffin Island, but that is the extent of its limited global breeding range.

In birdwatcher's parlance, the Iceland Gull and Glaucous Gull (and Ivory Gull) are generally referred to as 'white-winged gulls', as opposed to virtually all the other Laridae sp. which have some black in the primaries. Iceland Gull and Glaucous Gull superficially look much alike. In adult plumage they are all white, except for the back and wings which are a very pale grey. In the case of the Iceland Gull, the legs are pale flesh pink, while the bill is yellow with an orange spot on the gonys. At close range a brick-red orbital ring can be seen around the yellow eye. Its major distinguishing features, however, are probably size and shape, for the Iceland Gull is much the smaller bird, approximating to the Herring Gull. The bill is smaller and less heavy, while at rest it will be seen that the wings extend well beyond the tail, giving a long slender look. It was a bird in this plumage, the first I had seen, that surprised and delighted me and my friends at Radipole Lake, Dorset, England on 15 October 1960, an early date so far south.

The Iceland Gull looks less fierce than the Glaucous Gull and is indeed less predatory and possibly even more of a scavenger than its larger congener. In flight it is much more buoyant and the wings appear relatively longer than those of the Glaucous Gull, but differentiating between the species by this means requires considerable experience with both birds.

Like all the larger gulls, the Iceland Gull takes four years to reach maturity and each year there is a detectable change in its appearance. In the first or second winter, or the first or second summer, these differences can only be seen through very close,

This Iceland Gull is not quite fully mature and is probably about three years old.

detailed observation. In their first winter, Iceland Gulls are generally buffy to white, with wingtips irregularly washed with brown, while the eye is dark, the bill black and the legs greyish. The finer, and usually more even, pattern of grey-brown markings is only visible at close range, but in flight there is a distinct white terminal band on the tail.

In each succeeding year the plumage becomes whiter, the pale grey mantle forms and the colours of the leg and bill become brighter until full adult plumage is assumed by its fourth winter.

Iceland Gulls return to their low-arctic breeding areas in May, where they favour rocky coasts with high steep cliffs. Usually they nest above 656 feet (200 m), often mixing with kittiwakes, but choosing the roomier, flatter ledges. Occasionally they nest on lower cliffs, offshore stacks and islands. Their courtship is similar to a Herring Gull's, but very little study has been made of this species and little is known of its actual display rituals. The nest is a rather loose construction of seaweed, grass and mosses. The clutch usually comprises two to three eggs which are laid from May to July, though occasionally only one egg is laid. These are buff to olive brown in colour, much like those of a Glaucous Gull only smaller.

Incubation and fledging periods are, no doubt, similar to those of a Herring Gull, but again no specific data on this aspect of its breeding biology are available.

After nesting has been completed, birds disperse to different regions. Canadian-bred birds winter along the north American coast, from Newfoundland southwards to Virginia, and occasionally Florida. Small numbers also occur inland and on the Great Lakes.

In Europe it winters from Iceland to the Faeroes and Norway, with some occasionally seen south to Sweden, the Baltic, northern France, northern Belgium, the Netherlands and the British Isles. In a normal year, southern Britain and Ireland may have a winter population of possibly a hundred birds, but in some years this number is doubled or even trebled. It is more regular in Scotland, where 50 to 60 individuals are to be located most winters. Again, exceptional years can produce 200 or more, as in 1980/81 and 1982/83. It was in January 1983 that I saw five in Wick Harbour, along with two Glaucous Gulls, though I have to say the quarry was a Ross's Gull, which could not be found when I and Mike Warren, who was then researching his book *Shorelines*, went looking for it.

In the rest of Britain, Iceland Gulls are rarely noted before Christmas. In the English Midlands the species has become an increasingly regular visitor to larger reservoirs since the 1960s. Most have been recorded during January to March, with two or three being seen at favoured locations in good years. However, fewer have been noted over the last decade.

Generally its behaviour seems to differ little from that of a Herring Gull, though its voice is reported to be somewhat shriller. Its main diet comprises fish for which it will dive, completely submerging. It will also take any other form of marine life it comes across, especially molluscs and crustaceans. Equally, like a Glaucous Gull, it will scavenge and feed on carrion. In winter it can frequently be found at rubbish tips and sewage outfalls, as well as at more natural seashore and freshwater locations.

With its pinkish, black-tipped bill and flesh pink legs, mostly white head and otherwise streaked overall grey-brown feathers this bird displays the plumage of a first-winter Iceland Gull. This particular individual was photographed at Fairburn Ings, Britain, in February 1984.

GLAUCOUS GULL

LARUS HYPERBOREUS

Like the Iceland Gull, this is a 'white winged gull' which does not show black on the primaries at any age. Generally much larger than Iceland Gull, its size varies between that of Great Black-backed Gull and Herring Gull.

The adult bird is all white, except for the pale grey back and wings. The wings are relatively shorter than those of an Iceland Gull, and when at rest they do not project so far beyond the tail, giving it a less tapered look. The yellow bill, with a red spot on the gonys, is stouter and somewhat longer than an Iceland Gull's, a useful pointer to the identification of smaller Glaucous Gulls.

Close inspection of Glaucous Gull will reveal a yellow eye-ring (rather than red, as Iceland Gull). In winter, however, this is practically colourless. The legs are flesh coloured. The sexes are similar and there is no seasonal variation in plumage.

Along with the above features, the Glaucous Gull gives the appearance of a much more thick-set and powerful barrel-chested bird. It is much fiercer and generally more aggressive than the Iceland Gull, often attacking smaller shorebirds, especially if they are sick or injured.

Like the Iceland Gull, the Glaucous Gull also has a four-year cycle of plumage changes before reaching maturity. At a distance the juvenile looks a uniform coffee-coloured bird, always much paler than other large immature gulls. At close quarters it will be seen the plumage comprises fine, buffish, wavy barrings and mottlings. The first-winter bird, which is also coffee-coloured, has a diagnostic creamy flesh-coloured bill with a clearly delineated black tip. Iceland Gulls of the same age have darker bills with less clearly defined, but more extensive, dark tips. In its second winter the black in the bill is less distinct, with the extreme tip becoming white, while the base is often yellowish. By its second summer, the bill becomes pinkish yellow with a dusky tip. In its third year the bill and leg colouration is almost as an adult, but the bill usually lacks the red spot on the gonys. During each progressive moult over a three-year period the plumage becomes whiter until, by its fourth year, the bird has usually attained full adult plumage.

However, the possibility of albino or leucistic Herring Gulls should always be considered and any totally white gull could be an albino. Additionally, Herring Gulls and Glaucous Gulls hybridize. All

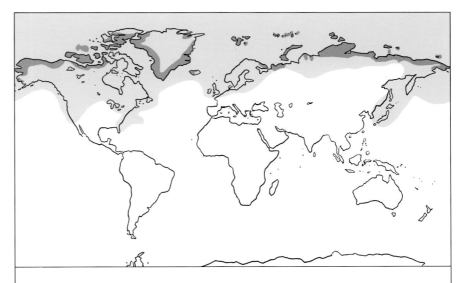

SIZE 26-30 in (66-77 cm)	EGG COLOUR Buffy to olive, blotched dark brown
WINGSPAN 52-56 in (132-142 cm)	INCUBATION 28 days
EGG CLUTCH Two or three, rarely four	FLEDGLING 45-50 days

Even at the early age of about four weeks since hatching, this Glaucous Gull shows all the signs of its fiercely predatory lifestyle to come.

hybrids, however, retain darker ear coverts, show faint secondary bars on the wing, have darker primaries and banded tails, or any combination of these features.

The Glaucous Gull is as omnivorous as the Great Black-backed Gull, being equally fierce and rapacious. Everything is fair game, and it preys upon virtually any other seabird. Most large arctic coastal seabird colonies will have attendant Glaucous Gulls that live off the eggs and young of nesting birds. Some adults will also be taken, particularly Dovekies, which they are able to catch in the air. Even the eggs and young of larger birds, such as geese and sometimes Loons, are prey. Additionally they will scavenge the tideline for fish.

Glaucous Gulls breed on coastal islands and along the cliff faces of arctic and sub-arctic coasts. They also nest on islands in freshwater lakes near the coast, or even some distance from the sea. The adult birds return to their breeding sites in March, or April in the case of those furthest north.

The courtship and display are similar to those of the Great Black-backed Gull, with a monogamous pair bond being formed. Most birds appear to return to the same nest site each year and colonies can be quite large, some with up to 1000 pairs.

The nest, which is built by both birds, comprises a substantial pile of seaweed, vegetation or other debris, lined with finer material and maybe a few feathers. The clutch is usually two or three eggs, rarely four, and these are laid in late May or early June. The eggs are buffy to olive and blotched and spotted dark brown. Incubation is by both sexes and lasts for approximately 28 days. The young, downy chicks are soon active and move away from the actual nest within a few days. However, they stay within the vicinity, being fed and cared for by both parents. The actual fledging period is not accurately known, but is probably in the region of 45 to 50 days, after which time the young become fully independent. They then tend to wander further afield than the adults in their first three years of life.

Circumpolar, the Glaucous Gull breeds mainly north of the Arctic circle, from Alaska east across Arctic Canada to Greenland, Iceland, Spitsbergen and in northern Europe from Murmansk, along the northern shores of the USSR to Wrangel Island and the Bering Straits. After breeding, birds disperse to their winter quarters.

An adult Glaucous Gull in non-breeding plumage has head, neck and sides of breast streaked and clouded brownish grey.

Those breeding in the Canadian Arctic and west Greenland are mainly resident, but some move south into eastern America. The eastern Greenland population appears to be more migratory and largely moves to Iceland, though some of these birds no doubt get as far as Britain and Ireland. The Icelandic breeding population is mainly resident. It is known to contain a large proportion of Glaucous x Herring Gull hybrids. Few such hybrids are reported in Britain so they presumably do not move very far. The northern limit of wintering Eurasian breeding birds is dependent on the weather, with severe wintry conditions no doubt pushing them south and south west. In Britain a few appear as early as September, but most of the winter population does not arrive much before December. A large proportion of birds are to be found in Shetland and the Orkney Islands. Indeed, Shetland invariably has 40 to 50 birds in total, with upwards of 100 or more in some years. In Britain as a whole, around 200 is the usual number, scattered about the country, but at times this might be doubled. In Ireland there is an average of 70 individuals each winter.

Some individuals return to the same stretch of beach or the same general area year after year, and can be seen to go through all the plumage changes to maturity. One well-known bird returned annually to the Dee in England for many years, whilst another regular visitor to Cley beach, Norfolk each winter, is affectionately known to local birdwatchers as 'George'!

An adult Glaucous Gull in full breeding plumage at its nest. It looks around to see if all is safe before settling down to incubate its eggs.

GREAT BLACK-BACKED GULL

L A R U S   M A R I N U S

This giant amongst gulls dwarfs virtually every other shorebird. Its massive bulk, black mantle and black wings, with bold white tips to the primaries, contrast with a snow-white head, neck and underparts. These features, along with its whitish-pink legs and huge yellow bill with a red-tipped gonys, make it an easily identifiable species in its adult plumage. Close views will also reveal a cold, calculating white eye surrounded by a red orbital ring, giving a fierce look. Not generally as noisy or vocal as its relatives, the usual note is a deep clipped 'owk', but it also has some longer 'Ow-ow-ow-ow' calls, particularly on its nesting grounds. This large, powerful and voracious bird eats anything that comes its way, from carrion scavenged along the tideline, to live birds up to the size of a Shag, which are killed on their nesting grounds. It preys on such species as Manx Shearwater and Atlantic Puffin, which it pounces upon as they leave their burrows. It kills rabbits and other small mammals and also takes the eggs or chicks from unattended nests. Equally, it will feed on all forms of marine life that it can find, especially fish, crustaceans and molluscs. It feeds at rubbish tips, fish wharves and in fact any location that offers any food.

Great Black-backed Gulls do not form large flocks and, despite a marked and widespread increase since the end of the last century, it is still the scarcest of all the breeding gulls in Britain. The Operation Seafarer survey 1969–70 revealed an estimated breeding population of 22,000 pairs thoughout Britain and Ireland. Of these, around 16,000 pairs were located in Scotland, with the largest concentrations in the Outer Hebrides, Orkney and West Sutherland. The biggest single colony of 2000 pairs was on North Rona in the Outer Hebrides. The increase of the species as a whole is considered to be part of a general expansion over most of its range on both sides of the Atlantic, while its spread northwards is possibly linked with climatic amelioration.

The North American breeding range extends from Labrador and Quebec, south along the maritime provinces almost to New York. In the North Atlantic it nests around Greenland, Iceland, Spitsbergen (where it first bred in 1930), and the Faeroes. In western Europe its range extends from Murmansk in the USSR, round the coasts of Finland, Norway and Sweden to the Baltic Sea, the British Isles and

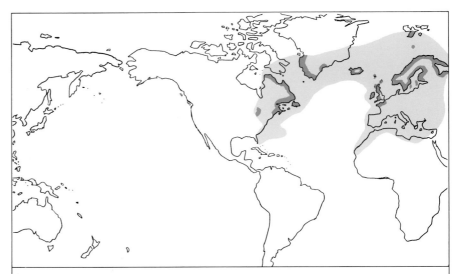

SIZE 28-31 in (71-79 cm)

WINGSPAN 60-66 in (152-167 cm)

EGG CLUTCH Two or Three

EGG COLOUR Pale buff to olive brown, blotched dark brown

INCUBATION 26-28 days

FLEDGLING 42-56 days

north west France. British breeding birds are mainly sedentary, but the Russian and Scandinavian populations move south to Britain, France and the Mediterranean in the winter. The North American population is joined by that from Greenland, with both wintering from eastern Labrador south to Florida.

In Britain the Great Black-backed Gull is almost entirely a west coast breeding bird, from the Shetlands to Cornwall, but it is also to be found nesting along the south coast, as far east as the Isle of Wight. In Ireland it occurs in coastal locations, predominantly along the western and southern coasts. Birds return to the nesting sites in March/April, where they strut around in upright posture, lower their heads in threat postures, and throw them back in long calling sessions. Bill nibbling, mutual preening and the presentation of food all contribute to the pair bonding. Considerable ag-

gression is displayed to other species and to any neighbours that enter its territory. Ritualized grass pulling may take place.

The nest is built by both sexes and comprises a large pile of grass, seaweed and any other handy vegetation, along with all manner of litter. The cup is often lined with finer materials. Nest sites are frequently at the top of a ridge or rock summit, especially on small islets, but may also be on grassy slopes. Often a solitary nester, in favourable localities it can be colonial, with perhaps 50 to 100 pairs breeding in close proximity. Nests may be only 6 to 10 feet (2–3 m) apart, but are spaced at greater distances if the site allows.

The two or three eggs are pale buff to olive brown, spotted and blotched dark brown. Incubation is carried out by both parents and takes 26 to 28 days. The week-old young will wander away from the nest, but they stay in the immediate

RIGHT *An almost fully grown, young Great Black-backed Gull with its well-marked chequered plumage showing clearly in this picture.*

LEFT *An immature Great Black-backed Gull, possibly well into its second year but showing the massive bill that should always aid identification when it is not possible to make comparable differences in size between this species and the smaller Lesser Black-backed Gull.*

An adult Great Black-backed Gull quietly incubates its eggs at a rather open nest site, for it has little to fear from other birds unless the nest is left unattended.

vicinity to be fed by either parent. After about six to eight weeks, the young are virtually independent and are soon flying. There is only one brood. Like most large gulls, the Great Black-backed takes four to five years to reach maturity. During this time it goes through a number of plumage changes, making identification difficult between it and the Lesser Black-backed Gull and the Herring Gull.

The Great Black-backed Gull's juvenile plumage shows a chequered pattern of blackish brown on the upperparts and whitish underparts. The legs are a dull, flesh colour and the bill is black. In first winter plumage the head is much whiter, while the upperparts and upperwing coverts are more distinctly

patterned black and white than either first winter Herring Gull or Lesser Black-backed Gull. By the second year the whiteness of the head and the uniformity of the dark mantle are intensified. When into its third year the bird shows almost adult plumage. Whatever the plumage, its large size and large powerful bill should aid identification.

In flight, the wing beats are slow and deliberate, while in strong winds it sails effortlessly above the waves, soaring to great heights. Its speed is deceptive and it can easily chase and overhaul other gulls, forcing them to disgorge their food.

Immature or adult, the Great Black-backed Gull is impressive at all times.

ROSS'S GULL

RHODOSTETHIA ROSEA

The first sighting of this beautiful little gull was made by James Clark Ross (1800–1862) in 1823. Then, as a lieutenant with the W. E. Parry Expedition to find the North West Passage, he collected two specimens of this bird, subsequently named after him, on the Melville Peninsula in the Canadian Arctic. Four years later, in 1827, Ross found the bird for a second time at latitude 82° North, north of Spitsbergen. He was again with Parry and together they noted at least six individuals in July that year. Ross's Gulls were subsequently noted by other Arctic explorers, usually as single birds, but occasionally two or more together. All these first sightings were in the polar basin and usually close to the pack ice, supporting the belief that they must nest somewhere in this icy region.

In 1879 quite large numbers of Ross's Gulls were discovered north of Siberia not far from the New Siberian Islands. Then in 1885 a nest was found in west Greenland at Disko Bay. This was an isolated breeding occurrence and no more were found in Greenland for many years. In 1894 the polar explorer Nansen found Ross's Gull north of Siberia and the following year noted others close to Franz Josef Island, continuing the belief they must nest somewhere in these icebound regions.

It was not until 1905, some 80 years after Ross's Gull had first been described, that the true breeding place of this mysterious bird was discovered. It proved to be not the frozen high Arctic, as expected, but the well-wooded, marshy river valleys in north east Siberia, from the Khatanga River to the Kolyma Delta region. In more recent times some small colonies have also been located in the Canadian arctic, at Bathurst Island near Churchill, Manitoba, and also in Greenland and Spitsbergen.

In its breeding plumage the bird is one of the most delightful of all gulls. It has a pearl-grey back and wings, and white underparts, rump and tail which are suffused with a soft rosy-pink colour. For this reason it is sometimes called the Rosy Gull. Around the head there is a narrow black ring. This ring is usually absent in winter, when there is then a dusky crescent extending from in front to below the eye and a dusky mark on the ear coverts. The bill is very small, thin and black and the legs and feet are bright red. The wings are very long and pointed and when the bird is at rest they project well beyond the tail. In this posture the round head,

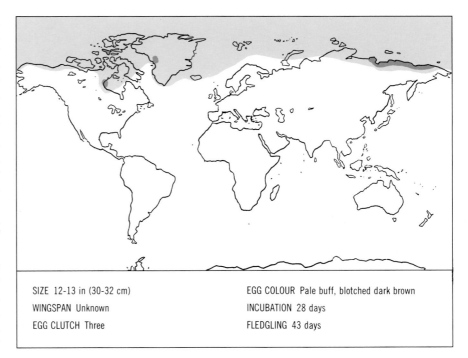

SIZE 12-13 in (30-32 cm)	EGG COLOUR Pale buff, blotched dark brown
WINGSPAN Unknown	INCUBATION 28 days
EGG CLUTCH Three	FLEDGLING 43 days

small bill and short legs give a dove-like impression. Although not always easy to see in the field, the tail is a most distinctive feature, for it is longish and wedge-shaped like no other small gull.

The young bird in its first year shows a striking 'M' pattern across the wings, like a Little Gull but the wedge-shaped tail is diagnostic. At this age only the tip of the central tail feathers are black, whereas a juvenile Little Gull shows a complete black band along the tip of its tail.

Ross's Gull has a very bouncy flight and at times it hovers and will frequently trail its legs in the manner of a Storm Petrel. On occasions it will feed along the water's edge in wader fashion. By such means it takes the small fish, crustaceans and insects that comprise its diet. On its breeding grounds it is especially insectivorous, taking beetles and dipteran flies.

Its variable and high-pitched calls are more melodious than other gulls, with a typical bubbling 'e-wo, e-wo, e-wo'.

In the spring birds return to their breeding grounds and by late May or early June, depending on the time of the thaw, they settle down to nesting. Not a great deal is known of their breeding biology, but it is presumed to be similar to other small northern breeding gulls. The nest is constructed of grasses and leaves, sometimes with a base of willow or other twigs. The three eggs are laid in early June and are pale buff, blotched with dark brown.

By later July/August, after nesting has been completed and the young are fledged, birds start to leave for winter quarters. Some move eastwards towards Chukchi and the Bering Seas, and are regularly noted at Point Barrow, Alaska in September and October. In some years thousands might be seen, but this seems to depend on the occurrence of strong north west winds, for at other times fewer birds are noted.

There is also some migration westwards along the coast towards the New Siberian Islands in the Arctic Ocean and thence further west through the Kara Sea to Franz Josef Land and Spitsbergen. Indeed, it is believed that many Ross's Gulls winter in the Spitsbergen area, though the precise limits of its range are not known.

In recent years Ross's Gull has virtually become an annual, though still rare, visitor to northern British waters, especially Shetland. Before 1958 it had only been recorded twice: in Yorkshire in 1846/47 and Shetland in 1936. Since 1958 there have been over forty records, mostly in January and February, but also some in April, May, June and August. There is one exceptional record of a bird that stayed on the south coast of England, at Christchurch Harbour in Dorset, from June to August 1974. These occurrences certainly lend credence to the Spitsbergen wintering grounds theory which hopefully will mean that British birders can look forward to continued visits by this delightful species from the high Arctic.

In the USA, apart from the regular occurrences along the Alaskan coast line, Ross's Gull is rarely seen. However, stragglers have occurred south to British Columbia and in Massachusetts and Illinois.

A Ross's Gull in full breeding plumage shows the pink flush of its underparts. This has given rise to the name of 'Rosy Gull'.

BLACK-LEGGED KITTIWAKE

LARUS TRIDACTYLA

During the non-breeding period of this bird's life, it is one of the most oceanic of gulls, haunting the northern region of the Atlantic Ocean and moving thousands of miles from where it was raised. After their early life at sea, Kittiwakes begin to drift back to their natal home at about three years old, though they may not breed until their fourth year. Having established an attachment with a particular colony, they usually return to nest there throughout their lives. This might be for twenty years or more, as ringing has shown them to be long-lived and still productive at such an age.

The adult Black-legged Kittiwake generally resembles a Mew Gull, but is slightly smaller and has solid black tips to the wings as if they were dipped in ink. The head, neck and underparts are white, with the upperparts deep grey (darker than the Mew Gull). The tail is slightly forked, but this is more noticeable in the juvenile, when it is then tipped with black. The legs are black and the bill yellow. The dark eye softens the expression, giving it a less fierce expression than is typical of most other gulls. If ever a bird is handled it will be noticed that there is but a vestige of a hind toe, hence its scientific name *tridactyla*.

Its more bounding flight and quicker wing action should also help to identify it from other 'grey'-backed gulls, even at some considerable distance. When feeding, it deftly takes food from the surface of the water or plunges, in tern-like fashion. Sometimes it settles on the water and then dives. It frequently follows ships, feeding in their wake. The food taken varies from small fish to crustaceans. Worms, molluscs, insects, aquatic plants and various seeds are also taken as the situation dictates.

Kittiwakes have been highly predated by man. In the early nineteenth century, along with other seabirds, they were shot for sport. Great decreases in their numbers were also undoubtedly brought about by the fashion dictates of the millinery trade, when the wings of young birds were used as an adornment for women's hats. The demand was such that at one time up to 700 birds a day were being taken from the colony on Lundy Island in the Bristol Channel. Other major nesting sites such as those at Flamborough and Ailsa Craig were much reduced and in some parts its breeding colonies were totally decimated. With the introduction of Bird Protection Acts at the turn of the century and

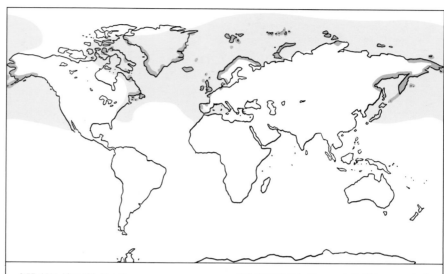

SIZE 15½-18 in (39-46 cm)

WINGSPAN 35½-36 in (90-92 cm)

EGG CLUTCH One to three

EGG COLOUR Pale blue grey to light brown marked with darker brown

INCUBATION 21-24 days

FLEDGLING 43 days

The clinging qualities of the Black-legged Kittiwake's nest are apparent from its location on the sheer cliff face shown here, which is typical of the species' nest site. Its two well-marked eggs can be seen in the deeply formed cup which will provide a safe nursery for the young birds.

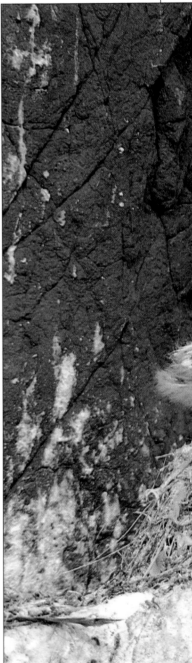

the change of fashion, the Kittiwake began to recover its losses and by the 1920s it had spread to other sites and began to establish new colonies. By 1959 the total breeding population of Britain and Ireland was estimated to be in the order of 180,000 breeding pairs. A decade later Operation Seafarer calculated the population to be almost half a million pairs. Scotland's share was put at 370,000 pairs, of which about 128,000 pairs were to be found on Orkney. Increased competition for preferred nesting sites has led to the use of buildings and during the last-half century Kittiwakes have nested regularly on warehouses and similar structures where vertical walls and window ledges substitute for the natural cliff face. This behaviour has been particularly well-documented along the Tyne, where as far up the river as Newcastle and Gateshead there are thriving colonies of Kittiwakes on the town's waterside buildings. At such locations it has been possible to reach the nests and study these more regimented and defined sites to great advantage, and many ringing studies have been carried out.

Individuals begin to return to their chosen colonies in February or March in the southern parts of the range, but not until April or May in more northerly latitudes. Various greeting displays establish the pair bond, including head bobbing, food begging and mock fighting. The nest is a neat construction, built by both birds, of compacted seaweed and sometimes grass and moss. Incredibly, it can be attached to a sheer rock face and has a much deeper cup than other gulls. This, no doubt,

is an evolutionary development to prevent young chicks from falling out of the nest. During the course of its use the whole structure becomes whitened and further strengthened by the birds' excrement.

Laying occurs in May and June and the usual clutch is two, though one or three eggs are sometimes laid. They are pale blue grey to light brown, marked with darker browns mainly at the large end. Incubation is carried out by both parents and lasts for 21 to 24 days. The young remain in the nest for four to five weeks and are fed on regurgitated food. During this period they develop their distinctive juvenile plumage pattern, which is most discernible in flight, and this they retain until their second winter. At this age they reveal a pattern of black diagonal bars in the wing which form an 'M' similar to the immature Little Gull but, unlike the Little Gull, the young Kittiwake, or 'Tarrock', as it is sometimes still called in Scotland, also has a black cervical collar. However, when in flight this collar may be hard to detect. A judgement may then have to be made in respect of size and mode of flight to differentiate between the two species.

At the nest the Kittiwake proclaims its name with incessant 'kitti-wa-ak, titti-wa-ak' calls, and a colony in full cry is quite overwhelming. At most other times the Kittiwake is a silent bird.

There are two races of Kittiwake. *L. t. pollicaris* breeds in the USSR from north east Siberia, south to Kamchatka and Commander Isles, then eastwards through the Bering Sea to the Aleutian

Islands. This race has slightly darker upperparts and more black on the wingtips. The nominate race *tridactyla* breeds along the coast of Arctic Canada including Prince Leopold Island, Bylot Island and Baffin Island, northern Labrador, the Gulf of St Lawrence, Newfoundland and Nova Scotia; and in Greenland, Iceland, Spitsbergen, Jan Mayen Land, the Faeroes, Novaya Zemlya and along the north coast of the USSR. In northern Europe it breeds from Murmansk south to Norway, the British Isles, the Baltic and northern France.

After nesting has been completed, birds disperse to sea. In the north Pacific they winter south to Japan and Baja California. In the west Atlantic they winter south to New Jersey with some occurring as far south as the Gulf of Mexico. In the east Atlantic most remain north of 40°N, but some reach the Mediterranean.

During periods of gales, particularly in October and November, thousands of Kittiwakes might be seen along the south western or eastern coasts of Britain. In recent years observation has shown a regular small passage of birds across inland Britain in spring and, more particularly, autumn.

An adult Kittiwake at a cliff-face nest site looks on while one of its two offspring stretches its wings. Even at this relatively early age the distinctive flight pattern in the wing is discernible.

IVORY GULL

P A G O P H I L A   E B U R N E A

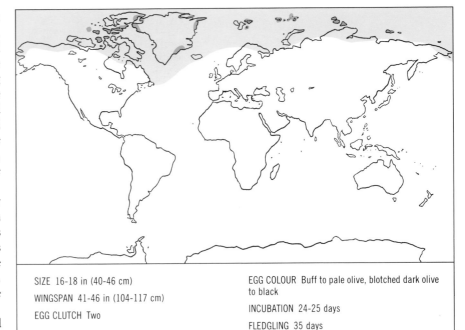

In its breeding plumage this bird of the high Arctic is wholly ivory white, hence the name. When perched its domed crown, plump body and short black legs give it a distinct, pigeon-like appearance, which is accentuated by its waddling gait. There is a short dove-like bill, which is slate blue at its base, becoming pale yellow and tipped with red. The iris is black/brown with a red orbital ring. The dark eye gives it a deceptively gentle expression, but it can be quite an aggressive species, able to hold its own in squabbles with birds the size of the Glaucous Gull.

The sexes are similar, but first-winter birds show irregular grey smudges on the face and chin, often with a small dark crescent round the eye. There is also a light sprinkling of spots on the underparts and sometimes the upperparts, black tips to the primaries and a very black terminal band to the tail. At all ages the legs are fully feathered down to the tibio-tarsal joint.

In flight the Ivory Gull looks long-winged and heavy-bodied, but it is nevertheless buoyant and

SIZE 16-18 in (40-46 cm)	EGG COLOUR Buff to pale olive, blotched dark olive to black
WINGSPAN 41-46 in (104-117 cm)	INCUBATION 24-25 days
EGG CLUTCH Two	FLEDGLING 35 days

A first-winter Ivory Gull shows only a scattering of black marking on its otherwise all-white plumage but the face is still rather dark at this age. This species demonstrates its scavenging ways as it feeds on a dead gull.

A first-winter Ivory Gull in flight showing black tips to the primaries and tail, typical of a bird at this age.

graceful in its actions, often flying with legs trailing, and revealing yellowish shafts to the primaries. It soars and glides with consummate ease and in strong winds will careen like a Kittiwake, skimming the sea, cliff or ice face with equal skill.

Fish and invertebrates are the main food, which it obtains by dipping the surface or surface plunging, but it is a capable scavenger on both land and ice. It attends polar bear kills to feed on the carcasses of whales and seals, after which its white face is often discoloured and stained. It also feeds on the faeces of seals, walruses and polar bears. Birds forage singly or in small groups, preferring the edge of the pack ice and areas of drift ice, but normally shunning ice-free waters outside the breeding season.

Its breeding range is to the north of the July isotherm of 5°C and includes a part of the Canadian Arctic, Northern Greenland, Spitsbergen, Franz Josef Land, Novaya Zemlya and Sverernaya Zemlya. In some parts of its range, notably Spitsbergen, there has been a marked decrease in its numbers since the nineteenth century, with colonies that were once 100 or more strong now down to twenty or so. In other areas numbers vary from thriving colonies holding upwards of 500 pairs, to those with only a handful of birds.

Favoured nesting sites are on bare ground, usually on an offshore islet where they are safe from the attentions of Arctic Foxes. However, some choose steep cliff faces, where they often mix with Kittiwakes. Cliff-nesting birds may select ledges up to 984 feet (300 m) or more high, often with an overhang for added protection.

Birds return to their nesting sites in May, where they establish a monogamous pair bond mainly through a series of bowing and calling displays. The nest is a bulky structure built by both sexes. It consists mostly of seaweed, but can include other locally obtained vegetation, with a lining of grass and perhaps a few feathers.

The normal clutch is two eggs, which are laid in June or July. They are buff to pale olive, spotted and blotched dark olive to black/brown. Incubation lasts for around 24 or 25 days, with both parents taking turns to sit for anything from a few minutes to several hours. After hatching, the young are brooded while they are small and are cared for by the parents for around 35 days.

When nesting is over, birds disperse to winter within the northern Atlantic and the Chukchi and Bering Seas. Moving with the pack ice, they drift generally southwards, but this is not true migration. Hundreds of birds have been reported off northern Newfoundland in late winter and early spring. A few stragglers reach Nova Scotia and have been recorded along the Atlantic coast to New York and inland to the Great Lakes. It is an uncommon visitor to northern and western Alaska.

In Europe vagrants have occurred in Denmark, France and Britain between 1958 and 1985, but with decreasing frequency in recent times.

GULL-BILLED TERN

GELOCHELIDON NILOTICA

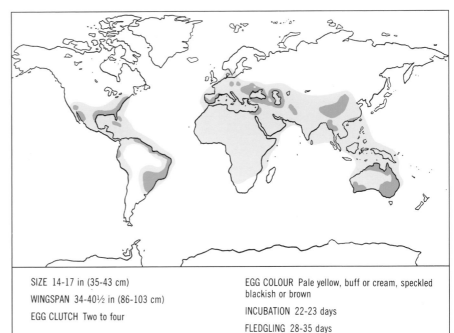

SIZE 14–17 in (35–43 cm)	EGG COLOUR Pale yellow, buff or cream, speckled blackish or brown
WINGSPAN 34–40½ in (86–103 cm)	INCUBATION 22–23 days
EGG CLUTCH Two to four	FLEDGLING 28–35 days

A visit to the Camargue in May 1960 provided one of those birding experiences which becomes etched into the memory for ever. It was an unforgettable three weeks of intensive birding, which at that time considerably added to my 'life list'. Many new birds were seen during this trip, including Gull-billed Tern.

At a place called Cacheret, there are some small islets out in the lagoon. These flat islets of dried mud and dotted with salicornia held breeding Black-headed Gulls, Red-crested Pochard (*Netta rufina*), Avocet (*Recurvirostra avosetta*), Little Tern and Gull-billed Tern. It was indeed a wonderland of noise and activity. We had previously seen Gull-billed Terns hunting over rice fields, but here was a colony of at least 60 pairs of these fine birds which we were able to study more closely. First impressions were of a Black-headed Gull sized bird, but with longer, broader wings, and other gull-like features such as a short tail and, particularly, a short, blunt, wholly black, gull-like bill from which the bird takes its name. After our initial intrusion to this colony, birds soon began drifting back to settle on their nests, while others stood around. Their much longer black-legged appearance was most obvious and it could be seen that the black crown and nape formed a deeper cap than the Sandwich Tern, with no hint of a crest. The neck and underparts are white, while the upperparts are ash-grey. A solid-looking bird, its gull-like flight lacks the grace and buoyancy of other terns, but shows a noticeably dark trailing edge to both the upper and under primaries. The silver grey rump and tail give it quite a different look to the wholly white rump and tail of the Sandwich Tern, the species with which it is most often compared.

The feeding habits of the Gull-billed Tern are also quite different to other Sternidae, for it is not a great fish eater. To the contrary, it shows a marked preference for terrestrial and aquatic insects, taking grasshoppers, crickets, dragonflies, earthworms, frogs, lizards and small mammals. It either hawks and swoops to catch insects in the air, or snatches prey from the ground or the surface of the water. As a consequence it is often to be seen feeding over dry ground, behaviour not usually associated with terns. In fact, the Gull-billed Tern appears to have very little affinity to the sea at all during the nesting period.

The breeding season begins in April or early May, when birds arrive back at their nest sites. Then their rather nasal 'rhaa-rhaa gahak-id' calls fill the air. This sound is quite unlike the 'kirri-kirri' notes of the Sandwich Tern.

The nest is a scrape in dried mud, sand or gravel, lined with pieces of grass and at times bits of dried seaweed and other debris. The clutch usually consists of two to four pale yellow, buff or cream eggs, with small spots, speckles and blotches of blackish or dark brown. Both parents incubate for 22 to 23 days. Shortly after hatching, the young leave the nest and hide in nearby vegetation, coming to their parents' call to be fed. The fledging period is 28 to 35 days and the young become totally independent after three months. Families generally stay together until the time they migrate. This often starts as early as July and lasts through to September, with birds usually following coastal routes to winter from Botswana to southern Africa.

The Gull-billed Tern also breeds in western North America at the Salton Sea, California, and from the coasts of Sonora, Mexico, south to Ecuador. It nests locally in eastern North America, too, from Long Island, New York through the Gulf States to Cuba and the West Indies. Others breed in south eastern America on the coasts of Brazil and Argentina, and in Australia, and from southern China south to the Malay Archipelago. In Europe, it breeds discontinuously in Denmark, Holland, Spain and southern France, and from eastern Europe across Asia Minor and eastwards to Mongolia and the Punjab. It also breeds in North and East Africa.

In Europe there have been marked fluctuations in the fortunes of this species and it has undoubtedly decreased in many areas due to habitat change. It is somewhat like the Sandwich Tern in being erratic in the choice of nest sites, readily deserting those favoured for some years for no apparent reason. It bred once in Britain, in 1950, where it is normally a very rare migrant averaging about four records a year. It is mainly noted on the south and east coasts of England, most usually in May, with fewer in summer and autumn.

RIGHT *With broad, more rounded looking wings than a tern, heavy body and shallow, forked tail, the Gull-billed Tern is more gull-like than others of its genus. The thick, gull-like bill gives the bird its name.*

LEFT *A Gull-billed Tern incubates its eggs. Sitting alert, the all black, thick gull-like bill is very apparent.*

CASPIAN TERN

STERNA CASPIA

This is a most impressive bird, a giant among terns. In flight it may show less grace than other terns, but it demonstrates its power and strength with deep strokes of its long wings as it patrols offshore waters, the coast or inland lakes. When feeding, it flies some 10 to 30 feet (3–9 m) above the waves with its huge bill held vertically downwards as it scans the depths below, and when prey is sighted, it makes a dramatic plunging dive, often disappearing completely below the surface. Occasionally it will alight on the water and take food in the same manner as a gull (Laridae). More rarely it will skim the water like a Skimmer (*Rhynchops* sp.) though this action may well be to clean its bill rather than another feeding technique. Its usual fare is fish of all sorts, herring especially, and these are invariably swallowed head first whilst in flight. Sometimes, though, it will settle on land to despatch a particularly large individual. On occasions invertebrates are taken and it is also reported to indulge in the most un-tern-like behaviour of sometimes eating the eggs and young of other birds.

In adult plumage, the Caspian Tern shows a similar mixture of black and whites as other terns (Sternidae) with a black cap, pearl grey upperparts and white underparts, while in flight the wingtips show a large dusky area. The rump and slightly forked tail are pale grey though the latter is sometimes almost white. The most noticeable feature, however, is the massive, dagger-like, blood-red bill, the bird sometimes being described as having a bill like a huge carrot!

There is a chance of confusion with the slightly smaller Royal Tern where the range of the two species overlaps, but the thinner, orange-red bill and general paler appearance of the latter bird should preclude the possibility of mis-identification. Additionally, the deep rasping 'kra-kra-kraa-uh' call that the Caspian Tern gives in flight is quite unlike the bleating 'kee-err' of the Royal Tern. This is sufficient in itself to identify the species if none of the aforementioned features have been seen. The Caspian Tern also has a short 'ra-ra-ra' alarm call. On the ground it waddles about on its relatively long black legs, with a carriage that is noticeably horizontal. In non-breeding plumage the black cap becomes streaked with white, but it never shows a fully white forehead as does a Royal Tern.

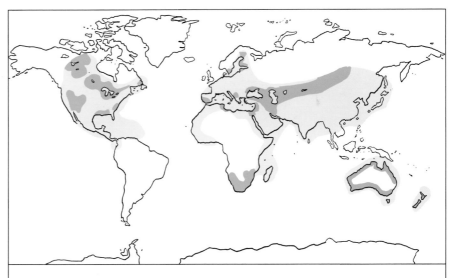

SIZE 19-23 in (48-59 cm)	EGG COLOUR Buff-coloured, blotched dark brown
WINGSPAN 50-55 in (127-140 cm)	INCUBATION 25 days
EGG CLUTCH Two or three	FLEDGLING 28-35 days

ABOVE *A Caspian Tern in full breeding plumage generally shows a blood-red bill with a distally black tip although often this can be yellow, orange or white.*

LEFT *The strong, swift flight of the Caspian Tern is as graceful as any other of the Sternidae, but its size and bulk give it a more gull-like dimension.*

Like the Sandwich Tern, the name 'Caspian' suggests a limited distribution, but this of course is not so. It is a cosmopolitan species, with a discontinuous breeding range that spans five continents and both hemispheres. However, it does occur most extensively in the area around and to the east of the Caspian Sea, from whence its name derives, and it was here that the eighteenth-century German naturalist Peter Simon Pallas, found the species during his travels in Russia.

Wherever it breeds, the preferred habitat would seem to be either sea coasts, estuaries, or the shores of inland lakes and seas, though occasionally it chooses rocky islands. The nest is a mere scrape in the ground on a shingle bank, dry mud or sand. This is sometimes lined with pieces of rotting vegetation. The two or three eggs are rather gull-like, buff-coloured, blotched and spotted with dark brown. The shell is rough to touch and lacks any

gloss. They are virtually indistinguishable from those of the Royal Tern.

Both parents take it in turn to incubate the eggs and this may take up to 25 days. When the young hatch, they are covered with a greyish down, speckled with dark markings. As they develop, the colour of the down fades to almost white to become juvenile plumage. Juveniles have a dull reddish orange, dusky-tipped bill and an almost complete black cap, its crown flecked with white. The upperparts are mostly pale grey, with brown tips to the feathers that give it a scaly look, especially on the scapulars. The fledging period is about four to five weeks.

Caspian Terns are most aggressive on their breeding grounds and will not hesitate to attack and kill the young of their neighbour. They can also defend themselves quite easily against marauding jaegers.

On the North American continent the Caspian Tern breeds along the Atlantic coast from Virginia, south to the Gulf States. It is to be found locally around the Great Lakes, west to California and south to Baja California. Breeding colonies here are generally larger than those in Europe, where they are often found nesting only singly or in small groups. American birds winter in the Baja California, the Gulf of Mexico and the Caribbean.

In Europe there have been decreases in its range and it is now either extinct as a breeding bird, or breeds less regularly than it did, in Denmark, West Germany, East Germany and Romania. The same is true of Tunisia, where I saw Caspian Terns feeding young on the wing at Lac de Tunis in October 1987. In contrast, there have been some increases in numbers in Sweden, Finland and Estonia.

The Caspian Tern is an accidental visitor to Britain and Ireland, where one or two are noted every year. Its migration patterns are still not totally understood, though generally it would seem that northern breeding populations winter in the tropics while those nesting nearer the Equator are probably sedentary. Those that migrate move from their breeding grounds during the months of July to October, when the young birds accompany their parents southwards. On spring passage, birds return northwards in April, May and June. The power of their flight is so great that they usually pass rapidly overland and rarely linger at inland waters for any length of time. However, it is not unusual to see such a migrant, as I did in Austria one May when looking through a flock of Black-headed Gulls resting along the shore of Zicke Lacke. How long it had been resting there I do not know, but after a short while it flew up and then very quickly disappeared from sight.

There are no known records of Caspian Tern wintering in Europe.

This picture shows an adult Caspian Tern in non-breeding plumage when the crown and forehead become finely streaked with white markings. However the huge, carrot-like bill is always diagnostic.

ROYAL TERN

STERNA MAXIMA

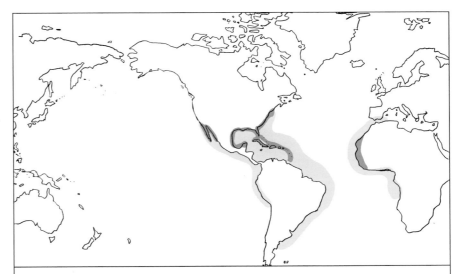

SIZE 18-21 in (46-53 cm)	EGG COLOUR White to medium brown, blotched red brown
WINGSPAN 42-44 in (106-112 cm)	INCUBATION 30-36 days
EGG CLUTCH One, rarely two	FLEDGLING 28-35 days

This large tern is approximately the size of a Common or Mew Gull and its dimensions are only exceeded by the Caspian Tern.

In general appearance it looks much the same as other terns, having white underparts, rump and tail; pale grey upperparts and a black crown. The full black crown, however, is acquired but briefly during the early part of the breeding period. For most of the year the bird's forehead and lores are white, the black not reaching the eye. The bill, which is almost as long as the head, comes to a much finer point than a Caspian Tern's and is usually deep orange in colour, but never shows a dusky subterminal tip as does the larger bird. The legs are black.

In flight, which is swift and strong, its long pointed wings and deeply pointed tail will be noticed. The underwing is white but shows dusky webs on the outer primaries which forms a diffuse wedge under the wing point, but this is less obvious than in the Caspian Tern. Like other Sternidae, it will dive when feeding, sometimes hovering before it does so. It catches fish, but especially favours crabs, and other crustacea. Occasionally birds indulge in aerial skimming but it is thought this may be only to clean the bill or perhaps to drink. Usually it feeds singly or in small groups, though sometimes small flocks of 100 or more might be encountered. A bird of the tropical and subtropical lower latitudes, it is to be found along coasts and on inshore and offshore islands, where it favours beaches, estuaries, lagoons and the mangrove coasts of north and central America.

The nominate race, *S. m. maxima*, breeds along the North American Pacific coast, from San Diego, California, southwards along the north west coast of Mexico, with the main nesting areas centred in Isla Raza, Gulf of California. On the Atlantic coast it nests from Virginia south to Texas, east Mexico, and in the West Indies and possibly also Venezuela. The race *S. m. albidorsalis* has recently been discovered breeding in north west Africa where large colonies are now known to exist on the Arguin Bank, northern Mauritania. Other colonies have been discovered in Senegal and the Gambia.

A highly gregarious species in North America, Royal Terns are found in vast colonies of many thousands of pairs, where they often breed in close proximity to Sandwich Terns, Caspian Terns and Laughing Gulls. A noisy bird on its breeding

A Royal Tern has a wholly black cap for only a short period during the breeding season. However some birds may still be incubating eggs yet show the white forehead of non-breeding plumage.

LEFT *A group of Royal Terns, some with totally black caps and some with white foreheads rest along a Florida coastline in early spring.*

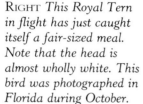

RIGHT *This Royal Tern in flight has just caught itself a fair-sized meal. Note that the head is almost wholly white. This bird was photographed in Florida during October.*

grounds, it has a number of calls similar to those of the Sandwich Tern, but lower pitched and louder. The alarm call is a hard 'keet-keet', or 'krit-krit', given either in flight or on the ground. Display and pairing is similar to other crested terns, with the monogamous pair bond believed to be for one season only.

Between April and June nesting takes place. The nest is no more than a depression in the sand created by both birds, though a few pieces of debris may be added during incubation. The clutch is usually only one egg, rarely two. These have a ground colour ranging from white to medium brown and are spotted and blotched red brown. There is only one brood. Incubation lasts from 30 to 36 days, and both birds take turns, though from time to time the eggs may be left unattended for several hours.

Twenty-four hours after hatching, the downy young of the nominate race are active and move from the nest site to form creches with other youngsters. By comparison, the young of the race *albidorsalis* remain in the nest for a week after hatching and do not creche for fifteen days.

The fledging period is between 28 and 35 days, but total independence of adults is not attained for probably five to eight months, which is an unusually long period among seabirds.

From August and September, North American breeding birds move to their winter quarters along the Pacific coast from central California south to Mollendo, Peru. On the Atlantic coast they are to be found during the winter from southern Carolina south through the Caribbean to Argentina.

The North African population appears to disperse in two directions. Some move north to Morocco and the western Mediterranean, while others move south to winter in the Gulf of Guinea and perhaps as far south as Namibia.

In their wintering areas, Royal Terns are equally gregarious as on their nesting grounds, often occurring in flocks up to 500, comprising both young and adults.

Royal Terns do not usually breed until their third or fourth year and in their first year they remain in their wintering area.

A vagrant to Britain, there have been just four records, all since 1954, with the latest in 1979.

SANDWICH TERN

STERNA SANDVICENSIS

This bird was first described from specimens collected in 1787 at Sandwich in Kent, but it is of course to be found much further afield than its common name suggests. In this respect it shares the same county association as the equally widely distributed and misnamed Kentish Plover and Dartford Warbler!

The Sandwich Tern is a colonial nesting species, breeding in isolated colonies in Britain and Ireland and along the north European and Baltic coasts, particularly in Holland (where it has declined considerably in recent years), Germany, Denmark and Sweden. A number breed in France, mainly round the Brittany coast, and some also in the Camargue. It has bred irregularly in Italy, Spain and Tunisia. Further east a considerable population breeds around the northern shores of the Black Sea and the southern and eastern shores of the Caspian Sea, with smaller numbers around the Sea of Azov.

In North America the subspecies *S. s. acuflavidus*, sometimes called Cabot's Tern, breeds along the Atlantic and Gulf coasts from Virginia to Florida and Texas, and in Mexico, Yucatan and the Bahamas.

The Sandwich Tern is a largish tern, somewhat smaller than a Royal Tern or Swift Tern (*S. bergii*), but about a tenth bigger and longer-winged than the Common Tern. In flight it is less buoyant and more gull-like, while the tail is less deeply forked than in some other terns. However, the long, narrow, pointed wings, black cap and longish black bill with yellow tips would aid identification.

When feeding, it patrols inshore waters, hovering briefly before plunge diving into the sea from a height of 20 to 40 feet (5–10 m) or more. Dives are mostly vertical, but sometimes at an angle. It tends to stay submerged longer than other terns that feed in a similar manner. Quite large fish are taken. Sand eels especially are a favoured prey and specimens measuring 8 to 9 inches (4–5 cm) long appear to present no difficulty to the bird. These are brought to the surface and immediately swallowed head first, unless they are intended for its mate or young.

At rest it will be seen that the black cap extends from the base of the bill to the nape, with the crown feathers elongated to form a distinctive crest. This becomes particularly obvious when the bird gets excited. The upperparts are pale grey and the underparts white, though in the breeding male these can, at times, have a creamy or pinkish wash.

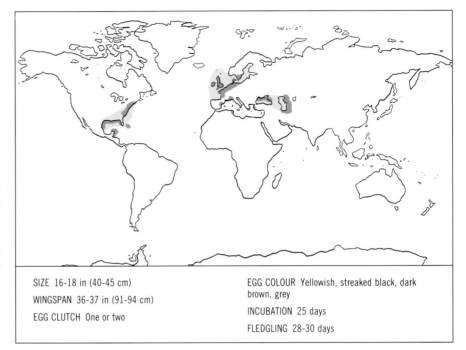

SIZE 16-18 in (40-45 cm)	EGG COLOUR Yellowish, streaked black, dark brown, grey
WINGSPAN 36-37 in (91-94 cm)	INCUBATION 25 days
EGG CLUTCH One or two	FLEDGLING 28-30 days

When standing, its black legs look comparatively long for a tern and, also in flight when its whiter appearance is more noticeable, it might be confused with Gull-billed Tern which also has longish legs. Winter plumage, when the front of the crown turns white, is assumed quite early on in the season, even whilst birds are still nesting in June and early July. By September or October the whole of the head has developed a streaky appearance. Juvenile birds look similar to winter adults, but can lack the yellow tip to the black bill.

The Sandwich Tern (like the Royal Tern) moults its dark head feathers at an early stage during nesting and as winter progresses the head becomes more streaky and white.

An adult Sandwich Tern and young chick at the nest in dunes, sheltered by marrams.

The Sandwich Tern is a noisy bird with a far-carrying, grating 'kirrick' call. When alarmed it utters an incessant 'krit', or 'krik'.

A migrant species, Sandwich Terns are first noted returning to their European breeding sites in late March or early April. Many birds arrive already paired, but their elaborate flight courtship continues to further establish the pair bond. The two birds will rise up for 200 to 300 feet (100 m) or more in a high spiral, returning earthwards in a spectacular glide. On the ground this is followed by much circling of each other, with wings held half open. During courtship food is often presented by one to the other.

The nest is a mere scrape in the ground into which the one or two (sometimes three) eggs are laid during May. These are much larger than those of other terns, mainly yellowish in colour and variably streaked, spotted or blotched with black, dark brown and grey. There is only one brood and incubation, which is undertaken by both parents, lasts about 25 days.

The preferred habitat for nesting usually comprises low-lying sand or shingly beaches, but sometimes rocky coasts or islands are chosen. In Ireland it also nests on lakesides a considerable distance from the sea.

Sandwich Terns are very erratic in their choice of nesting sites, and areas favoured one year can be ignored the next. They are prone to disturbance and whole colonies have been known to suddenly desert their nests and eggs for no apparent reason. They are easily disturbed by humans, whilst the attention of such predators as rats, stoats, weasels, foxes and Short-eared Owls can quickly contribute to total nesting failure.

The Scolt Head colony in Norfolk, however, has been successful for most years due to protection and efficient wardening. Here one can see the nesting terns in full breeding clamour with no danger to the birds.

After breeding has taken place, adults and young generally move south, but migration is considerably protracted. Along the North Sea coast of Britain they can still be seen in late September and early October, and sometimes even into November or later. In Britain occurrences inland are regular and small numbers are noted most years during spring and autumn at the larger reservoirs.

The winter quarters of the European population extends from Portugal to South Africa, but most are to be found along the tropical West African coast. The Black Sea population, on the other hand, tends mainly to winter in the western Mediterranean, while those from the Caspian Sea area spread from the Persian Gulf east to the Indian Ocean.

In North America, *S. acuflavida* winters from Florida south to Uruguay on the Atlantic coast and from the Gulf of Mexico, south to Peru on the Pacific coast.

ROSEATE TERN

S T E R N A   D O U G A L L I I

Though globally a widespread breeding species, the Roseate Tern nests in comparatively few places. The nominate race breeds locally in North America from Nova Scotia discontinuously south to the West Indies, the Central Americas and Venezuela. It also breeds in Europe, with its main strongholds in Britain and Ireland. There are also some small colonies in Brittany, while sporadic breeding has been reported in Denmark and Germany. In Africa, some birds have been found nesting off the west coast of Mauritania; it is suspected of having nested in Tunisia; nesting occurs in South Africa and there are large colonies on the islands off the Kenyan coast.

The race *S. a. arideensis* breeds in the Seychelles, Mauritius and Cargados Carajos in the Indian Ocean. The race *S. a. gracilis* breeds in the Moluccas Sea and northern Australia, while *S. a. bangsi* breeds in Riukiu, the Solomon, Philippine and Kei Islands.

In its tropical range it nests throughout the year and is almost certainly resident in this region.

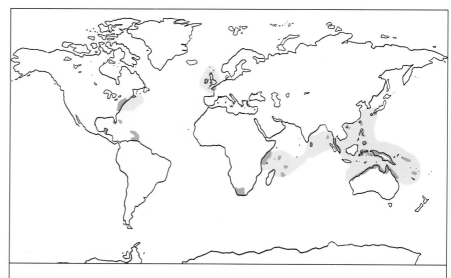

SIZE 14-17 in (35-43 cm)	EGG COLOUR Creamy buff, blotched black-brown
WINGSPAN 30-31 in (76-79 cm)	INCUBATION 23 days
EGG CLUTCH Two	FLEDGLING 27-30 days

LEFT *An almost fully grown, young Roseate Tern still retaining a few wispy, down feathers here and there. This bird carries an identification ring on its right leg which may well be recovered off the West African coast where, unfortunately, many Roseate Tern meet their death by the sport of local boys.*

PREVIOUS PAGE *A mixed flock of mainly Sandwich Terns, but including Crested and Caspian Terns, in their winter quarters in the Oman.*

Differences between the races are slight, and mainly involve the size of the wings and bill and the colour of the bill, with those found in tropical areas being smaller and showing more red on the bill.

In overall appearance the Roseate Tern is much like a Common Tern and Arctic Tern in size. However, its much whiter appearance and shorter wings should make it possible for the species to be singled out amongst a mixed flock of all three species. Also its noticeably long, 'whipping' tail streamers, long, rasping 'aaak' call, and at times soft very characteristic 'chu-ick' note further assist in its specific identification.

Like other Sternidae, there is a black cap which is long but rather shallow, while the back and wings are pearl grey or pale blue grey – noticeably paler than on a Common Tern. Another distinction is the bill, which is long, pointed and usually almost wholly black, except for the base which in summer is red. In the case of tropical breeding birds, the whole bill can be red. The legs are red. Additionally, when the bird is at rest it will be seen that the tail streamers extend far beyond the folded wingtips, whereas on a Common Tern they just reach the folded wingtips and on an Arctic Tern only slightly beyond them. The distinctive rosy tinge to the breast, from which the bird gets its name, only shows for a short period of time during the early part of the breeding season and soon disappears as the summer progresses.

The Roseate Tern is one of the rarest breeding seabirds in Britain and Ireland, with only about a dozen or so colonies that are regularly in use. In total there are possibly well under 2000 pairs at all sites. Nevertheless its status has in fact improved in recent years, despite pressures on its nesting areas. Disturbance is a major problem in its success or failure, as it is with other coasting nesting species, and its recent improvement is undoubtedly due in part to the intensive protection and wardening of traditional nesting areas. More breed in Ireland than Britain, but there are major colonies in the Firth of Forth and on Anglesey. It was in fact at this latter site, on the Ynysfennig rocks at Rhosneigr that I first really got to know this bird, where it shares the site with Arctic Terns.

It is not unusual for Roseate Terns to nest in mixed colonies with other species, but when doing so they generally form 'discrete' groups. Often they choose dunes covered with marram grass, where this forms part of the breeding area. Like some other Sternidae, breeding is sporadic and uncertain and on occasions whole colonies may fail, or shift to a new site half-way through the breeding season.

Roseate Terns arrive back at their chosen nest sites quite late and then usually *en masse*, with many birds already paired. They do not generally settle down to nesting until the end of May. Meanwhile

The graceful, buoyant flight of the Roseate Tern makes this a most attractive member of the Sternidae family.

A Roseate Tern settles down to incubate its eggs at a sand dune nest site. Note the almost totally black bill with just a hint of red at the base, quite the reverse colouring of those subspecies breeding in the tropics.

the pair bond is reinforced and the territory established by aerial display flight or by the male strutting about with wings drooped and the long tail streamers raised as it offers a sand eel to its mate. The nest is a shallow scrape, often in the shelter of vegetation, in a hollow or a rabbit burrow. There is little or no lining to start with, but pieces of grass may be added during incubation.

The normal clutch of two eggs is not usually laid until early June. They are more oval in shape than those of other terns, being creamy-buff and variably spotted, blotched and scrawled with black-brown. Both parents take turns to incubate, but the female takes the larger share of the 23 or so days before hatching takes place. The chicks are quite distinctive, appearing rather hairy because the filaments of their downy feathers are joined together in groups rather than being separated and fluffy like those of the Common Tern or Arctic Tern chicks.

The adults are strongly defensive of their young and will attack intruders, calling loudly with a chittering 'ke-ke-ke-ke', then ending with a sharp barking note as they dive onto the trespasser. However, they do not strike home their attack as an Arctic Tern would. The fledging period is usually

27 to 30 days, but the young tern is dependent on the adults for at least another eight weeks.

Families depart from the breeding grounds in August and September. By the end of September most of the European population is in its main wintering quarters off the coasts of North West Africa, between the Equator and 10° North.

In winter plumage the forehead is white, while the bill darkens and the legs become orange red. The juvenile bird, which is smaller than the adult, has even blunter, more rounded wing points and a slightly blunter bill. The head is wholly dark, while the saddle is brownish. The upperwing also shows a dark carpal bar along its length and the secondaries are noticeably white. First-summer birds remain in their winter quarters, but some second-year birds return to the breeding areas, though they will not nest before they are at least three years old. The North American population winters south to the Caribbean and the adjacent Atlantic, occasionally reaching as far south as Brazil.

The Roseate Tern is the most marine of the Sternidae and is rarely noted overland. For this reason it is least often recorded at migration times.

COMMON TERN

STERNA HIRUNDO

For most British birders this is probably the first *Sterna* or 'sea tern' they will encounter. This may be at a coastal breeding site or at inland water, where passage migrants pause to feed or rest during April/May or September/October. As the name suggests, it is the most widely distributed nesting tern in Britain, though not as numerous as the Arctic Tern.

Identification of Common and Arctic Terns can be difficult, especially when they are not seen very clearly. This is particularly so in the autumn, when juveniles are also to be encountered. Indeed, the problem has led to the expression 'Commic' Tern being coined to cover sightings of those birds which cannot be specifically identified. The Common Tern is a graceful, medium-sized bird with white underparts, pale grey back, black cap, red legs and a red bill with a black tip. The long, pointed wings and forked tail with projecting streamers have given rise to the vernacular term 'Sea Swallow', though of course it is no relation whatsoever to the Swallow (*Hirundo rustica*).

At close range the Common Tern can be readily identified by its scarlet bill with black tip. But this feature is reliable only in the breeding season, as at other times of the year the Arctic Tern might be seen with the black-tipped bill of its winter plumage. Through the winter the black cap is incomplete and both Common and Arctic Terns show a white forehead at this time. When at rest certain differences between the two are more obvious. For example, the folded wing of the Common Tern extends to virtually the same length as the tail, but the Arctic Tern's tail extends well beyond its folded wing. The Common Tern has slightly longer legs. In flight the best distinguishing feature is the wing-tips. When viewed from below only the innermost primaries of the Common Tern show up as a translucent panel or 'window', whereas all the primaries are translucent on the Arctic Tern. From above, the upperwing tip has dark streaking on the Common Tern, but is a pale clear grey on the Arctic Tern.

Towards the end of April, Common Terns begin to return to their nesting sites and within a few days of their arrival males are staking out their breeding territories. These might be on the mainland, or on an island, among dunes or salt marshes and, at times, on the shores of lakes, or along rivers or, in

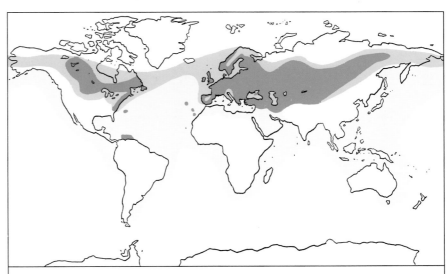

SIZE 12½ in (32-38 cm)	EGG COLOUR Cream to dark brown, blotched dark brown. Sometimes pale green or blue unmarked
WINGSPAN 31-32 in (79-81 cm)	INCUBATION 22-26 days
EGG CLUTCH Two to four	FLEDGLING 28 days

A juvenile Common Tern at rest. Note the gingery forehead which will be white later in the autumn. The dark carpal bar is partly hidden on this bird but in young birds it is especially noticeable at this age, particularly in flight.

ABOVE *An adult Common Tern in flight shows proportionately broader, shorter wings, heavier body and shorter, broader tail than Arctic Tern. However the black-tipped, red bill visible in this picture is diagnostic.*

LEFT *An adult Common Tern comes in to land at its nest site holding a small sand eel to feed the ever-hungry youngster.*

RIGHT *A group of Common Terns have discovered a shoal of small fry trapped in the shallows of a falling tide. They excitedly call to each other as they plunge in one after another to secure their share of the prey.*

more recent years, at inland sand and gravel workings. At one such site in Warwickshire, England, there is now a well-established colony about as far from the sea as you can get in Britain. Birds first nested there in 1969. Numbers have steadily increased and by 1987 a total of twenty pairs nested, raising 56 young, an excellent average per pair.

The male displays to prospective mates both in the air and on the ground. Once the pair bond has been established it is reinforced by the presentation of fish.

The nest is a scrape or hollow in sand, shingle or soil, lined with varying amounts of local materials, especially thrift or marram stalks. At times the nest might be on tideline debris or in old gull nests. Occasionally floating nests are constructed, sunken boats or old piers are also utilized, and they readily take to floating platforms especially launched to attract them to nest.

The two to four eggs, which are laid in May and June, vary from cream to dark brown, usually with spots and blotches of dark brown. The eggs can sometimes be unmarked, while pale green or blue eggs do occur. Incubation begins when the first egg is laid and lasts from 22 to 26 days, with fledging completed 28 days or so after hatching. There is only one brood.

The early juvenile is brownish above and white below, with a mostly dark bill, and white forehead. In flight it shows a prominent dark shoulder bar, as do all winter plumaged birds.

The Common Tern is extremely noisy on its breeding grounds especially when there are young about. The usual call is a long grating 'keeeee-yaah' with downwards inflection, but it also has a frequently uttered 'kik, kik, kik' note. The principal food is small fish and sand eels, which it secures by flying methodically above the waves, plunging in to secure its prey. The young are fed on the same diet and often some items are larger than the young bird itself, but somehow or other they eventually manage to swallow it!

Some birds are quite late in leaving their summer home and a number can still be around in October. The majority of Common Terns nesting in Britain favour the west coast of Scotland, but in England they are concentrated particularly along the East Anglian coastline. It is in Norfolk that I have watched most of the Common Terns that I have seen, spending long hours observing them at the famed National Trust reserve, Blakeney Point. This was in the days when the colony was under the watchful eye of Ted Eales. There are no doubt others of my generation who will recall similar happy times and other characters of the day, such as Reggie Gaze whose book *Bird Sanctuary* first

An adult Common Tern on the nest calls to its mate out of picture as it returns to take its turn at incubation.

alerted me to the existence of this incredible area.

Other places in Britain where the Common Tern nests include the Hampshire and Dorset coast, the Isles of Scilly, Anglesey and the Isle of Man. A fair number also breed inland in north east Scotland, and the East Midlands of England. It also occurs at suitable localities in Ireland. The total British and Irish breeding population is somewhere around 20,000 pairs.

Globally the Common Tern nests throughout most of Europe, Asia and North America between 30° and 65° N. There are also some isolated populations in the Caribbean, the north Atlantic islands and Africa. Throughout most of its world range it does perhaps surprisingly breed away from the sea coast.

In North America it is a common bird, breeding across most of Canada from Newfoundland, New Brunswick and Prince Edward Island, mainly north of the Great Lakes westwards to Alberta, east of the Rocky mountains. In the USA it nests in north eastern Montana, South Dakota, southern Michigan, northern Ohio, northern New York and south to North Carolina. It also nests in south eastern Texas and Florida. It does not breed on the Pacific coast, but some winter from southern Baja California and south Carolina southwards to the straits of Magellan.

North American birders not only have to consider the differences between Common and Arctic Terns, but also have to distinguish these species from Forster's Tern and the Siberian subspecies of Common Tern (*S. h. longipennis*). This latter bird, seen regularly on the islands of western Alaska, is dark overall and has a black bill and legs.

ARCTIC TERN

STERNA PARADISAEA

The first Arctic Tern I ever saw was at a disused gravel pit near Coventry in April 1950. It provided a friend and me with the distinction of obtaining a note in *British Birds* magazine (March 1951) for the second earliest record of an Arctic Tern in the British Isles since 1911.

That particular bird stayed all day, allowing plenty of time and opportunity to view every distinguishing feature. What brought the early migrant to central Britain at that time is one of those continuing puzzles of migration which still awaits explanation today. However, one thing that is known about the species is that its movements are indeed prodigious. It is probably the most travelled of all migratory birds, enjoying more hours of daylight than any other living creature.

The first indication that Arctic Terns, breeding in the northern hemisphere, travelled southwards to the opposite Pole came about when specimens were obtained by Antarctic explorers. Subsequent ringing recoveries have further shown that this species does make such lengthy journeys annually.

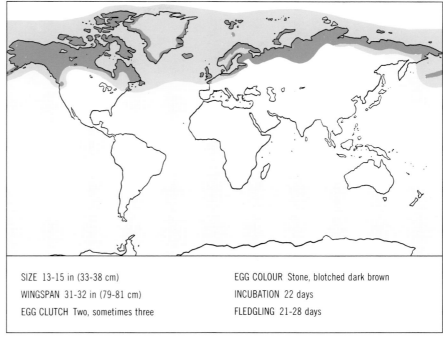

SIZE 13-15 in (33-38 cm)	EGG COLOUR Stone, blotched dark brown
WINGSPAN 31-32 in (79-81 cm)	INCUBATION 22 days
EGG CLUTCH Two, sometimes three	FLEDGLING 21-28 days

An Arctic Tern at its tundra nest site in northern Canada, incubates its egg amongst the spongy moss and dwarf vegetation typical of the region.

One particular individual, ringed in Britain and washed up off the shore of New South Wales, Australia, is the farthest any ringed bird has ever travelled, about 12,500 miles (20,117 km) by the shortest sea route. Another that was ringed in Russia also turned up in Australia, having travelled an almost equal distance to the British ringed bird.

Very similar in size and appearance to the Common Tern, the Arctic Tern has white underparts, a grey back and a black cap. Potentially it can present many birders with an identification problem. However, if given the opportunity to make a more detailed examination of this bird, it will be seen to have a more buoyant, airy flight, longer tail streamers and relatively slimmer wings. There are also other subtle differences to further aid the separation of the two species. In its breeding plumage the Arctic Tern has generally greyer-looking underparts, which make the contrasting white cheeks a more prominent feature. In some instances this contrast is almost strong enough to suggest Whiskered Tern. In flight the Common Tern shows a translucent panel only on the innermost primaries of the underwing, whereas all the primaries of the Arctic Tern are translucent. On the upperwing, the Common Tern shows darker wingtips. At rest it will be noted that the folded wing does not reach the end of the tail as it does in the Common Tern. The red legs are also much shorter, though the longer-legged Common Tern will adopt a squatting stance which makes this a less positive identification feature. In breeding plumage the wholly blood-red bill should clinch the identification.

In all other ways the behaviour of both birds is generally similar, but the Arctic Tern is if anything a much more aggressive species. Certainly on its breeding grounds it will press home aerial attacks more vehemently when an intruder invades its nesting territory. In fact it will draw blood from the unprotected head of a trespassing human. At such times it utters a high, whistling 'kee-kee', which rises in pitch. It also has other notes much like those of the Common Tern.

The Arctic Tern has a circumpolar breeding distribution. In the Arctic and Sub-Arctic regions of North America it is to be found from Alaska and Canada south to British Columbia on the west coast and Massachusetts on the east coast. It also nests along most of coastal Greenland, north to about 83° north in Iceland, the Faroes, Britain (mostly in the north), Ireland and France, where small numbers nest in Brittany. Its range then continues round the Baltic and Scandinavian coasts, including Spitsbergen, and across north Russia to the Bering Sea. Migration usually commences late April, with the majority of birds reaching their chosen breeding territories by late May. Its preferred habitat is similar to that of the Common Tern, but it is inclined to a more maritime location and normally does not nest at any great distance from the coast. In general it also tends to nest further north than the Common Tern, though mixed colonies of both species occur over quite a large part of their respective ranges.

In its northern-most colonies it will nest on bare rocky ground, which is only free of ice for a few weeks during the Arctic summer. The Arctic Tern does in fact have the distinction of being the most northerly breeding bird of all.

The nest is usually a mere scrape in sand, shingle or turf. This is lined with marram grass, or shells into which two, sometimes three, eggs are laid. These are indistinguishable from those of the Common Tern, having the same general stone colour, blotched and spotted with rich dark brown. Incubation takes around 22 days, with both birds sharing this duty. For a few days after hatching one or other of the parents, usually the female, broods the chicks while the other parent fetches food. Small fish and sand eels are the usual fare. After around three to four weeks the young can make short flights and soon afterwards they begin to make their own fishing trips, sometimes alone, sometimes accompanied by a parent.

A colonial species, many will nest in close proximity to one another in suitable situations. Its stronghold in Britain is in the north and west of Scotland, but Shetland has the largest concentration. At one time there were believed to be in

BELOW LEFT *An Arctic Tern has chosen quite a stony setting for its nest, but it is more likely to pick this type of terrain than the Common Tern which much prefers a more sandy location.*

BELOW RIGHT *Two Arctic Terns showing the pure white underwing with narrow black tips forming a thin, dark, trailing edge to the primaries most of which are otherwise translucent. In this picture the totally red bill can be seen clearly.*

An adult Arctic Tern at its nest site on the Inner Farnes, England, calls with its usual harsh nasal 'kee-aar' note. When at rest, it looks much shorter-legged than the Common Tern, though the all-red bill is diagnostic.

excess of 25,000 pairs there, though in recent years disturbance by people and cattle, and the additional problem of Skua predation, has considerably reduced the total number of breeding pairs. During 1988 and 1989 a considerable reduction in breeding numbers has occurred and this is possibly caused by the shortage of sand eels in that area.

Though it is believed to be holding its own in most other parts of Britain, it no longer nests on the Isles of Scilly, where in the nineteenth century it outnumbered Common Terns. Also many sites in Ireland have been deserted this century.

Dispersal from the breeding grounds begins in late July, but more southerly nesting sites may still hold birds in August. North American breeding birds move south after nesting on both the Pacific

and Atlantic sides of the country, usually well offshore. In America it is only irregularly noted inland in the fall and even less so in the spring, but in Britain it is quite a frequent migrant at inland waters, especially in spring. Over most of the more extensive land masses of Europe, however, it is but rarely encountered.

In today's world of greater interest in wild birds and their protection, it is hard to believe these beautiful creatures were once slaughtered for their plumage, yet many accessible colonies in North America were decimated to satisfy the millinery trade in the nineteenth century. Nowadays, many Arctic Terns and other seabirds face the threat of death from pollution or poisoning by toxic substances spilled or wantonly dumped on land or sea.

FORSTER'S TERN

In its breeding plumage, Forster's Tern is very similar indeed to the Common Tern, and for this reason it long remained unknown and unrecognized. Indeed, it was in its distinctive winter plumage that it was initially described. Essentially a bird of inland marshes during the summer, in winter it is coastal in its range well to the north of most other species of tern.

Like the Common Tern it has orange-red legs and an orange-red bill tipped with black. Structurally it differs subtly in its heavier bill, longer legs and longer tail, the streamers of which extend past the wingtip when the bird is perched. The most important distinctions from Common Tern, however, are the snow-white underparts, grey tail with narrow white sides, the paler and more silvery inner primaries which often appear strikingly paler than the rest of the wing, and less black on the outer wing.

In non-breeding plumage, which is assumed from August onwards (rather earlier than Common and Arctic Terns), Forster's has a black mask through the eye, giving it a distinctive and rather piratical appearance, somewhat resembling the larger Gull-billed and Sandwich Terns. Although there may be some streaking over the nape, the eye patches are not joined, unlike a winter-plumaged Common Tern. The legs remain reddish, but the bill becomes black.

The juvenile Forster's Tern is scaly on the upperparts, the feathers of the mantle and wing-coverts being white with a subterminal dark line and gingery fringe. It has the dark ear-coverts of the winter adult, but the rest of the cap is gingery brown, richer and browner than that of a juvenile Common Tern. It also lacks a dark bar across the inner wing-coverts to the carpal joint. The first-winter bird resembles the winter adult, except that the centre of the crown is more streaked, the nape is greyer and the inner rim of the shallowly forked tail has a neat black edge.

Forster's Tern breeds in interior North America. It inhabits freshwater marshes, especially those bordering lakes, and its range stretches from Alberta, Saskatchewan and Manitoba south to southern California, Colorado and Michigan. It also breeds on the Atlantic coast, though much less commonly, from Long Island south to North Carolina, and on salt marshes along the Gulf Coast in Texas and

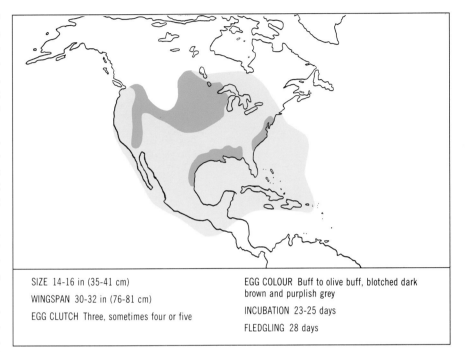

SIZE 14-16 in (35-41 cm)

WINGSPAN 30-32 in (76-81 cm)

EGG CLUTCH Three, sometimes four or five

EGG COLOUR Buff to olive buff, blotched dark brown and purplish grey

INCUBATION 23-25 days

FLEDGLING 28 days

ABOVE *In winter plumage the conspicuous black patch from the lores through the eye to the ear coverts of the Forster's Tern readily identifies the species. Additionally, at this time of year, the bill is generally all black, though there may be some red at its base. Note the long legs and tail streamers, extending beyond the folded wings.*

LEFT *A summer-plumaged Forster's Tern closely resembles a Common Tern, though its longer, more robust bill can be determined with practice. Hopefully however it will utter its diagnostic call 'tzaa-ap' to proclaim its identity.*

Louisiana. Its diet at breeding time includes many flying insects, especially dragonflies and caddis flies, which it catches on the wing with great agility, sometimes at a great height. It also takes fish and other small marine creatures picked from the surface of the water.

Birds return to their breeding colonies in May. The nest is built on floating vegetation, small islets or even on muskrat houses. It is sometimes a large, well-built, indeed elaborate structure consisting of a pile of dead sedge and grass with a neat cup woven in the top. In other cases it is simply a depression in the mud, lined with grass, or a hollow in the half-decayed material of a muskrat house. The normal clutch is three eggs, but four or even five is not uncommon, though these larger clutches may involve more than one female. They are laid in June and July, being buff or olive-buff with small dark brown and purplish-grey spots and blotches. Both sexes incubate for a period of 23 to 25 days. The chicks remain in the nest for a few days, but quickly learn to run and swim, hiding from potential predators in marsh vegetation. The calls include a 'kit-kit-kit', a 'kyarr' and a diagnostic 'tzaa-ap', which are more nasal than those of other terns.

In winter and on migration Forster's Tern may be found anywhere on the coast, and on rivers and lakes. The main migration takes place through the interior, with birds less frequently seen on the West coast as far north as British Columbia. Those breeding on the Atlantic seaboard disperse northwards prior to migration, reaching Quebec, New Brunswick and Nova Scotia.

Forster's Tern generally winters further north than other Sternidae, being found on the Pacific coast from central California, but then south to Guatemala, and on the Atlantic coast from Virginia southwards through the Gulf to Veracruz in Mexico. It is occasionally found in Costa Rica, the Bahamas and Greater Antilles. The number of birds seen in winter on the Atlantic seaboard has increased recently, and this may explain the greater incidence of trans-Atlantic vagrancy. The first to be recorded in Britain appeared in 1980, but since then there has been an average of two a year, including several wintering birds. In the last two years there have been six further records of Forster's Tern in Britain. There may be more in future as it spreads northwards along the east coast of the USA. Being more coastal in winter, its feeding habits then resemble other terns and it often plunge-dives into the water from a considerable height.

LITTLE TERN

STERNA ALBIFRONS

For some time now there has been considerable concern in Britain about the future of this species, for in recent years its breeding numbers have decreased alarmingly. Following an increase in status at the turn of the century, which possibly peaked in the 1920s and 1930s, the Little Tern population has regrettably seen another downturn in its fortunes. This is believed to be due to increased disturbance, particularly by holidaymakers on its nesting beaches. Land development and egg collecting have also added to the problems of this delightful bird.

At the present time the breeding population in Britain and Ireland, where it is exclusively a coastal nesting species, is probably no more than 2000 pairs. In other parts of its range it nests beside lakes and rivers far from the sea. Even so, there have still been marked decreases in some European countries where this type of habitat is used, again through disturbance and loss of habitat.

Interestingly though, in some areas where the natural habitat has been lost through development,

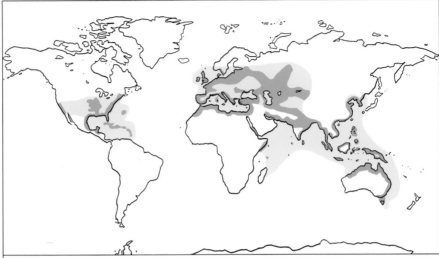

OTHER NAME Least Tern	EGG COLOUR Pale stone, green or blue with light brown blotches
SIZE 8-11 in (20-28 cm)	
WINGSPAN 19½-21½ in (50-55 cm)	INCUBATION 22 days
	FLEDGLING 28 days
EGG CLUTCH Two	

Little Terns have adapted to nesting on the man-made artifacts that have replaced the original setting. In North America, particularly in Florida, birds are now nesting on the tops of flat, gravelled roofs in areas where they once nested in more natural sites. In Britain, concern for this species' plight has singled it out for special protection. Even such simple measures as a single strand of wire between posts to cordon off sensitive areas, with notices saying 'Please keep off – nesting birds' have proved to be quite successful in most instances. Such action does invariably require the presence of wardens to ensure the desired effect.

As the common name implies, this is a tiny bird. It is the smallest of the 'sea terns' and this alone makes it easily distinguishable. Its white forehead, sharply pointed yellow bill with a black tip, and yellow feet mean there is no mistaking this bird in its summer plumage. Even at a distance, when it is not so easy to pick out all the detail, the size and mode of flight are all that the practised eye needs to put a name to it. The only possible confusion might be with the subspecies, *S. a. saundersi*, so-called Saunders' Tern in those areas where both occur, such as Iran and the Gulf Coast of Saudi Arabia. The Little Tern flies with rapidly beating wings as it patrols the shore, sometimes rising vertically and stopping momentarily to hover, head on into the wind before plunging into the waves. Often it completely submerges to secure small fish. After rising from the water, it continues along its intended flight path, perhaps making sudden dives, sideways turns and backward twists.

An excitable and noisy bird, it calls frequently with a high rasping 'kree-ik' or a sharp repeated 'kitt', whilst at times it will utter a rapid chattering 'kirri-kirri-kirri'. As well as fish, it will take various crustacea, marine molluscs, and, at times, whatever insect larvae are available.

A summer visitor to Britain, birds begin to arrive at their breeding grounds in late April. By the middle of May, following preliminaries such as those carried out by other *Sterna* terns, like the presentation of small fish, pairing is complete. The nesting site can be in either fine sand, shingle, or even dried mud left by the evaporation of lakes and marshes. I have seen examples of the latter in the Camargue.

The nest itself is a scrape to which bits of shell, straw or grass are added. The two eggs, which are laid at the end of May or early June, are pale stone, green or blue, with blotches and fine spots of light brown on an ashy underlay. Incubation begins after the first egg is laid and takes up to 22 days. The chicks leave the nest within a day of hatching and are flying within four weeks, though they continue

to be fed by the parents for some time afterwards. There is only one brood. Once nesting is over, birds soon move totally away from the nesting area and by the end of July they have begun their migration back to winter quarters. Most have left by the end of August.

In winter plumage the back of the crown becomes ash grey, merging to black at the nape. The immature bird, though resembling the winter-plumaged adult, has a darker bill and legs and a dark fore-edge to the wing.

European birds move mostly to the west coast of Africa. During both spring and autumn some birds move overland across Britain and small numbers are regularly noted at lakes and reservoirs.

The Little Tern breeds from Europe east to central Asia, and south to Morocco, Egypt, the Middle East, northern Pakistan and India. It also breeds in west and central Africa, south and eastern Asia, through the Philippines and Indonesia to New Guinea and in northern and eastern Australia. There are nine subspecies breeding in various parts of the world, but these show only slight variations and all races are virtually inseparable in most field sightings.

In the USA, the subspecies *S. a. antillarum* is known as the Least Tern. It is a fairly common, though local bird of the east and Gulf coasts, but is less common and declining at inland locations and on the west coast. North American breeding birds winter from Central America southwards.

ABOVE *A Little Tern hovers on rapidly beating wings just above the waves before plunging in to secure some small fish or sand eel. Note the white forehead and the sharp, pointed, yellow, black-tipped bill.*

LEFT *A pair of attentive Little Terns stand by as the tiny chick attempts to swallow a sand eel almost as big as itself.*

WHISKERED TERN

CHLIDONIAS HYBRIDUS

This is the largest of the so-called 'marsh terns', looking bulkier and longer-winged than either of the other two *Chlidonias* species. Its behaviour, however, is more akin to the Sternidae and in breeding plumage it shows certain similarities with the Arctic Tern, and even more so with White-cheeked Tern. In this plumage it looks paler than the other marsh terns, but shows a distinct black cap extending down the nape. This contrasts with the white face and dark grey underparts, creating a combination which at a distance gives the distinctive 'whiskered' look from which the bird gets its name. This feature is especially noticeable when observed head-on.

The upperparts are ash-grey, while the vent, undertail coverts and underwing are white, and fairly conspicuous features. The tail is slightly forked, while the bill and legs are dull red.

Both White-winged Black Tern and Black Tern have a distinctive fluttering and dipping flight as they feed over water. By comparison the Whiskered Tern flies in a more leisurely, less erratic style and

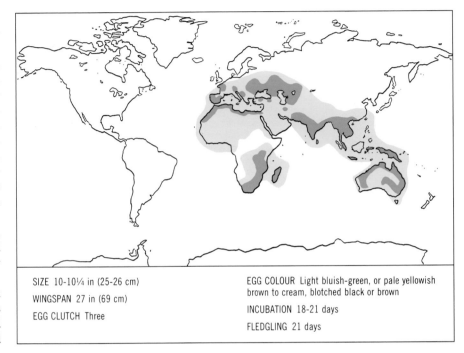

SIZE 10-10¼ in (25-26 cm)

WINGSPAN 27 in (69 cm)

EGG CLUTCH Three

EGG COLOUR Light bluish-green, or pale yellowish brown to cream, blotched black or brown

INCUBATION 18-21 days

FLEDGLING 21 days

plunges into the water for most of its food. This comprises mainly insects and their larvae, especially dragonflies, mosquitos and beetles, though it also takes freshwater shrimps, frogs and other amphibians as well as small fish. In its winter quarters in Africa, it also eats locusts and grasshoppers.

Spring passage occurs in April through to May and most are nesting by the end of that month, or at the latest, early June. The breeding haunt of the Whiskered Tern is freshwater, marshland and areas of scattered pools, particularly where the vegetation is grazed by cattle or horses. It prefers water 2 to 3 feet (60–90 cm) deep, upon which it builds a floating nest. This is invariably out in the open amongst crowfoot or pondweed and not hidden in reeds or rushes. Generally a colonial species, as many as 50 to 100 pairs may nest in close proximity to each other, but at times perhaps only a dozen or so will be found together. The nest is an untidy platform of broken or uprooted sedges or rushes, which are sometimes brought from quite a distance. If cattle are present to trample the vegetation it makes the acquisition of nest material much easier for them. The nest is generally larger in area than that of the Black Tern, but is flimsier and merely heaped, rather than woven. There is no real cup or lining, but material is constantly being added during the nesting period.

Noisy at the nesting site, the usual call is a rasping 'kyick' or 'cherk', similar to a Corncrake (*Crex crex*). It is mostly silent at other times.

The usual clutch comprises three eggs, sometimes only two and occasionally four are laid. These are light bluish green, or pale yellowish brown to cream, spotted and blotched with blacks and browns. In the more northerly parts of its range the eggs are rarely laid before the end of May or early June, and sometimes even later. There is only one brood. The eggs hatch after 18 to 21 days. The chicks stay in the nest for around a week, but after that they begin to wander about, being tended by the parents for at least three weeks. After this period of time the young birds can fly and feed themselves. Departure for the winter quarters begins about the end of July, but families sometimes remain together at the nesting grounds until September.

The juvenile has a white forehead and pale cap. The upper wing is pale with no dark carpal bar, while the leading edge is pale. Young birds of the year are very difficult to separate from similar-aged Black Terns and White-winged Black Terns, but generally the dark saddle of Whiskered Tern is more variegated than that of White-winged Black Tern, while the comparatively pale leading wing edge and less distinctively marked upperwing are features to be looked for. The forehead is whiter and the cap paler than in either juveniles of the two other species of marsh tern.

The adult Whiskered Tern in winter plumage is probably best separated from the Black Tern by its paler, more uniform upperparts, less black on the crown, and especially by the lack of dark patches at the sides of the breast. Differences between Whiskered and White-winged Black Tern are the greyish nape, longer bill and more uniform upperparts with a grey, not white, rump. All three in either juvenile or winter plumage offer serious difficulties of identification and great care is needed when putting a name to any of them.

The Whiskered Tern breeds locally in southern Europe and northern Africa, from Spain to Morocco and discontinuously eastwards through the Balkans and Tunisia to south west Asia. It winters in East and West Africa. There are other races, inseparable in the field from the nominate race, to be found breeding in South Africa and Madagascar, from Kenya south to Tanzania, from Iran to India, and in southern China, Taiwan, Indo-China, Sri Lanka, Malaysia, Java, Celebes, Moluccas, New Guinea and Australia. It is unknown in the USA.

Most birds are migratory and start south from the end of July onwards, when large movements pass through Suez and the Mediterranean.

LEFT *A Whiskered Tern on its nest amidst water crowfoot of a low-lying, marshy area of southern France. With its more pronounced* Sterna-*like bill and gonys, this is possibly a male bird.*

RIGHT *A pair of Whiskered Terns at their floating nest which tends to be an untidy heap of marsh vegetation rather than the woven structure created by the Black Tern.*

BLACK TERN

C H L I D O N I A S   N I G E R

This is the most widespread of the so-called three 'marsh terns' that breed in Europe, the others being White-winged Tern and Whiskered Tern. It is also the only marsh tern that nests in North America.

In its breeding plumage the species is unmistakable, being dark slate-grey to black all over, except for the white undertail coverts, which are most conspicuous and contrast markedly with the dark body. This simple colour combination, plus its characteristic feeding flight just above the surface of the water, make it relatively easy to identify even at some considerable distance. In winter plumage though, identification is a different question altogether!

During the spring, often as early as April, Black Terns are on the move, but more frequently it is May before migration begins in earnest. Then they might be seen hawking for food above lakes or reservoirs and even along the sea coast, which they do not normally visit in the breeding season. At such times they flutter, dive, turn and swoop to pick prey from the surface of the water occasionally uttering a quiet, weak 'kik-kit' or similar note. Though their chief food is aquatic insects and their larvae, and small fish are sometimes taken in an occasional plunge dive, they never totally submerge. Tadpoles and very small frogs are also readily taken whenever available. Always head on into the wind, they keep up their incessant search for food, sometimes skimming the water surface, sometimes rising up to hang motionless for a second then continuing their slow, methodical and undulating course. They rarely settle on the water, but quite frequently perch on posts or floating objects, when it can be seen that the short legs are reddish black and that the slender bill is totally black. Though often seen singly or in twos and threes, Black Terns are very gregarious and frequently occur in considerable numbers. Indeed, flocks of several hundred birds are not an uncommon sight. On occasions as a flock feeds over a stretch of water all the birds appear to be seized by a sudden panic or dread. In complete silence, they bunch together in the middle of the water, and fly round very rapidly close to the surface. Then, suddenly, they will all rise up to fly off and disappear into the distance.

In the Old World the Black Tern breeds in

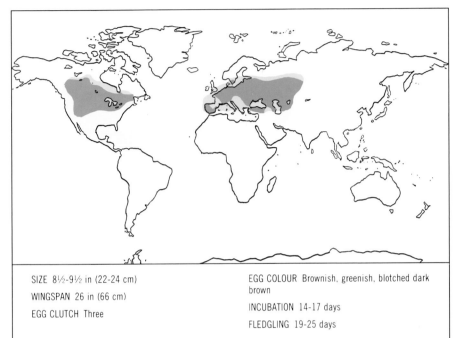

SIZE 8½-9½ in (22-24 cm)

WINGSPAN 26 in (66 cm)

EGG CLUTCH Three

EGG COLOUR Brownish, greenish, blotched dark brown

INCUBATION 14-17 days

FLEDGLING 19-25 days

Europe and West Asia, from Sweden and Spain eastwards to south west Siberia and the Caspian Sea. Its European breeding locations are scattered and it is said to have decreased in number in many areas. It no longer breeds at all in some parts, probably due to the loss of suitable nesting habitat. Small numbers did breed in some areas of eastern and south eastern Britain up until the end of the nineteenth century but virtually none have since then, though in more recent times a few pairs may have bred spasmodically in the Ouse washes.

Nesting requirements are fresh or brackish water, with plenty of emergent vegetation. Small pools, lakes, ditches, overgrown canals, quiet reaches of rivers, marshes and swampy meadows are favoured. The nest, which both birds construct, is a floating heap of locally found vegetation lined with finer stems. Occasionally a thinly lined scrape is made on dry ground. The eggs, usually three in number, are smooth and slightly glossy. They are brownish or greenish in colour, heavily streaked or blotched with dark brown. They are laid in late May or early June and incubation lasts from fourteen to seventeen days. The chicks are looked after by both parents in the first week, but they leave the nest after only two or three days to hide in nearby

RIGHT *A juvenile Black Tern on its first migratory flight to winter quarters rests awhile* en route.

BELOW *In its overall dark breeding plumage the Black Tern is unmistakable. This picture shows the bird on its nest in Ontario, Canada.*

vegetation. Then, after about nineteen days, they move totally away from the nesting area and by the 25th day they are capable of flight.

During its moult the Black Tern looks mottled and patchy, but once in full winter plumage it no longer lives up to its name. Instead it looks grey on the back and has a white forehead, neck and underparts. It also has small, blackish patches on the sides of the breast, in front of the wings, which the two other winter plumaged 'marsh terns' do not have. Immature birds are like winter adults, but have a darker saddle on the back. In this plumage, differences between this species and immature White-winged Tern and Whiskered Tern are not easy to detect.

Dispersal and migratory movements begin in July as birds begin to move their winter quarters.

In August and September thousands of Black Terns pass westwards through the Straits of Gibraltar to winter mainly along the coasts of Ghana and Nigeria, with some reaching Angola, Namibia and South Africa. During the winter months they feed mainly at sea.

In North America the Black Tern breeds throughout much of the interior, from central British Columbia and Saskatchewan east to New Brunswick and south to Nevada, Colorado, Nebraska, Ohio and New York.

Nesting time and behaviour are similar to those of European birds. Similarly, dispersal from the nesting grounds begins in July. Birds moving south are commonly seen along the east coast, but rarely on the west coast. The winter range is along the coast, from Panama south to Chile and Surinam where they congregate offshore in large numbers.

WHITE-WINGED TERN

CHLIDONIAS LEUCOPTERUS

This most elegant of the 'marsh terns' is unmistakable in its breeding plumage, when its black head and body plumage contrasts with its white tail coverts and white forked tail. The wings have blackish grey outer primaries shading to white on the lesser coverts, from which the bird's name is derived. The underwing coverts are also black, not grey, which is a further distinguishing feature. The bill is black, tipped with crimson, and when at rest it will be seen that the short legs are bright red.

A small, compact bird, it looks slightly heavier in build than Black Tern, with which it often associates when on passage, but in comparison it will be noted that the wings are proportionately shorter, broader and more rounded at the tip, the flight appears somewhat slower, with shallower wing beats, and it also hovers less frequently than a Black Tern.

Like all marsh terns, it is skilful on the wing, dipping, wheeling and stalling just above the surface to take aquatic invertebrates and very occasionally small fish. It lands readily on the water and at times may even feed by wading or walking in

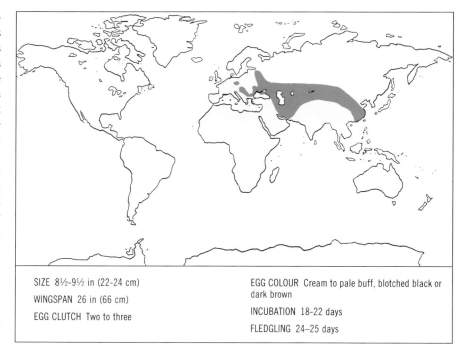

SIZE 8½-9½ in (22-24 cm)	EGG COLOUR Cream to pale buff, blotched black or dark brown
WINGSPAN 26 in (66 cm)	INCUBATION 18-22 days
EGG CLUTCH Two to three	FLEDGLING 24–25 days

muddy areas to pick up flies.

The White-winged Tern prefers to feed over freshwater at all times, but is quite adept at catching aerial insects over land. As a breeding species its range extends eastward from Hungary with an uneven distribution across Asia to central Russia. There is a large gap in central Siberia, but farther east it is to be found in southern China.

A late migrant, the White-winged Tern does not arrive back at the nesting site much before the end of May. It favours naturally flooded grasslands, or similar swampy conditions, and in some parts of its range does not breed in years when drought conditions prevail and suitable nesting requirements do not exist. It appears to avoid fish ponds, rice fields or ornamental waters.

Not a great deal is known about this bird's courtship but it does include communal circling, weaving flights above the colony, when a hundred or more birds may perform in this manner. It is also very vocal on the breeding ground, uttering a variety of harsh rattling and churring sounds. On migration, however, it is generally silent. The monogamous pair bond, once established, results in the construction of a nest of water-weed sited on a mat of floating vegetation. Exceptionally the nest

ABOVE *A flock of White-winged Black Terns in flight above Lake Mikhael, Israel, in September. The different degrees of individual plumage patterning is well worth close scrutiny.*

LEFT *A White-winged Tern in its distinctive summer plumage, revealing the white forewing and white undertail coverts, flies above the waters at Eilat, Israel during its May-time migration.*

may be on a dry shoreline, when an unlined scrape is made. The eggs, which are laid in June, are smooth, slightly glossy, and coloured cream to pale buff, with large black or dark brown spots and blotches. Incubation is carried out by both parents, but the female undertakes most of this duty. After around 18 to 22 days the young hatch. Only a few days later they are ready to leave the nest and hide in the surrounding vegetation. Both parents continue to feed and tend their young for a further period of 24 to 25 days.

Birds begin their southwards migration from August onwards and by October all the breeding grounds are deserted. Most of the Eurasian population winter in central and southern Africa, mainly on the large lakes and along the major rivers, where tens of thousands of birds may occur together. Many of these pass through the Nile Valley and the Rift Valley in autumn, returning by the same route in spring. Asian nesting birds winter in southern China, India, the Malay archipelago, Indonesia and northern Australia.

The White-winged Tern is a rare visitor to the North American east coast. Some stragglers have found their way to Alaska and occasionally inland. It is a regular, but scarce, visitor to Britain, more so

in the autumn when the identification problem of separating juvenile White-winged Terns from Black Terns and from Whiskered Terns is especially acute.

The juvenile White-winged Tern has a diagnostic combination of a dark saddle, pale midwing panel and a whitish rump. It has no dark mark on the side of the breast. Some adults may be seen in autumn still with varying amounts of their breeding plumage. They then have a mottled or patchy appearance, but in winter plumage, which has generally been attained by late October, they are overall pale grey-looking birds, with a distinct white collar and a noticeable contrast between the grey upperparts and the white or very pale grey rumps. In most situations, jizz plays an important role and the general *Sterna* look of the Whiskered Tern may alert one to the other differences when it comes to differentiating between these two species.

In Britain, almost all occurrences of White-winged Tern have been between March and November, with just a few in some years but double figures in others. The increase in sightings over recent years undoubtedly reflects the increase in the number of observers able to identify winter-plumaged marsh terns.

BLACK SKIMMER

R H Y N C H O P S   N I G E R

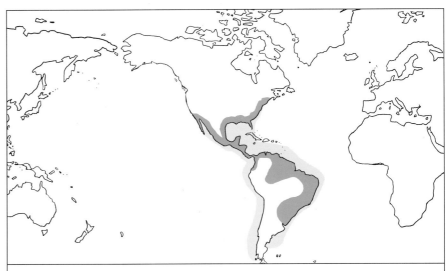

SIZE 16-19½ in (40-50 cm)	EGG COLOUR Buff to blue-green, heavily blotched purplish-black
WINGSPAN 42-50 in (107-127 cm)	INCUBATION 23 days
EGG CLUTCH Two to five	FLEDGLING 28 days

An unmistakable bird with a distinctive feeding technique, the Black Skimmer at first sight may suggest a large tern, though it is not at all closely related to them as was once thought. Rather the bizarre bill, with its knife-like mandibles compressed to thin blades, of which the lower one is longer than the upper, is unique to the Skimmer family. Globally there are two others species of Skimmer, all looking very similar. They are the African Skimmer and the Indian Skimmer which are to be found in the continents after which they are named.

In North America, the Black Skimmer breeds locally along the Atlantic coast south from Massachusetts, through the Gulf coasts to northern Brazil. On the Pacific coast it breeds from north west Mexico southwards to Ecuador. There has also been a recent expansion of its range north to the Salton Sea, where it first nested in 1972, and to San Diego Bay, California. More recently Black Skimmers have appeared in the San Francisco Bay area where they are thought to be breeding.

There are also two subspecies of the Black Skimmer that are found only in South America. *R. n. cinerascens* breeds along the coasts and rivers in the north and north east, including the Amazon basin, while *R. n. intercedens* breeds along the rivers and coasts of the east and south east, south to the Rio de la Plata, and in central Argentina.

In breeding plumage the Black Skimmer has a black crown, nape, hindneck, back and wings, while the forehead, face and underparts are white. The unique bill is bright vermilion, with the terminal half of the upper mandible and most of the lower mandible black. The legs and feet are also bright vermilion. Though both sexes are similar in appearance, the female is distinctly smaller than the male, an example of sexual dimorphism not normally found in seabirds.

Whilst the Black Skimmer spends long periods inactive, its mode of flight is graceful and buoyant. Flocks of Black Skimmers often perform bouts of synchronous flight, twisting and turning in unison. However, it is when feeding that it lives up to its name, revealing its special skills. At such times it flies straight and low over the water, beak wide open, with the tip of the longer, lower mandible ploughing the surface. When the lower mandible strikes any prey, such as a fish or shrimp, the short-

hinged upper mandible snaps down on to it. Simultaneously the angled head is brought sharply backwards and, with bill clear of the water, the prey is swallowed. Skimming is immediately resumed, with no evident interruption of the flight path. Feeding mainly takes place around dawn, at dusk and on calm moonlit nights when planktonic food rises to the surface of the water. In these half-light conditions another evolutionary development by this bird comes into play. Uniquely among birds, it has eyes like a cat, with a vertical pupil which closes in bright light to protect the sensitive retina from harmful direct and reflected sunlight. In poor light the pupil becomes round, giving better vision during its half-light feeding activities.

Its preferred breeding locations are the broad sand bars of large river systems or low coastal sandflats. These sites are all unstable, as tide or flood conditions can render them untenable at any time. As a consequence Black Skimmers frequently move to colonize new areas as conditions dictate. They are adaptable to changing circumstances and on parts of the east coast, where human disturbance has driven them from traditional sites, they have taken to nesting in areas of wet eel grass and on artificial islands created during land drainage or filling operations. Also, like Little Terns in Florida, they have even nested on flat roof tops!

Black Skimmers are colonial nesters and will quite often nest among other birds, such as the Gull-billed Terns at Salton Sea or Common Terns on the Atlantic coast. They have a long nesting season which starts in May and ends in September, long after other species have finished. Courtship includes various aerial displays which are similar to the high flights of terns and long, calling sessions, as with various gulls, when they utter a series of drawn-out, barking notes.

Birds may arrive at the breeding grounds in mid-April, but will take two or three weeks to settle down before nesting begins in earnest. They make a simple scrape into which two to five eggs are laid. These are buff to blue-green and heavily blotched with purplish black. Incubation lasts for around 23 days, with both parents taking turns. In the intense heat of mid-summer the adults will frequently soak their body feathers and wet their feet to reduce heat stress. Equally the newly hatched young require special care and during their first few days they are carefully shielded from intense heat. They are immobile at this early age and are fed on regurgitated food, which is dropped onto the ground. Later on they take food from the parents, mainly small fish such as silverfish or blennies which are held crosswise in the parent's beak. After about 28 days the young birds can fly, but they continue to be fed by the parents for at least another two weeks. It is during this period that they no doubt learn their feeding skills from their parents, but it is some months before the bill length is fully developed.

The juvenile bird is a mottled, ginger brown in the upperparts, while the bill is a dusky red with a blackish tip and the legs are dull red.

Black Skimmers winter on the Pacific coast from San Diego Bay south to Chile, while on the Atlantic coast they are to be found southwards from the northern shores of the Gulf of Mexico and east Florida. It is not known if any of the birds breeding in their southerly limits are joined by migratory birds. The movements of these South American birds is linked to annual flooding, when they disperse to feed over vast areas of inundated land. On occasions, wind-blown individuals have occurred in North America beyond the limits of their range.

ABOVE *A Black Skimmer lives up to its name, flying straight and low over the water, beak wide open, the longer, lower mandible ploughing the surface as it seeks out prey such as shrimp or small fish.*

LEFT *A Black Skimmer stands in the shallows, its bizarre red- and black-tipped bill with the lower mandible longer than the upper one unique amongst birds.*

COMMON MURRE

URIA AALGE

Among the huge colonies of seabirds that are to be found in northern latitudes many contain the group we call the 'auks'. These are birds belonging to the family Alcidae, collectively called 'alcids'. There are twenty-two species in thirteen genera, ranging from medium-sized to some of the smallest seabirds in the region. Generally they are all black and white and look similar to each other when given only a cursory glance. When standing upright on their breeding cliffs they look very much like Penguins. In particular, this species and Thick-billed Murre (called respectively Guillemot and Brunnich's Guillemot in Europe) require some 'sorting out' from each other and from the Razorbill, especially when observed at some distance floating on the sea.

The Common Murre, is probably the most familiar of the auks that breed around the coasts of Great Britain and North America, where it nests on both the Pacific and Atlantic shores.

It is most likely to be confused with the Razorbill and in North America with Thick-billed Murre, or

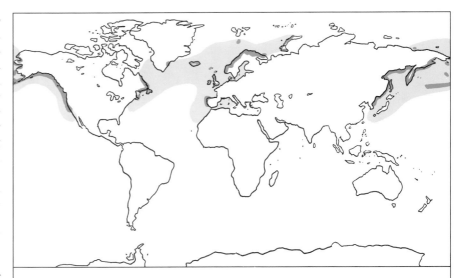

OTHER NAME Thin-billed Murre	EGG COLOUR Creamy white to pale or deep blue-green to buff, blotched brown or black
SIZE 16-17 in (42 cm)	
WINGSPAN 28 in (71 cm)	INCUBATION 28-37 days
	FLEDGLING 15-17 days
EGG CLUTCH One	

A pair of Common Murres either side of their single chick on the cliff-ledge nest site, the sea hundreds of feet below.

Brunnich's Guillemot, as it virtually matches both species in size and superficially resembles each in appearance. Nevertheless, the slender, pointed bill, thinner neck and browner looking upperparts of the Common Murre, especially on the neck and head, should aid identification when in breeding plumage. However, birds in the more northerly parts of their range may have bodies as dark as a Razorbill. These belong to the nominate race, which is found in northern Scotland, whereas the race *U. a. albionis* extend from southern Scotland south west into England, Wales and Ireland. At sea the Common Murre sits lower in the water and the tail is not cocked like that of the Razorbill. When diving for food, it can stay under water for at least a minute, at times reaching depths of up to 30 feet (9 m) and propelling itself with its wings as if flying under water. All its food is obtained in this way, though most of the fish that are caught are obtained relatively near to the surface.

The so-called 'Bridled' or 'Spectacled' Murre is not a subspecies, but a variant which has a white ring round the eye and a white line running back from this over the sides of the head. The number of bridled birds increases progressively northwards, with one per cent or less in the population of south west England to as much as 25 per cent in those of the Shetlands. In Iceland and Bear Island it can be as high as 50 per cent or more. The bridled form is not found in the Pacific.

After spending the early winter at sea, Common Murres begin to return to their nesting sites before Christmas, although often not until January and February. However, these early visits are brief and it is March or April before a greater attachment to their nesting ledges begins to form. During these comings and goings there is much squabbling, jostling and a great deal of quarrelling between the sexes. As the pair bonds are strengthened, this is replaced by mutual preening, followed by mating.

Around mid-May a single egg is laid on the bare rock. These are extremely variable in colour, ranging from creamy white, through pale or deep blue-green, to shades of buff, and they are patterned with brown or black blotches interlaced with thin lines. In such crowded conditions, with so many eggs in close proximity, it is this variety of colour and pattern that allows each parent to recognize its own egg. The egg is pear-shaped which makes it less likely to roll into the sea if it is accidentally bumped or knocked as the birds fly to and from their crowded nest sites. Even so, many are lost in this way. Both sexes share the incubation, which takes from 28 to 37 days. On hatching, the chick is quite well advanced, with a covering of down and its eyes open. It is cared for by both parents, being

regularly brooded until they leave the nesting ledge after 15 to 17 days. At this stage it cannot fly, but after a lot of hesitation and calls from its parents, it throws itself to sea. Many hit the rocks below, but usually survive and scramble to the water, where they join their parents and swim out to sea. This performance usually happens in the fading evening light, thus lessening the chance of predation by large gulls. For several weeks the young are fed at sea by their parents, eventually attaining their independence and power of flight after 50 to 70 days.

In winter plumage the Common Murre loses much of the black around the head and neck, with its chin, throat and cheeks becoming white with a dark post-ocular stripe across the ear coverts. In its first winter, the young Common Murre's head is darker with no stripe and the bill is proportionately shorter. For a short time between August and October the adult is flightless during its wing moult, after which it heads out to sea. The winter range is determined by weather and the extent of ice.

As well as the nominate race *U. a. aalge*, which breeds from Labrador and Greenland to Norway and north Scotland, there are six subspecies distributed as follows: *U. a. inorata* breeds from the Bering Sea and North Pacific Ocean south to Hokaido, Japan; *U. a. californica* breeds along the Californian coast south to Hurricane Point; *U. a. hyperborea* breeds on Bear Island, North West

ABOVE *Designed more for swimming than flying, a Common Murre steers on thin, narrow wings to land using the webbed feet as air brakes.*

OVERLEAF *Common Murres stand around penguin-like on the Staple Rocks of the Inner Farnes, England, a regular nesting site. Left and right of the picture are some Kittiwakes.*

Territories; *U. a. spiloptera* breeds on the Faroes; *U. a. intermedia* breeds around the Baltic Sea and *U. a. albionis* breeds in south Scotland, England, Wales, north west France and south to Portugal.

Operation Seafarer revealed the Common Murre to be the most numerous British seabird, with a population in excess of half a million pairs. Of these, maybe 80 per cent were in Scotland, with Orkney holding the largest single colony, 70,000 pairs on Westray.

As with many other colonial seabirds, the Common Murre has suffered from the predation of man. Before the Bird Protection Acts and changing fashions, many eggs and adult birds were harvested annually for food, though in some of the more remote island communities this appears to have had little effect on numbers. More serious, and profoundly more threatening to the stability of auk populations, is the danger of pollution, especially from oil spillages. Large numbers of seabirds, including a high proportion of Common Murres, die annually from the effects of oil. In Britain the *Torrey Canyon* disaster of 1967 was a major incident that is remembered today. More recently, in Alaska the long-term effects of the *Exxon Valdez* oil spillage in 1989 remain to be seen.

The wondrous sight, sound and smell of a major Common Murre colony, with row upon row of birds coming and going against a backdrop of precipitous cliffs and a surging sea, is surely one of those marvels of the natural world that deserves to be protected and treasured for all time.

LEFT *The Common Murre has a dark chocolate-brown head and sharp, pointed bill.*

ABOVE *A bridled form of the Murres perched on a cliff ledge on Craigleith, adjacent to the Bass Rock in the Firth of Forth. The* *further northwards Murres occur the greater the percentages of bridled birds there are recorded.*

THICK-BILLED MURRE

URIA LOMVIA

This bird is named after Morten Thrane Brunnich (1737–1827), a Danish naturalist who first described a number of northern birds, including this species. He gave it the scientific name *U. troile*, which at the time was already being used in Britain for the Common Murre (*U. aalge*). It was Edward Sabine, of Sabine's Gull fame, who proposed the name *U. brunnichii* to clarify the matter. This name has remained in the English vernacular ever since, but in North America the species is known as the Thick-billed Murre.

A bird of the higher latitudes in both the Pacific and Atlantic Oceans, its range overlaps in some parts with both Common Murre and Razorbill and similarities in appearance can pose identification problems.

An altogether darker bird than the Common Murre, the upperparts and throat of the adult Thick-billed Murre are blacker looking, with the white underparts usually forming a sharp point on the foreneck. Thick-billed Murre is also slightly larger and has a shorter, thicker neck. However, it is the shorter and much thicker bill that is its main identifying feature. Even at a distance this is quite obviously larger than a Common Murre's. At close range the observer may also perceive a white line along the side of the bill, though this white tomium stripe is absent on some birds. In their winter plumage, the two species are harder to separate, but as their moults are staggered this problem fortunately only arises for a limited time. The Common Murre begins its post-nuptial moult as early as July and by mid-August most of the population have diagnostic white sides to the face and dark post-ocular stripes. Thick-billed Murre, on the other hand, can still be in summer plumage at the beginning of October, so any dark-headed alcids in late autumn should be looked at closely. Indeed, I have seen birds off Monterey, California, where it is but a casual visitor, that in early October were still in almost full breeding plumage. In the spring the situation is reversed. Then the Common Murre, which begins its prenuptial head moult as early as December/February time, will have a dark head early in the year. Equally, therefore, any pale-headed alcids seen in March and April should be carefully scrutinized. The winter-plumaged Razorbill may also trap the unwary into believing they see a Thick-billed Murre, especially as young Common Murres

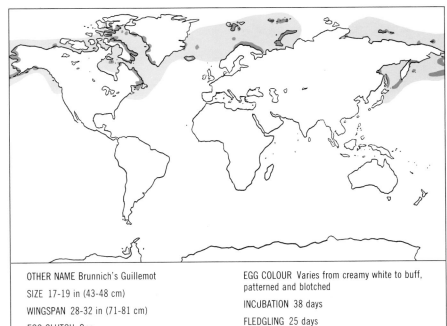

OTHER NAME Brunnich's Guillemot	EGG COLOUR Varies from creamy white to buff, patterned and blotched
SIZE 17-19 in (43-48 cm)	
WINGSPAN 28-32 in (71-81 cm)	INCUBATION 38 days
EGG CLUTCH One	FLEDGLING 25 days

have smaller bills. Adult and juvenile together will show different bill size, which could lead to mis-identification. However, both adult and juvenile Razorbills have white extending upwards onto the ear coverts behind the eye, which gives them a more white-headed look. In any event, at any age the Thick-billed Murre looks more like a Common Murre than a Razorbill.

There are two subspecies of Thick-billed Murre, which are not separable at sea. The nominate race breeds from the Gulf of St Lawrence, Labrador and Hudson Bay in Canada to Greenland, Iceland, Jan Mayen Land, Spitsbergen, Franz Josef Land and Novaya Zemlaya in the USSR. Breeding has also been recently proved (1964) in Norway. The race *U. l. arra* breeds on Wrangel Island and along the Chukchi Sea coast from Cape Lisburn south throughout the Bering Sea to the Aleutian Islands, the Gulf of Alaska and the Commander Islands. There is also a small colony at Cape Parry in the Canadian North West Territories.

Thick-billed Murres begin to return to their nesting sites as early as March at lower latitudes, but not until April or May in the more northerly parts of the range, where occupancy depends greatly on the nesting ledges being snow-free as

A Thick-billed Murre, with chick. Very like the Common Murre, the stouter bill and the white tomium stripe readily identify the species at relatively close range.

well as on sea ice conditions. It chooses steep cliff faces for nesting, using ledges up to 1476 feet (450 m) above sea level which it frequently shares with, but never in such dense ranks as, Common Murres. Thick-billed Murre's display, courtship and nesting is the same as a Common Murre's. Similarly, it lays a single pyriform egg on the bare rock. This shows tremendous variation in the colour and pattern of its blotches and scrawls.

The parents share incubation, which lasts around 38 days. On hatching, the chicks are down-covered, but within 25 days this is replaced with their first feathers, though they are still unable to fly at that age. During this short fledging period the young are fed a diet of small fish, such as capelin and arctic cod. Only one fish is brought at a time and this is carried head first in line with the bird's bill. Food for the young is rarely regurgitated. Like other alcids, Thick-billed Murres feed mainly on fish, which they secure by diving, often to considerable depths, 246 feet (75 m). Normally, food is obtained much nearer the surface, with the bird diving at a shallow angle and propelling itself underwater with its wings. Sadly, they frequently get caught in fishing nets and many die this way. The adult birds also feed on zooplankton and crustaceans as available. Like the Common Murre, Thick-billed Murre is highly vocal during the breeding season, having similar growling and crowing calls.

By the end of August nesting is virtually over and the vast colonies, or 'looneries' as they are sometimes called, fall silent for another year, as the birds move far out to sea. They are much more pelagic than Common Murres. Winter dispersal is largely governed by the presence of sea ice, but Thick-billed Murres regularly winter in the Chukchi Sea north to Point Hope and Cape Thompson. Apparently the Cape Parry population moves west to winter in the Bering Sea. It is also to be found in the North Pacific, south to Hokkaido where it is common, while in the east it occurs off south east Alaska, British Columbia and occasionally further south to Washington and California.

In the Atlantic it can be found from Greenland south to the Hudson Bay, along the Atlantic coast to Long Island and occasionally off the South Carolina coast. In northern Europe it is mainly found in open waters adjacent to its breeding areas and, casually, further south to Britain and Ireland. Of the twenty or so records in the British Isles, most relate to tideline corpses. Happily, Thick-billed Murre is still one of the most numerous of breeding seabirds in the northern hemisphere. However, half a million get caught in salmon fishing nets off Greenland every year. Additionally, some three-quarters of a million are harvested for various uses. One wonders how long this can go on, for it will only take one or two marine disasters to bring this population crashing down. Such exploitation needs to be carefully monitored.

RAZORBILL

ALCA TORDA

The Razorbill generally looks much blacker than the Common Murre and appears more compact and plumper-looking, with a thicker neck and heavier-looking head. The tail is also longer, pointed and often cocked. On the sea it dives for fish with more of a splash than other auks, giving a distinct kick of the legs and a flick of the partly opened wings as it does so. Before diving it often dips its head into the water several times, in order to spot its prey. Underwater the wings are used to propel itself to depths of 30 feet (9 m), thus equalling the Common Murre's diving ability. Generally its dives at around 45 seconds are shorter in duration than the other species.

At close range the laterally compressed bill, crossed by a white line, is a distinctive feature. This specialized beak is the ideal tool, perfectly adapted to hold several fish at a time. The biting edges are indeed razor-sharp, hence the bird's name, and these are turned inwards with both mandibles having backward-pointing projections. Fish are the staple diet, with sand eels a major prey item and occasion-

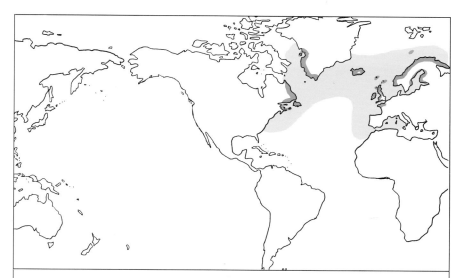

SIZE 15½-17½ in (40-45 cm)	EGG COLOUR Patterns of brown blotches on white, greenish or light brown background
WINGSPAN 25-26 in (63-66 cm)	INCUBATION 30 days
EGG CLUTCH One, rarely two	FLEDGLING 14-21 days

LEFT *A young Razorbill calls to be fed. Soon it will make its hazardous way to the sea.*

ABOVE *A Razorbill with its single egg at a cliff ledge. The large, deep, black bill with its* transverse white bar and narrow white line to the eye is most diagnostic.

BLACK GUILLEMOT

CEPPHUS GRYLLE

An alternative name for the Black Guillemot that finds favour with many birders is 'Tystie'. This is a corruption of the old Norse 'Teiste', meaning pigeon or dove, and is still in use in Orkney and Shetland. This connection is further reflected in other archaic local names for the species, such as Sea Pigeon, Sea Dove, Greenland Dove, Turtledove and Turtur. These should not, of course, be confused with the Pigeon Guillemot of the North Pacific, which is a separate species of the same genus dealt with elsewhere in this book.

A Holarctic species with an almost circumpolar distribution, there are seven subspecies, none of which has been shown to be easily separable at sea. The nominate race is to be found in the Baltic Sea area; *C. g. mandtii* along the high Arctic coasts from Spitsbergen eastwards to northern Alaska; *C. g. ultimus* along the high Arctic Canadian coasts; *C. g. arcticus* in northern America and southern Greenland, western Sweden, Denmark, Norway, Murmansk and the White Sea; *C. g. islandicus* in Iceland; *C. g. faeroensis* in the Faeroes and *C. g.*

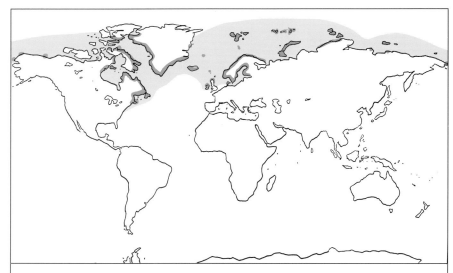

SIZE 12-14 in (30-36 cm)	EGG COLOUR White, tinged cream, buff, blue-green, blotched black, brown, grey
WINGSPAN 23 in (58 cm)	INCUBATION 28 days
EGG CLUTCH Two	FLEDGLING 35-38 days

A newly hatched, down-covered Black Guillemot nestles against an, as yet, unhatched egg. The brood of this species usually comprises two youngsters.

atlantis along the east coasts of the North Atlantic, including Britain and Ireland. As the name implies, this bird is almost completely black, but with a large, conspicuous, white wing patch which readily identifies it when in summer plumage. Confusion with the similar Pigeon Guillemot may occur in the Bering and Chukchi Seas, where the species overlap. When at rest the bright red legs can be seen, and when revealed the bright red gape further adds to the attractiveness of this bird.

The flight is swift, on rapidly beating wings which are comparatively short and broad, providing greater manoeuvrability than larger auks. When on the wing, the contrast between the white wing patches and the dark body is even more apparent than when at rest on the sea. Also the underwing shows an even larger area of white, extending onto the primary coverts and axillaries. However, it should be noted that the Icelandic race shows a broken brown line across the lower edge of the white wing panel, while in all races there is a rare variant that has no wing panel at all. In winter plumage the Black Guillemot looks quite different, the neck and head become predominantly white from late July onwards. Furthermore, the white, fringed feathers of its upperparts give a heavily mottled appearance, while the white wing patch is much less distinct. The juvenile is similar to the winter adult, but is dusky on the crown and at close range the white wing patch shows a row of dusky spots.

In Britain and Ireland the Black Guillemot is at the southern limit of its range, which is much more restricted than that of either Common Murre or Razorbill. There are concentrations in Shetland and Orkney and breeding continues down the western coast of Scotland, in the Isle of Man and as far south as Anglesey. It also nests at suitable places around most of Ireland.

In the breeding season the Black Guillemot is to be found along rocky and boulder-strewn coasts, particularly in sea lochs and harbours, narrow inlets and fjords with relatively shallow water. Prior to nesting in late April and May, groups gather on the sea to perform communal displays, when perhaps twenty, thirty or more birds, but rarely more than a hundred, will take part in a complex water dance. One bird will swim round another, almost touching, as it emits a weak whistling note and shows its bright red gape. The prospective mate shows little response, but may utter squeaky sounds. Several pairs may participate in processional swimming, followed by chases just above, and at times under, the water during which the white wing patches and red legs are predominantly displayed. When the pair bond has been established a suitable site is selected, usually among boulders, scree or in cre-

vices in low cliffs. A wide range of 'artificial' sites have also been recorded, such as holes in harbour walls, under discarded fish boxes, piles of driftwood and drainage holes. Colonial to solitary, it is not such a gregarious nester as the Common Murre. Its location is also more difficult to determine, though a strong smell of guano from the latrine area adjacent to the nest will give the position of the nest away to those with a nose for such things.

The Black Guillemot can be quite noisy at the nest site, on the sea and occasionally in flight. It utters a shrill 'peeeeee' note, either high-pitched and plaintive or shrill and feeble, and this can be another means of detecting its nest site.

There is little in the way of nest construction and the two eggs are usually laid on the bare ground, or rock. They are oval, smooth and white, often tinged cream, buff or blue-green and spotted or blotched black, brown and grey. Incubation is

At 56 days old this Black Guillemot chick photographed on Orkney is fully grown. Though there is a hint of the white wing patch diagnostic of the adult bird it does not look much like its parent at this age.

Perched on a rock, the Black Guillemot with its wholly blackish plumage, except for prominent white wing patches, is unmistakable but has to be distinguished from similar Pigeon Guillemot where range overlaps.

carried out by both parents and lasts around 28 days. On hatching, the young are covered in a rich brown down, being paler underneath. Brooded when small, they are cared for by both parents. Fish for the young are brought singly, with butterfish a major ingredient of the diet. The fledging period is around 35 to 38 days, by which time juvenile plumage is attained and they make for the sea to fend for themselves.

The Black Guillemot's diet comprises all manner of marine fish species as available, but it possibly

feeds more on crustaceans in the Arctic areas of its range.

British breeding birds are quite sedentary and spend most of the winter months around or near the coastal areas where they nest. Indeed, most recoveries of ringed birds have been no more than 30 to 745 miles (50–1200 km) from the point of origin.

On the North American east coast it is casual south to Long Island and New Jersey. Uncommon in Alaska.

PIGEON GUILLEMOT

CEPPHUS COLUMBA

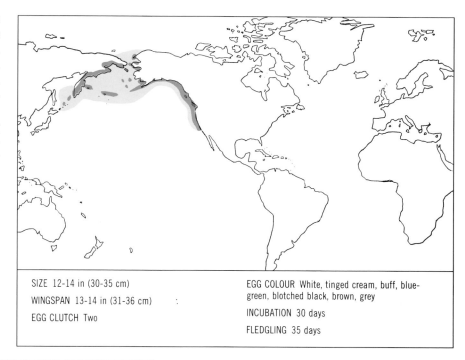

Very much the North Pacific equivalent of the Black Guillemot, the Pigeon Guillemot is quite common, breeding from northern Alaska south through the Bering Sea to the Aleutian Islands, and then south along the Pacific Coast, to southern California. It also breeds in the USSR from the Chukotskiy Peninsula south to the Kurile Islands. The species does not move far in winter, being found throughout the breeding range, except in the ice-bound northern-most parts, and only dispersing slightly southwards in Asia to Sakhalin Island in the USSR and to Hokkaido in Japan.

Pigeon Guillemots have the same jizz as Black Guillemots, though they are slightly larger. They can be seen bobbing about high on the water and then diving, their coral-red feet flashing for a moment before they are gone. They also swim with head submerged, apparently looking for food or even fishing. Underwater, they pursue their prey using their wings to 'fly' through the water. Their diet includes small fish, molluscs, crustacea and other invertebrates. At times the birds haul them-

SIZE 12-14 in (30-35 cm)

WINGSPAN 13-14 in (31-36 cm)

EGG CLUTCH Two

EGG COLOUR White, tinged cream, buff, blue-green, blotched black, brown, grey

INCUBATION 30 days

FLEDGLING 35 days

Pigeon Guillemots are similar to Black Guillemots but close inspection reveals a blackish bar across the white patch in the wing.

selves out on the rocks to bask in the sun, either standing upright with their tails touching the ground or sitting in a more relaxed position with their breast on the ground. They are generally rather silent, but a faint, shrill whistle, like the chirping of a sparrow, has been recorded, as well as an angry hiss when breeding birds are disturbed.

Adults in breeding plumage are black, with the same white wing-coverts as the Black Guillemot. However, unlike that species, the white patch is invaded by a black wedge. The bill is blackish and the feet are red. In winter plumage the adult undergoes a dramatic change, becoming pale over-all. The crown and face are sullied with sooty-black, with a more distinct dark line through the eye to the bill. The upperparts are mottled sooty-black, and the wings are black, though still with the same pure white wing-coverts invaded from below by a black wedge. Because the contrast with the whitish body is much reduced, the white wing patch is less noticeable. Juveniles are essentially similar to winter adults, though their plumage is even more marbled with sooty brown, especially on the coverts patch and breast. First-winter birds are similar to adults, though slightly darker.

In the Chukchi Sea region of north west Alaska,

the Pigeon Guillemot overlaps with the Black Guillemot, so in the north it should not be assumed that a black auk is a Pigeon Guillemot. Identification of perched birds requires a relatively good view, but in flight, separation of Pigeon and Black Guillemots is easy. Black Guillemots have pure white underwings, with a neat, dark trailing edge, whilst Pigeon Guillemots have entirely dusky-grey underwings. Another pitfall is the first-summer Black Guillemot, which may show the dark wedge on the wing-coverts for a while. Immatures and winter adults could be mistaken for one of the Murrelets, especially non-breeding Marbled Murrelet, but that species has white scapulars, not wing-coverts, and in any case Pigeon Guillemot is much larger, with a longer and more slender bill and paler head and body than any Murrelet.

The species breeds singly or in loose colonies in crevices in cliff faces or amongst tumbled boulders on the shore. In the breeding season, birds are generally found close to shore, often around kelp beds or even in harbours. It is opportunistic, taking advantage of man-made structures such as abandoned wharves and piers. Sometimes it will excavate its own burrow, and holes in clay banks 200 feet (60 m) above the sea have been recorded. Birds return to their colonies in March, when there are squabbles and fights between males. There is no nest, the eggs simply being placed on the rock, sand or whatever substrate there is, though they may make a collection of any small pebbles or rock chips that lie within reach. The two eggs, which are laid between May and July, are very similar to those of a Black Guillemot, though they are slightly larger and more heavily marked. Incubation lasts for 30 days, and both sexes take part.

Fledging and dispersal of the young takes place in August and September, though, as already noted, birds do not move far in winter, being found along rocky sea coasts and out to sea. However, their precise winter range is not clearly understood and many southern breeding birds may actually move north for the winter, as the Californian breeding areas are deserted for several months.

A Pigeon Guillemot in winter plumage rides the Pacific swell off the coast of California in early October.

DOVEKIE

ALLE ALLE

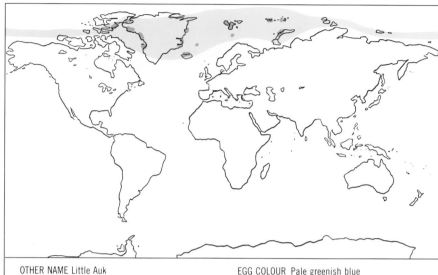

This tiny seabird is possibly the most abundant of all the alcids, with a world population estimated to be in the region of 30 million. Even so, there may well have been a decline in its overall numbers in recent historical times for some of its more southerly breeding colonies have either become smaller or have disappeared altogether.

A bird of the high Arctic for most of the year, its main breeding areas are Greenland, Iceland, Novaya Zemlya, Spitsbergen and Jan Mayan Land. It is also said to nest on Ellesmere Island, Canada. The slightly larger subspecies *A. a. polaris* which is not separable at sea, breeds only in Franz Josef Land. Britain and Ireland are at the southern edge of the Little Auk's wintering range, though individuals have been reported further south in Portugal, Spain, Italy, Malta, Madeira, and the Azores.

Dovekies noted in Britain are most likely to come from the Spitsbergen colonies, or possibly further east. Some large specimens are considered to be *A. a. polaris* and it is also possible that some American north east coast birds reach European waters at times.

The best chance British birders have of observing the species is in Shetland, where flocks or 'flights' of hundreds and at a times thousands may be seen, or along the east coast of Britain as far south as north Norfolk during October and early November. In the right conditions it is not uncommon, especially at times of strong onshore winds. Stormy conditions particularly can also bring birds to inland locations but such 'wrecks' are not frequent.

The small size, the short stubby bill and the neckless appearance of the Dovekie, or Little Auk as it is known in Europe, should preclude confusion with other black and white alcids. Breeding plumage is acquired in late winter or early spring when the head, neck and upperparts are black, and the underparts are mainly white, except for a blackish upper breast. At close quarters a distinctive feature is the white streaking on the scapulars. On land it either sits upright on its tarsus, like a tiny penguin, or squats full length on its breast, as Atlantic Puffins do. On the water it sits very low, so that its identification over any great distance requires some deliberation. This is especially so in winter plumage, when the ear coverts, throat and upper breast become white.

OTHER NAME Little Auk

SIZE 8-10 in (20-25 cm)

WINGSPAN 12-13 in (31-33 cm)

EGG CLUTCH One

EGG COLOUR Pale greenish blue

INCUBATION 29 days

FLEDGLING 28 days

However, when on the wing, its fast furious, whirring flight is fairly distinctive while the dark underwing should prevent confusion with the juvenile Atlantic Puffin or other similarly plumaged auks, all of which have pale underwings.

During a winter spent at sea, most Dovekies tend to remain near the edge of the pack ice, where they feed on the small planktonic crustaceans which are abundant in those cold waters. In any event, they rarely stray south of the Gulf Stream's influence.

Birds move back to their breeding grounds at variable times. Those nesting in Franz Josef Land return as early as February or March, but those nesting in Spitsbergen do not arrive back until around April, while Greenland nesting birds do not show up until the first half of May. On arrival they will make spectacular, circling flights over and around the nesting area and collect together on the sea forming huge 'rafts' just offshore. The preferred nesting sites are on mountain slopes of loose talus rocks or scree, ranging from sea level to an elevation of 1640 feet (500 m). Most colonies, if not facing the sea, are within easy flying distance of it, though they could be several miles away up a valley or fjord. Dense, noisy colonies will at times produce the effect of 'flock singing', an incredible sound which suggests a co-ordinated variation in frequency and amplitude.

Study of breeding pairs has indicated there is a marked 'mate fidelity' and a tendency to return to the same nest site over a number of years. Much of the birds' courtship comprises head wagging, which at times is preceded by or followed by 'butterfly flights', and accompanied by trilling calls.

The nest site is usually well-hidden among boulders, scree or in a crevice of a rock or cliff face. To this chosen location the pair will bring small pebbles or occasionally a piece of lichen or straw, which serves as the nest. One pale greenish blue egg is laid in early June with both birds taking turns to incubate with the egg positioned under one wing. Incubation lasts around 29 days. Change-over may take place up to four times a day, but the egg might be left unattended for several hours if a sitting bird is disturbed. Predation by Glaucous Gulls and Arctic Foxes accounts for considerable losses within a colony during the nesting period. The young are fed by both parents until, some four weeks after hatching, the chick has developed its juvenile plumage and looks not unlike its parents. The family then moves to the sea and the young is fed for a further period.

Most feeding actually takes place in the twilight hours, when the plankton rise nearer the water surface. Food is then obtained in shallow dives, during which the Dovekie may travel some distance

using its feet and wings and remaining submerged for up to 40 seconds.

Immediately after the breeding season the adults moult and are flightless for a few weeks.

Then, at the mercy of the ocean currents, they drift westwards then southwards. In the north Atlantic they are to be found in Baffin Bay and Davis Strait as early as July and they reach Newfoundland by September in some years. In October many may be found off the New England coast and less frequently south to Long Island, New York. As in Britain and Europe, autumn gales on shore can 'wreck' these birds well inland along the US eastern seaboard.

LEFT *A Dovekie in breeding plumage stands on lichen-covered tallus typical of its nesting sites; and* ABOVE *dwarfed by steep cliffs of its high Arctic summer home.*

PREVIOUS PAGE *This tiny alcid, in winter dress, may be mistaken for a Puffin but note the white-streaked scapulars which Puffins do not have.*

ATLANTIC PUFFIN

FRATERCULA ARCTICA

This is perhaps the most popular of all seabirds and certainly the best-known member of the auk family, especially to Europeans, birders and non-birders alike. It is remarkable for its coloured, parrot-like beak, which gives it such a comical and appealing appearance. However, as T. A. Coward so astutely states in his *Birds of the British Isles and Their Eggs*, 'it is not the parti-coloured bill, nor the black and white plumage, or the upright carriage or the orange red legs that give the Puffin its quaint look, but its eye!' This is set deeply above the round, full cheek, from which a conspicuous groove curves backwards. Around the eye there is a crimson ring and above it a small, triangular, blue, horny plate and below it a small, similarly coloured bar. All these features are discernible only at relatively close quarters, but the Atlantic Puffin is usually obliging enough to allow close scrutiny when on its breeding grounds. One can then see clearly that it is indeed the expression created by the eye that makes the 'Sea Parrot', as it was once widely called, so endearing.

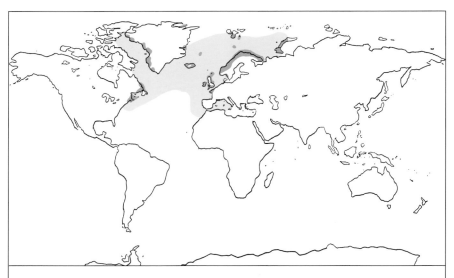

SIZE 11-12 in (28-30 cm)	EGG COLOUR Dull white with grey, reddish spots
WINGSPAN 21-23 in (53-58 cm)	INCUBATION 40 days
EGG CLUTCH One	FLEDGLING 38 days

It is a well-worn cliche, but one cannot help repeating the phrase that the Atlantic Puffin is indeed the 'clown' of the bird world with brightly coloured, conical bill and quizzical expression.

The Atlantic Puffin is found on both sides of the North Atlantic, with the nominate race breeding in southern Greenland, Iceland, and from Labrador south to Maine, and northern Norway.

The subspecies *F. a. grabae* breeds in southern Norway, Sweden, the British Isles and islands off north west France, while *F. a. naumanni* occurs in northern Greenland, Spitsbergen, Novaya Zemlya and Jan Mayen Land. The difference between the subspecies is solely a matter of size with *F. a. naumanni*, by the very slightest amount, the larger.

It is only during the breeding season that the Atlantic Puffin sports its colourful red, yellow and blue beak. Once nesting is over, it is lost, along with the yellow ritual tubercles and other horny appendages round the eye. During the winter months the face of the adult looks a dirty grey, while the juvenile's is even darker, but with a smaller beak. In both, the legs are a dirty yellow at that time of year. From September through to February Atlantic Puffins are truly pelagic and are spread widely across the north Atlantic and into the Mediterranean. Storm-driven birds blown inland turn up on lakes and reservoirs miles from the sea. However, they seem less prone to such 'wrecking' than some other seabirds such as Dovekie or Manx Shearwater.

On the sea they swim easily, riding the waves in the roughest weather, whilst on the wing their rapid whirring flight carries them low over the water. It is in flight that identification can be a problem, with the differences between it, the Razorbill and the Common Murre hard to determine.

In the breeding season Atlantic Puffins especially favour turfy island and grassy cliff tops, where they nest in underground burrows which they mostly excavate themselves. At times they will take over those previously dug out by rabbits. Birds often start to arrive back at their nesting areas at the end of February or early March, certainly at lower latitudes. They collect together in restless 'rafts' just offshore, only occasionally coming, briefly, to land. During these early days they will disappear en masse to return a few days later.

Most birds would seem to be paired on arrival, but as the season advances and more time is spent on land, further courtship ensues, with much billing and cooing and neck and head nibbling. Further establishment of the pair bond is determined by the ritual presentation of feathers or pieces of grass by the male to the female. When these ceremonies take place, other nearby birds may attempt to join in. Quite often squabbles break out and birds become locked in battle using feet, wings and bill to drive away would-be interlopers to these private affairs. However, during courtship Atlantic Puffins are quite promiscuous birds.

Both male and female share in the excavation of the burrow, the strong legs and feet, with their ¼ inch (6 mm) claws, well able to scratch away the earth. It is at this time that Atlantic Puffins are most vocal, when their low growling 'arr' takes on a whole range of different 'meanings and emotions' according to the way it is uttered. In soft soil, the burrow may be 3 to 4 feet (1 m) long, with perhaps more than one entrance and exit. In harder terrain it may be no more than a cavity under a pile of rocks. At some sites where constant burrowing has taken place over the years, whole areas have collapsed, rendering them untenable. The extinction of the colony on Grassholm, Wales, is a classic example of such a situation.

The nest itself may be little more than a few bits of grass and the odd feather, whilst at times the egg can be deposited on bare soil. The single egg, laid during the second half of May, is dull white with a rough texture and is usually faintly marked with grey or reddish spots. Incubation lasts for about forty days. The newborn chick is covered in black down above and white below. It grows rapidly on a diet of small fish, especially sand eels, during which time the adult birds can be seen returning from their fishing trips with, amazingly, often a dozen or more sand eels held in their bill. When feeding their young the adults are particularly vulnerable to predation by large gulls and skuas. The Great Black-backed Gull, particularly, preys on the Atlantic Puffin and can swallow them whole.

ABOVE *A two-week old, down-covered Atlantic Puffin emerges from its underground nesting burrow to assess the dangerous world it will shortly move into.*

OVERLEAF *At favoured nesting sites, before breeding properly gets underway, crowds of Atlantic Puffins stand about preening, displaying and pair forming. At such times, quite fierce fights take place.*

The young Atlantic Puffins are fed for about 40 days and then abandoned by their parents. Eventually, after about a week, they are driven by hunger to emerge from the nesting burrow and make their way down to the sea. This journey is fraught with the danger of predation by gulls or skuas, and quite a number for one reason or another fail to reach the comparative safety of the ocean. Those British birds that succeed spend the winter months in the waters of the Atlantic, in the North Sea or Bay of Biscay. The North American population appears only to move from its breeding sites to adjacent offshore waters, but occasionally some are to be found south to Long Island, New York.

In Britain the major concentrations of nesting Atlantic Puffins are to be found in Orkney, Shetland and the Western Isles of Scotland. There are numerous other scattered colonies, particularly round the western shores of Britain and Ireland, whilst the Farne Islands especially have a notable population. In British waters the Atlantic Puffin was once numbered in millions. Indeed, it is believed that at one time St Kilda alone held over a million pairs. This century has seen a marked reduction in the overall population, with pollution of the sea from oil spillages undoubtedly contributing to this decline. The present British population is estimated to be in the region of half a million pairs.

All the features of an adult Atlantic Puffin in full breeding plumage are seen clearly in this unique shot of the bird coming into land.

HORNED PUFFIN

FRATERCULA CORNICULATA

The Horned Puffin is the North Pacific equivalent of the Atlantic Puffin. It breeds off the coasts of eastern Siberia from the northern Kurile Islands, Sakhalin Island, the Kamchatka Peninsula and the Commander Islands in the USSR, north around the shores of the Bering Sea to the Diomede Islands and the Chukchi Sea, and on through the Aleutian chain and along the coast of Alaska. It has spread south to Queen Charlotte Island in British Columbia and, in recent summers, numbers have also been seen around Vancouver Island, where the species may well be found to be breeding.

The Horned Puffin is indeed very similar to the Atlantic Puffin, but fortunately their ranges do not overlap so there can be no confusion. A plump, medium-sized auk, in breeding plumage the Horned Puffin is black above, including a black cap and collar, and white below. Its face is greyish-white with a swollen, red eye-ring and a small, fleshy 'horn' projecting upwards from the eye, from which the species gets its name (incidentally, the Atlantic Puffin has a similar, though smaller, horn). The thin black line running backwards from the eye across the Horned Puffin's cheeks gives it a rather oriental expression. The feet are reddish orange and the huge swollen bill is yellow, with a reddish tip and an orange wattle at the gape. Just like its Atlantic cousin, in winter it loses the colourful sheath around the bill, which becomes smaller and much darker, with a reddish tip. It also loses the fleshy horn above the eye and the cheeks become heavily washed grey, giving the whole bird a duller and drabber appearance. The juvenile is even duller, with a smaller and darker bill.

When seen clearly the Horned Puffin is unmistakable but it does need to be distinguished from the Tufted Puffin. The latter has an all-black body and never shows clean white underparts. In winter, when the colourful facial decorations are shed, Horned Puffins can be separated from murres by their stubbier appearance, proportionally larger head and deeper bill. At long range, the dark chin is an important distinction from winter-plumaged murres, and in flight the lack of a white, trailing edge to the wing can also be seen. In flight, which is strong and usually quite high above the surface of the sea, the reddish feet are also conspicuous, while the dusky flanks and underwing might be seen, although the bird beats its wings so fast that no

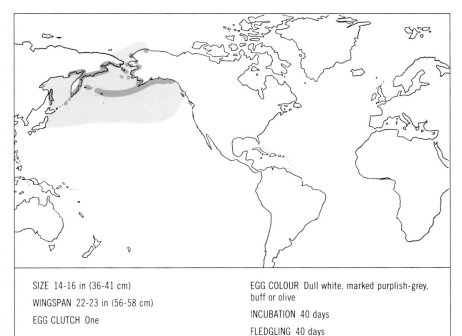

SIZE 14-16 in (36-41 cm)

WINGSPAN 22-23 in (56-58 cm)

EGG CLUTCH One

EGG COLOUR Dull white, marked purplish-grey, buff or olive

INCUBATION 40 days

FLEDGLING 40 days

The Horned Puffin is the counterpart of the closely-related Atlantic Puffin, and is similar at all ages, but problems of specific identification between these two should not apply as their ranges do not overlap.

more than a fleeting impression of the underwing colour may be gained. Indeed, its short, rounded wings and large head may invite confusion with one of the smaller auklets or murrelets.

On the water the Horned Puffin swims high and buoyantly, and when fishing it normally jumps clear of the water's surface before diving, rather like a Shag. A gregarious species, it is often found in large numbers throughout the year. It feeds largely on small fish, which may be brought back to the nest neatly stacked crosswise in the bill, just like an Atlantic Puffin.

Birds arrive in the breeding colonies from mid-May onwards, depending on the date the ice melts. They breed in holes and crevices in cliff-faces and amongst boulders on rocky islands, only more rarely using burrows in the ground, which are the common nest sites of their Atlantic cousins. The single egg is laid in June or July, and is dull white, faintly marked with purplish-grey, buff or olive. It is placed on the ground, on a simple mat of grasses, sticks or small stones. Both sexes take part in incubation, and are courageous in defence of the nest, being able to inflict a good nip on any intruder with their large bill. They are aggressive towards each other. Breeding birds have a whistling call, as well as a variety of low growling or grunting calls. The young vacate the nest before being able to fly, leaving under the supervision of the parents, even to the extent of the adult catching the chick by the wing and flying with it in a shallow dive to the water.

The centre of gravity of the population shifts southwards in the winter, with post-breeding dispersal beginning in September. Birds are then found from the Aleutians and the Bering Sea south to Japan and British Columbia, and, more rarely, to southern California and even Baja California. There are also records from Hawaii. In the winter, however, it is largely pelagic, only infrequently being seen from land. Indeed, it is more likely to occur on the West Coast, in late spring and summer, when non-breeders may be found south to southern California and north to Wrangel Island, often around the breeding colonies of other species of auk. Vagrants have been recorded in Mackenzie in northern Canada, and inland in Washington State.

The Horned Puffin can be separated from the Tufted Puffin by its clear white underparts, while breeding adults lack the head plumes of this other species.

TUFTED PUFFIN

LUNDA CIRRHATA

If there is another contender as the comic of the seabird world, it is surely the Tufted Puffin. In Alaska, it is one of the most abundant of seabirds, with an estimated population of four million birds, and it is certainly very conspicuous. Around the Aleutian Islands the sea may be populated with thousands of Tufted Puffins, against a backdrop of snow-capped islands shrouded in the perpetual mists of the region. Around the colonies the air is full of Puffins, flying a few feet above a veritable seabird city.

The adult in breeding plumage is unmistakable, being almost entirely black, except for a white face and a bright reddish-orange bill and legs. In detail, the bill has a massive sheath which is largely reddish-orange with the basal third of the upper mandible olive-yellow. The iris is yellow and the eye is surrounded by a red orbital ring. There are a pair of conspicuous, pale-yellow plumes, which sprout from behind the eye and curl down over the back of the head. The sexes are similar.

In winter plumage the bright adornments are shed, the bill becomes slimmer and duller, grey at the base and reddish at the tip. The plumage also becomes duller, the cheeks being heavily washed with grey, the plumes brown and almost vestigial, and the body blackish grey above and brownish grey below. The juvenile has a smaller bill than the non-breeding adult's, coloured largely yellowish-horn. Its upperparts are dull blackish brown, while the underparts are dirty white, heavily washed brownish grey, with a more distinct dark area on the sides of the breast. It has a dark eye, a dark cap, paler cheeks and a dark bridle from the bill, under the chin to the sides of the breast. After the post-juvenile moult, the first-year bird remains in a plumage similar to the juvenile's until the spring moult. As in other species of Puffin, each individual takes several years before it reaches the glories of full adult plumage.

At close range the breeding adult is distinguished at all times from the Horned Puffin by its lack of clean white underparts. Out of breeding plumage it may be mistaken for the Rhinoceros Auklet, which is about the same size. Juveniles and especially sub-adults invite confusion, as they share a yellowish bill with the Rhinoceros Auklet. However, the bill is a different shape, being much heavier and less pointed, and the Tufted Puffin has a much larger

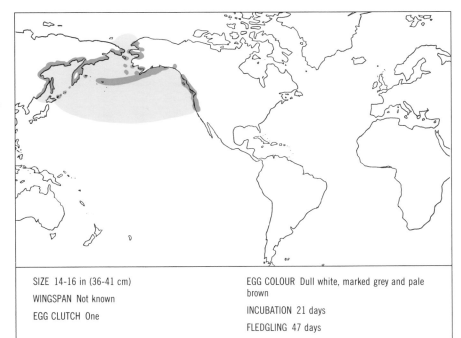

SIZE 14-16 in (36-41 cm)

WINGSPAN Not known

EGG CLUTCH One

EGG COLOUR Dull white, marked grey and pale brown

INCUBATION 21 days

FLEDGLING 47 days

PREVIOUS PAGE *A Tufted Puffin in winter plumage loses the colourful bill sheath, white face and plumes, and appears generally blackish grey. A Rhinoceros Auklet is similarly patterned but head and bill shape are different.*

ABOVE *A group of Tufted Puffins in full breeding plumage at their Alaskan breeding grounds, make a colourful sight; with their large, orange bills, white faces and plumes they cannot really be confused with any other species at that time of year.*

and more bulbous head. In flight, the Tufted Puffin also has more rounded wingtips and rather darker underwings than the Rhinoceros Auklet. In addition, it lacks a white trailing edge to the wing which separates it from guillemots, while the reddish feet are rather conspicuous. Being a plump species with short wings, it seems to require a good run before it can take off from the water. Once airborne, however, it is a strong flier, keeping high above the waves.

The Tufted Puffin is a North Pacific species. In eastern Asia it breeds from northern Japan northwards through Sakhalin, the Kurile, Commander Islands and the Kamchatka Peninsula to the Bering Straits. In western America it breeds in Alaska from the Diomede, Pribilof and Aleutian Islands south along the Pacific coast to central California. In the Aleutians, both birds and eggs were widely eaten by the local people, who used to catch them in flight with large, long-handled nets. The skins were also used to make parkas. Forty-five birds produced a good warm coat when worn with the feathers on the inside.

Birds return to the colonies in April or May and, like the Atlantic Puffin, the Tufted Puffin breeds in burrows in the ground on seaside slopes. Less

commonly it uses crevices amongst boulders and piles of rock, or even hides the nest in dense vegetation. The nest itself is an accumulation of grass, leaves and sometimes feathers, on which the single egg is laid in June or July. The egg is dull white, often marked with greys and pale browns. Both male and female incubate the egg over a period of about 21 days, and in the south of the range it is reported that two broods are raised. The chick is fed in the burrow until it is fully feathered.

A rather pelagic species, the adults keep well out to sea even in the breeding season, feeding far from shore and occasionally following trawlers or other small fishing boats. They are good divers, feeding on shellfish and small fish.

In the winter there is a slight southward shift, with birds being found from Kamchatka Peninsula to the USSR, to southern Japan, and from southern Alaska to central, or even southern, California. They are most common in the north, however, even in winter.

Outside the breeding season, Tufted Puffins seldom come within sight of land unless they are unwell or injured. They also tend to be rather solitary, occurring singly or in pairs. Vagrants have been recorded in Hawaii and Maine.

APPENDIX

The following is a list of seabirds that are irregular or scarce visitors in North America or Europe.

BLACK-BROWED ALBATROSS
Diomedea melanophris
LENGTH: 32 in (81 cm)
Also known as Mollymawk

Breeding on islands in the southern oceans, this huge Fulmar-like bird normally winters only as far north as the tropics. However, has been noted off the US coast of New England and the Maritimes. There have also been a number of sightings around Britain, but some of those no doubt relate to the bird which has annually summered at the Hermaness Gannetry, Unst, Shetland since 1972 and which returned yet again in 1989. Adult can be identified by its dark underwing with a broad white central strip, wholly white head (except for black brow) and yellow bill.

YELLOW-NOSED ALBATROSS
Diomedea chlororynchos
LENGTH: 32 in (81 cm)
Also known as Yellow-nosed Mollymawk

Can be confused with Black-browed Albatross but it is a slimmer, longer-necked bird having a dark bill and predominantly white underwing with a dark border. Breeds south Atlantic and Indian Oceans. Accidental off the Atlantic and Gulf coasts of USA.

BLACK-FOOTED ALBATROSS
Diomedea nigripes
LENGTH: 32 in (81 cm)

A bird of the south Pacific, it breeds north west of Hawaii. Almost a dark-plumaged bird overall, it shows some white around the bill and quite extensive white undertail coverts in older birds. It is to be seen off the US west coast the year round, and is quite common in summer. Often follows ships.

LAYSAN ALBATROSS
Diomedea immutablis
LENGTH: 32 in (81 cm)

Breeding on islands of the north Pacific, its habit of colonizing aircraft runways, particularly on Midway, resulted in costly bird strike damage and the subsequent slaughtering of many thousands of birds in a futile attempt to prevent such happenings. Regularly noted off the west coast of USA, though rare. Sometimes recorded inland in spring in south eastern California. Quite numerous off Alaska. It has dark upperwing with white flash in primaries and white underwing showing irregular black markings, making it fairly easy to identify. There are, however, Black-footed Albatross x Laysan hybrids which can pose more of an identification problem.

SHORT-TAILED ALBATROSS
Diomedea albutrus
LENGTH: 36 in (91 cm)
Formerly known as Steller's Albatross

It was once quite common off the US west coast, but now extremely rare with world population around 250, but increasing. Breeds only on the Japanese island of Torishoma. Its large size, massive pink bill and pale feet of adult make it readily identifiable.

MOTTLED PETREL
Pterodroma inexpectata
LENGTH: 14 in (35 cm)
Also known as Scaled or Peale's Petrel

The grey belly contrasts with its mostly white breast and there is a broad diagonal bar on the leading edge of the wing. In breeding plumage the back is slightly mottled with white, hence the name. It also has a distinctive rapid bounding flight. Breeds on islands off New Zealand. Regularly noted off Alaska from May to late October but rarely elsewhere off US Pacific Coast.

PROVIDENCE PETREL
Pterodroma solandri
LENGTH: 16 in (41 cm)
Also known as Solanders or Brown-headed Petrel

A grey-brown bird overall, it has a conspicuous white patch on underwing at base of primaries. Has a pale area around entire base of bill. Breeds on islands off Australia. Some are noted west coast of USA, but well offshore.

BLACK-CAPPED PETREL
Pterodroma hasitata
LENGTH: 18 in (46 cm)
Also known as Diablotin or Jamaica Petrel

A mid-Atlantic breeding species, nests Hispaniola, also possibly Dominica and Martinique. Fairly common along edge of Gulf Stream to North Carolina from spring to late fall when up to 40 a day seen off Cape Hatteras. Accidental inland after hurricanes. It has a white forehead, white collar and white U-shaped band on rump. There is a white wing lining with a variable dark diagonal bar on leading edge. Wing shape and white forehead distinguish it from Great Shearwater, but dark birds cannot be separated from Bermuda Petrel. Recorded twice in Britain, one in 1850, the other in 1984.

COOK'S PETREL
Pterodroma cookii
LENGTH: 10.5 in (27 cm)
Also known as Blue-footed Petrel

Upperparts uniform grey, dark bar on upperwings extends across back forming distinct 'M'. Wing lining almost entirely white. Flight rapid and erratic with fluttery wing beats and bounding swooping movements. Breeds on offshore islands off New Zealand. Regularly noted off US west coast, but rare.

STEJNEGER'S PETREL
Pterodroma longirostris
LENGTH: 10 in (25 cm)

Almost identical to Cook's Petrel, but has dark cap contrasting with grey upperparts. Breeds islands off Chilean coast. Accidental off Californian coast.

CORY'S SHEARWATER
Calonectris diomedea
LENGTH: 21 in (53 cm)
Or Mediterranean Shearwater

A large, grey-brown shearwater with pure white underparts but greyish mottlings on sides of breast, though lacking dark smudges on flanks and belly which occur in Great Shearwater. Flight action recalls Fulmar with typically five to eight flaps followed by long glide. At relatively close quarters, thick yellow bill is prominent. Mainly breeds Mediterranean area.

In autumn occurs in small numbers off south west England. Also noted off east coast of USA primarily in summer and fall.

BULWER'S PETREL
Bulweria bulwerii
LENGTH: 10–10.5 in (25–27 cm)

Breeds Atlantic and Pacific Oceans. Almost wholly black, with long, wedge-shaped tail and very fast, swooping flight. Three records in Britain and Ireland, the latest in 1975 off Cape Clear Island, Cork, Ireland.

STREAKED SHEARWATER
Calonectris leucomelas
LENGTH: 19 in (48 cm)
Also called the White-faced Shearwater

Bears some resemblance to light phase Northern Fulmar as the finely streaked head looks white at a distance. Underparts have a scaly look while the axillaries are white and underwing primary coverts are dark. Bill mostly pink. An Asian breeding species, it is casual off the Californian coast in the fall.

FLESH-FOOTED SHEARWATER
Puffinus carneipes
LENGTH: 19.5 in (50 cm)
Also known as Pale-footed Shearwater

Larger than Short-tailed or Sooty Shearwater, entirely dark above and below except for paler flight feathers. At close quarters pale base to bill and pale legs can be seen. Breeds Australia and New Zealand. Winters in north Pacific and regularly seen July to December from British Columbia south to California.

PINK-FOOTED SHEARWATER
Puffinus creatopus
LENGTH: 19 in (48 cm)

Dark above, the underparts and wing linings are variably mottled. Slower in flight it soars more than Sooty Shearwater. Pink bill and feet distinctive at close range. Breeds on islands off Chile – common along the west coast of USA in summer through to fall, though usually well off-shore.

GREATER SHEARWATER
Puffinus gravis
LENGTH: 19 in (48 cm)
Other name Greater Shearwater

Distinguished from Manx Shearwater by larger size, dark cap sharply contrasting with pure white throat and almost complete white collar. Upperparts dark brown and shows narrow white patch at base of tail. Underparts white. Breeds on Tristan de Cunha Islands. Fairly common off east coast of USA, especially spring. Most frequently noted in British waters August to October, but casual.

BULLER'S SHEARWATER
Puffinus bulleri
LENGTH: 18 in (46 cm)
Also known as the Grey-backed Shearwater or New Zeland Shearwater

Its most distinctive wing pattern shows a dark bar across the leading edge and across the back forming an 'M'. Gleaming white underparts and winglinings, dark cap and long, dark, wedge-shaped tail also readily identify this bird. Its flight is graceful and buoyant, soaring for long periods. It breeds on islands off New Zealand. Irregularly noted, mainly August to September, off west coast USA from Washington to central California.

SOOTY SHEARWATER
Puffinus griseus
LENGTH: 18 in (46 cm)

Looks all black at a distance, gliding close to waves in typical shearwater fashion. Near views reveal pale areas in under-surface of wings to form an indistinct stripe along centre of wing. Almost identical to smaller Short-tailed Shearwater, it also resembles Pale-footed Shearwater. However, it is by far the most numerous of the dark Shearwater occurring off Oregon and Californian coast throughout summer, often in hundreds of thousands together; also quite common off east coast USA. Occurs in European waters especially August to November where up to 3000 daily have been seen off north west Spain. Small numbers also noted along south and east coast of Britain at this time of year.

SHORT-TAILED SHEARWATER
Puffinus tenuirostris
LENGTH: 14 in (36 cm)
Formerly called Slender-billed Shearwater

Very like Sooty Shearwater but much smaller and has shorter bill and steeper forehead. Wing linings generally more uniform in colour. Breeds south Australia, Tasmania, winters in north Pacific, when occurs along west coast USA from British Columbia to California. Some non-breeding birds present at other times. Originally known as the 'Mutton bird' as used for food by early mariners.

BLACK-VENTED SHEARWATER
Puffinus opisthomeias
LENGTH: 14 in (36 cm)

Formerly considered to be subspecies of Manx Shearwater, it is dark brown above and white below with dark undertail coverts. There is variable dusky mottling at the sides of the breast, often extending right across. Breeds on islands off Baja California, dispersing north and south after nesting. Can often be seen from shore along Californian coast from August through to May.

LITTLE SHEARWATER
Puffinus assimilis
LENGTH: 12 in (30 cm)

Resembles small Manx Shearwater but is blacker above and shows more white on the face. Flies with fast whirring wing beats and seldom glides. Various races breed Atlantic, Pacific and Indian Oceans. Accidental off the Atlantic coast of USA in summer and fall.

Before 1958 only five records for British Isles. Since then there have been over sixty occurrences, mostly from south west Ireland, all those subspecifically identified have been the Madeiran race. *P. a. baroli.*

AUDUBON'S SHEARWATER
Puffinus l'herminieri
LENGTH: 12 in (30 cm)
Or Dusky Shearwater

Has a complex taxonomy and some authorities treat this species and Little Shearwater as conspecific. Also there are nine or ten subspecies. Has a rapid fluttering flight but not as fast as Little Shearwater. Occurs in Gulf Stream along Atlantic coast to North America. In September totals have peaked at 1500 birds off Virginia, where some remain until November. Noted as far north as New York.

WILSON'S STORM-PETREL
Oceanites oceanicus
LENGTH: 7.5 in (19 cm)

Very similar to Storm Petrel but larger. Skims waves with fluttery flight on short, rounded wings in swallow-like fashion. Feet trail behind tip of tail, which is square or roundish. Yellow webbing between toes is visible at close range. Breeds south Shetlands, south Orkney Islands and South Georgia where populations are estimated in millions. Considered by some to be the most numerous seabird in the world. Common off US Atlantic coast May to September. Rare central Californian coast but annual Monterey Bay. Only a handful of records in British waters until recently, when during pelagic trips off south west Cornwall and Scilly 50 or more birds have been located on occasions.

WHITE-FACED STORM-PETREL
Pelagodroma marina
LENGTH: 8 in (20 cm)
Sometimes called Frigate Petrel

A small petrel with distinctive wholly white underparts. Upperparts slaty brown. Shows conspicuous white supercilium and dark eye stripe and dark crown. Pale rump contrasts with blackish tail. Long, dark legs with orange webs extend beyond tail. Flies with stiff, shallow wing beats and short glides. At times swings from side. Breeds islands sub-tropical north Atlantic and southern oceans. Very rare off Atlantic coast from North Carolina to Massachusetts. There is one British record from the Inner Hebrides in 1897.

LEAST STORM-PETREL
Oceanodroma microsoma
LENGTH: 6 in (15 cm)

A tiny Storm Petrel, appearing almost tailless in flight, which is indirect and low over the water with deep wing beats. Breeds only on islands off western Baja California and on northern islands in Gulf of California. Fairly common to abundant off coast of southern California in late summer and fall.

FORK-TAILED STORM-PETREL
Oceanodroma furcata
LENGTH: 8.5 in (22 cm)

Breeds from Kuril and Commander Isles through Aleutian chain east to Sanak Islands, also perhaps south east coasts of Kamchatka. Also breeds southerly Alaska, Washington, Oregon and northern California. Distinctively bluish grey above and pearl grey below. Shows dark grey forehead and eye patch, wing linings also dark. Wing beats rapid and shallow, often followed by long glide. Looks long tailed in flight.

Now rare off Californian coast but becomes more abundant further north.

ASHY STORM-PETREL
Oceanodroma homochroa
LENGTH: 8 in (20 cm)

Grey brown overall, being darkest on crown, leading edge of wings and upper surface of flight feathers. Pale mottling on underwing only visible at close range. Looks long tailed side on. Flight fairly direct but wing beats fluttery but not as swallow-like as Wilson's Storm-petrel. Breeds on islands off central and southern California, where fairly common but rare in winter.

BAND-RUMPED STORM-PETREL
Oceanodroma castro
LENGTH: 9 in (23 cm)
Also called Harcourt's Storm-petrel or Madeiran Storm-petrel

Larger than Wilson's Storm-petrel and stouter and darker than Leach's Petrel. The white band which crosses the rump is not as bold and broad as on undertail coverts of Wilson's Storm-petrel. Tail is squarish or slightly forked. Flight is shearwater-like with deep wing strokes followed by long glides. Breeds tropical and sub-tropical Atlantic islands and Pacific Oceans. Winters at sea within these regions. Scarce off Gulf coast and rare off Atlantic coast of USA. There are two accepted records for British Isles, one 1911, the other 1951.

WEDGE-RUMPED STORM-PETREL
Oceanodroma tethys
LENGTH: 6.5 in (17 cm)
Also known as Galapagos Petrel

Almost as small as Least Petrel but shows distinctive bold white, wedge-shaped patch on tail giving the appearance of a white tail with dark tips at the corners. Breeds on the Galapagos Islands and other islands off Peru. Occasionally noted off Californian coast August to January.

BLACK STORM-PETREL
Oceanodroma melania
LENGTH: 9 in (23 cm)

Largest of all the dark storm petrels it is blackish brown overall with pale bar on upper surface of the wing. The tail is forked and fairly long. Its flight is graceful with slow, deep wing beats. Breeding on islands off the coast of southern California and the Baja. Commonly to be seen off the southern California coast to Monterey from late summer through to fall.

MATSUDAIRA'S STORM- PETREL
Oceanodroma matsudairae
LENGTH: 10 in (25 cm)

One identified in the western approaches beyond Scilly on 3 August 1988. This will be the first record for British waters if accepted by BOU. Its only known breeding location is Volcano Island south of Japan.

RED-BILLED TROPIC BIRD
Phaethon aethereus
LENGTH: 19.5 in (50 cm) without tail streamers

The adult bird has black barring on back and wings which have black primaries. The tail streamers are long and white, the bill is red. The immature bird is much like adult but with black collar and lacks streamers, bill yellow to reddish. A tropical species, it is rarely noted well off southern California coast and even rarer off Atlantic coast to North Carolina.

RED-TAILED TROPICBIRD
Phaethon rubricauda
LENGTH: 18 in (46 cm) without tail streamers

Mostly white, flushed pink in breeding plumage. Wing shafts of outer primaries black. Long tail streamers red, as is bill. Juvenile lacks streamers, upperparts barred, bill black. A bird of southern Pacific Ocean, accidental off California coast.

WHITE-TAILED TROPIC BIRD
Phaethon lepturus
LENGTH: 16 in (41 cm) without tail streamers

Smaller and slimmer than Red-tailed Tropicbird, wings show distinctive black stripes, bill usually yellow. Immature has boldly barred upperparts and lacks tail streamers. A tropical species annual in spring on the Dry Tortugas. Rare but regular in summer along Gulf and Atlantic coasts to North Carolina.

RED-FOOTED BOOBY
Sula sula
LENGTH: 28 in (71 cm)

Smallest of the boobies, there are two colour phases. One phase is brown with a white tail, the other white with black primaries and secondaries. All birds have a bright pink bared skin at base of bill. The adults of both phases have bright red feet. Young birds are pale brown with yellowish feet. Breeds islands in tropical oceans. Occasionally noted on Florida's Dry Tortugas and accidental on the Gulf and California coasts.

MASKED BOOBY
Sula dactylatra
LENGTH: 32 in (81 cm)
Also called Blue-faced Booby

Distinguished from Northern Gannet by yellow bill and extensive black facial skin, black tail and black secondaries. Immatures have yellowish bill, brown underparts with white on wing coverts. There is a white patch on the upper back and often a white collar.
    Breeds on islands of tropical oceans.
    In USA rarely seen from mainland, but fairly common in Gulf of Mexico in summer and occasionally offshore to North Carolina.

BLUE-FOOTED BOOBY
Sula nebouxii
LENGTH: 32 in (81 cm)

Adults have streaked pale heads, while in flight shows white nape patch and white rump. Wings dark, underparts white. Adults have bright blue feet, darker in young birds. Breeds tropical and subtropical waters of western coasts off south and central America. Irregular wanderer in late summer and fall to inland waters of the south west USA, particularly the Salton Sea and occasionally to the Pacific coast.

BROWN BOOBY
Sula leucogaster
LENGTH: 30 in (76 cm)

A dark brown bird, shows sharply contrasting white underparts and white wing linings. Male has whitish head and neck. Pantropical, it is possibly the commonest and most widespread Booby in east Pacific. There are four subspecies with *S. i. brewsteri* breeding in the Gulf of California south along Mexican mainland. Casual at Salton Sea and along Colorado River valley in late summer. Accidental along Atlantic coast to New Jersey (dark headed eastern form).

RED-FACED CORMORANT
Phalacrocorax urile
LENGTH: 31 in (79 cm)

In breeding season has bright red facial skin, hence the name. Throat pouch is bluish and the partly yellow bill distinguishes it at all ages from very similar Pelagic Cormorant. Breeds Moyariri Island, Japan and in Commander Islands and Aleutian Islands east along coast of Alaska. Alaskan population said to be around 130,000 birds. Disperses to surrounding seas after nesting.

OLIVACEOUS CORMORANT
Phalacrocorax olivaceous
LENGTH: 26 in (66 cm)
Other name Neotropic Cormorant

A small, long-tailed cormorant with pale border to dull yellow throat patch tapering to a sharp point behind the bill. In breeding plumage acquires conspicuous white tufts to side of face and short white filoplumes on sides of neck. Habitat ranges from high mountain lakes to offshore islands, from Panama south to Cape Horn.

PYGMY CORMORANT
Phalacrocorax pygmeus
LENGTH: 19 in (48 cm)

A very small active cormorant with long tail and small round head. In breeding plumage both sexes have dark red-brown heads and glossy greenish-black plumage spotted with white except for dark-grey saddle across centre of back and wing coverts. Breeds Yugoslavia, Romania, Greece, Turkey, Crimea, Iran, and Caspian and Aral Seas. In serious decline due to loss of marshy habitat. Vagrant outside breeding range.

DALMATIAN PELICAN
Pelecanus crispus
LENGTH: 63–70 in (160–178 cm)

Very like the Great White Pelican (*Pelecanus oncocrotalus*), though usually slightly larger. In flight shows dusky secondaries and black wingtips above and all dirty white below. Now rare in southern Europe, breeding only Romania, Danube Delta, Greece, Albania, Turkey, USSR east to Chinese border, also possibly China, Mongolia and Iran.

MAGNIFICENT FRIGATEBIRD
Fregata magnificens
LENGTH: 40 in (102 cm)

One of five similar species of large dark predator seabirds with long wings and long, forked tails, the male Magnificent Frigatebird is glossy black with an orange throat pouch that becomes bright red and inflated in courtship display. Breeds tropical and subtropical Atlantic and Pacific Oceans, also Marquesas Key of South Florida. Occasionally noted along both coasts. Rare but regular in Salton Sea.

In Britain there have been three records since 1960.

SOUTH POLAR SKUA
Catharacta maccormicki
LENGTH: 21 in (53 cm)
Also called McCormick's Skua, see Great Skua.

GREAT BLACK-HEADED GULL
Larus ichthyaetus
LENGTH: 27 in (69 cm)

Size of a Great Black-backed Gull, but with a pale mantle and wings colour of Herring Gull. Adult in summer has a black hood with a broken white eye ring. The bill is heavy, yellowish with a black subterminal band and a red tip. Juvenile and immature like Herring Gull, but separable by size and bill structure. Breeds Russia and west and central Asia. There have been five records in Britain but none since 1932.

SLATY-BACKED GULL
Larus schistisagus
LENGTH: 25 in (64 cm)

A north eastern Asiatic species. Adult has very dark grey back and wings with broad, white trailing edge, legs bright pink, eye yellow. An uncommon summer and rare fall visitor to the Aleutians and western Alaska. Resembles darkest race of Western Gull, also compare with Siberian form of Herring Gull, *L. a. vagae*, which is widespread in western Alaska.

THAYER'S GULL
Larus thayerii
LENGTH: 23 in (58 cm)

This gull is very much like an Iceland Gull or Herring Gull. (It may yet be shown to be conspecific with either.) The adult has a smaller head and bill, brown eyes and has little or no black on the underwing tips. It is darker than an Iceland Gull. Breeds on Baffin Island and vicinity. Winters mainly along the Pacific coast. Uncommon elsewhere in North America.

YELLOW-FOOTED GULL
Larus rivens
LENGTH: 27 in (69 cm)

Formerly considered a subspecies of Western Gull which it closely resembles but, as name implies, has yellow legs and feet. Bill also more massive. Breeds on islands in Gulf of California wintering mostly within its breeding range.

RED-LEGGED KITTIWAKE
Rissa brevirostris
LENGTH: 15 in (38 cm)

Distinguished from Black-legged Kittiwake by short red legs and shorter thicker bill. The mantle is darker and in flight shows a broader white trailing edge on wings, underside primaries dusky. Immature bird lacks black 'M' wing pattern of Black-legged Kittiwake and in first-year plumage resembles Sabine's Gull but with all white tail, the only gull to do so at this age. Confined to Bering Sea and adjacent waters off the north Pacific, it is rarely noted away from its breeding grounds.

LESSER CRESTED TERN
Sterna bengalensis
LENGTH: 15–17 in (38–43 cm)

Mainly a bird of the Indian and west Pacific Oceans, it approximates a Sandwich Tern in size and shape, but has a bright orange bill. It has a slightly darker grey mantle and wings, grey rump and tail. First recorded in Britain at Anglesey in 1982. There have been a handful of other occurrences since then, including one on the Farne Islands in May 1985 which was identified by many birders watching a live television broadcast being made at the time!

ELEGANT TERN
Sterna elegans
LENGTH: 17 in (43 cm)

Confined to California and Mexico, it mainly breeds along the coast of Baja California. Much like Royal Tern, the bill is longer and thinner and with colour ranging from reddish orange to yellow on some juveniles. Smaller and slimmer overall than Royal Tern, its sharp 'kee-rick' call is reminiscent of Sandwich Tern. After breeding, some move north in late summer and are commonly found in San Francisco Bay area. Most, however, depart south to reach Ecuador, Peru and Chile. There is one record of this species in County Down, Eire, on 1 August 1982.

ALEUTIAN TERN
Sterna aleutica
LENGTH: 13–15 in (33–38 cm)

A bit of a mystery bird, its migrations and wintering range is unknown but breeds Siberia, USSR and Alaska. Dark grey above and below with a white forehead and black cap, black bill and legs, it resembles a small Bridled Tern but with a white tail which is deeply forked. In flight, which is graceful, strong and direct, shows a white-edged bar on the secondaries. The call is a most untern-like squeaky 'twee-ee-ee'. There is only one Western Palearctic record for this species: on the Farne Islands, Northumberland, 28–29 May 1979.

WHITE-CHEEKED TERN
Sterna repressa
LENGTH: 14 in (35 cm)

An adult summer-plumaged bird was identified at Dungeness, Kent, England on 13 May 1989, the first record for the species to be claimed anywhere in Europe. It has yet to be ratified by the BOU. Breeds north west Indian Ocean, Red Sea from Gulf of Suez, Gulf of Aden, Somali and Persian Gulf east to Malabar coast, western India and Laccadine Islands; also in East Africa south to Klunga islands, Kenya.

BRIDLED TERN
Sterna anaeathetus
LENGTH: 15 in (38 cm)
Also known as Brown-winged Tern

Circumequatorial in its distribution, some breeding colonies in the Pacific are immense. Adults resemble a slightly larger Sooty Tern, but slimmer looking with more pointed wings which show more white on the underside. The white forehead patch extends behind the eye. US birds come from Bahamas and West Indies, which summer in Gulf of Mexico to North Carolina, though well offshore. Storm driven birds have reached New England. Of the dozen British records, all have been of birds found dead, except for the latest record of a bird at Cemlyn Bay, Anglesey on 2 July 1988.

SOOTY TERN
Sterna fuscata
LENGTH: 16 in (41 cm)
Also known as Wideawake

About Sandwich Tern size, it is blackish above and white below, lacking the white collar of Bridled Tern, while the deeply forked tail is edged with white. The white forehead patch which stops at the eye is another distinguishing feature. Widespread throughout tropical oceans, there are also large breeding colonies located on the dry Tortugas, Florida. Also nests on islands off Texas and Louisiana. Tropical storms can carry individuals far inland and some as far north as New England and the Maritime provinces. In Britain, has been recorded 26 times.

BLACK NODDY
Anous minutus
LENGTH: 13.5 (34 cm)
Also known as Lesser Noddy

A tropical species rarely noted in North America but with the occasional occurrences among Brown Noddies on the Dry Tortugas, Florida.

BROWN NODDY
Anous stolidus
LENGTH: 15.5 in (39 cm)
Also known as Common Noddy

An overall dark grey-brown bird with a whitish grey cap. Unlike other terns, the Brown Noddy has a long, wedge-shaped tail with only a small notch at the tip. Breeds tropical and subtropical islands in Atlantic, Indian and Pacific Oceans. In USA, nests on the Dry Tortugas, Florida. As other noddies and some pelagics, might be seen along Gulf coast of Texas or as far north as North Carolina after storms.

MARBLED MURRELET
Brachyramphus marmoratus
LENGTH: 9.75 (25 cm)

An intriguing species, little is known about it. To date only four nests have ever been found, two on the ground and two in trees. In breeding plumage this tiny alcid is dark above and heavily mottled below with brown. In winter the underparts are mostly white and the upperparts blackish grey with white scapulars. Precise limits of breeding areas unknown but occurs in hundreds of thousands off Alaska and in smaller numbers south to California.

KITTLITZ'S MURRELET
Brachyramphus brevirostris
LENGTH: 9 in (23 cm)

Equally enigmatic as Marbled Murrelet, it is very similar in both summer and winter plumage, but dark bill is shorter. In winter plumage, it is much whiter of face making eye conspicuous. The few nests found have been on dry, stony ground some distance inland. During breeding season tens of thousands on Prince William Sound, Alaska, considered to be its major breeding area.

XANTUS' MURRELET
Endomychura hypoleuca
LENGTH: 9.75 in (25 cm)

Slate black above and white below, a southern Californian form, *S. u. scrippsi*, has a partial white eye ring. The form that breeds on islands off Baja California, *S. h. hypoleucas*, has more white in the face. Both forms distinguished from Craveri's Murrelet by lack of partial collar and white wing linings visible when birds flap wings before taking off. Nests in colonies on rocky islands. Uncommon to fairly common regular late summer and fall, adjacent to breeding localities, but some wander as far north as Washington. Rarely noted close inshore.

CRAVERI'S MURRELET
Endomychura craveri
LENGTH: 10 in (25 cm)

Very like Xantus's Murrelet, but has dark partial collar extending onto white breast. More readily distinguished by variably grey wing linings. Breeds on rocky islands off Baja California. After nesting disperses to adjacent waters, some south along west coast of Mexico, others northwards to southern California and, some years, Monterey Bay. Usually only to be seen many miles offshore.

ANCIENT MURRELET
Synthliboramphus antiquum
LENGTH: 10 in (25 cm)

Black crown and nape contrast with grey back. There is white streaking on the head and nape in breeding plumage, hence the 'ancient' look and name! Chin and throat are black, and the bill yellowish. In winter less black under chin and white streaking hardly discernible. Immature has throat mostly white and no head streaking. Breeds from Commander Islands and Kamchatka south through Kurile Islands to Korea. In USA breeds from Aleutian Islands eastwards to Alaskan Peninsula and south to British Columbia. There are about 40 Alaskan colonies with an estimated population of 400,000 birds. Winters as far south as California. Rarely noted inland in North America.

CASSIN'S AUKLET
Ptychoramphus aleuticus
LENGTH: 9 in (23 cm)

Breeding from the Buildir Islands in the Aleutians eastwards through Gulf of Alaska, then south to Guadelupe Island and the Baja California, it is one of the most widespread of the Pacific alcids. A small, plump, grey bird with a short, stout bill, at close quarters the pale eye, with prominent white crescent above and below, and pale spot at base of lower mandible might be seen. The juvenile is paler looking overall with a whitish throat. Winters southwards from about Washington to Baja California. Feeds far offshore moving into sheltered bays at night for roosting.

PARAKEET AUKLET
Cyclorrhynchus psittacula
LENGTH: 10 in (25 cm)

A large, white-breasted auklet, with an upturned orange-red bill, it has a white plume extending back from behind the eye. The upperparts are dark slate grey and sides are mottled grey. In winter bill is duller and underparts, including throat, become white. Breeds on rocky shores and sea cliffs from Cape Lisburne, Bering Strait through Bering Sea including St Lawrence, Pribilof Islands, Aleutian Islands, west to Commander Islands and east through Kodiak archipelago to Prince William Sound. In winter occurs off US coast, well out to sea, in pairs or small numbers sometimes as far south as California.

CRESTED AUKLET
Aethia cristatella
LENGTH: 10.5 in (27 cm)

In summer plumage is sooty black overall with a prominent crest which curves forward from forehead and a narrow white plume trails from rear of yellow eye. The bill is enlarged with bright orange plates. In winter bill is smaller and browner, crest and plume much reduced. Juvenile has no crest or plume. Nests in crevices of sea cliffs and along rocky shores, mainly area from Bering Sea, through Pribilof and Aleutian Islands to Alaska. Also nests westwards into Eastern Siberia. Winters within breeding range.

WHISKERED AUKLET
Aethia pygmaea
LENGTH: 7.75 in (20 cm)

Confined to the Aleutian Islands and perhaps the Commander Islands and Kurile Islands, it is the rarest of the alcids in Alaska. A little known species, it is not much larger than the Least Auklet, but similar to the Crested Auklet having a conspicuous forward-curving crest but showing three white facial plumes which are retained all the year round. The short, stubby bill is orange, otherwise the plumage overall is dark grey. After breeding, disperses to adjacent seas, and some have wandered to Japan.

LEAST AUKLET
Aethia pusilla
LENGTH: 6.25 in (16 cm)

Smallest of all the alcids, it is sooty black above with the underparts variable, heavily mottled with grey or nearly all white. The stubby bill is dark red with a pale tip. Close views show the forehead and lores to be streaked with white bristly feathers whilst in summer plumage a streak of white plumes extends back from the eye. In winter the underparts are entirely white. Juvenile resembles winter adult.

Nests on boulder-strewn beaches and islands in countless numbers. Alaskan population estimated at six million. Winters mainly within breeding range.

RHINOCEROS AUKLET
Cerorhinca monocerata
LENGTH: 15 in (38 cm)

More closely related to the Puffins, this large, heavy-billed bird is blackish brown above, being paler on the sides, neck and throat. In breeding plumage has distinct white plumes and pale yellow horn at the base of the orange bill. In winter loses horn, and plumes less distinct. Breeds north Paupi discontinuously from Korea, Japan, Sakhalin, Kurile and Aleutian Islands to southern Alaska through British Columbia to the Farallon Islands, California, where nests in self-excavated burrows.

Winters at sea adjacent to breeding areas and can often be seen along most of west coast USA during fall and winter.

GLOSSARY

Allopatric A term used to designate closely allied species and families of birds living in different geographical areas.

Axillaries The feathers at the base of the underside of the wing – in the armpit of the bird.

Alcid (Alcids pl.) Shortened version of Alcidae, a family of diving seabirds also generally referred to as auks.

Bird strike A collision between birds and an aircraft.

BTO Initials of the British Trust for Ornithology, premier scientific ornithological body in Britain, whose headquarters are at Tring in Hertfordshire.

BOU British Ornithologists Union: on whose decision acceptance of birds to the British list depends. (AOU: American Ornithologists Union.)

Carpal Small bones of the 'wrist' in a bird's wing, the carpal joint being on the bend of the wing.

Colony A number of birds nesting in close proximity to one another. Colonial nesting species include many seabirds.

Culmen The dorsal ridge of the upper mandible of the bird's bill from its forehead to the tip.

Filoplume A hair-like feather.

Gonys The prominent ridge formed by the fusion of the two halves of the lower jaw towards the tip of the bill, especially evident in many gulls (*Larus* sp.).

Guano The excrement of fish-eating seabirds which, in large accumulation, forms a valuable organic fertilizer. Certain seabird islands in the Pacific are commercially managed for this product.

Gular (pouch) Pertaining to the throat.

Jizz An expression of uncertain origin used by birders to convey the rather indefinable overall impression given by a bird when observed in the field.

Life list A list kept by some birders of all the bird species they have seen. Each new bird is 'ticked off', hence another term often used is 'tick list'.

Lore (lores, pl.) The area between the base of the upper mandible and the eye on each side of the head).

'Lumper' A vernacular term used by birders to describe a taxonomist who is less inclined to classify small variations in a species across its range into a subspecies (see 'splitter').

Leucistic A pale-coloured version of a normally darker pigmented bird is said to be leucistic – sometimes also called 'dilute albinos'.

Mirror Term used for the small white patches on the primaries of some gulls (*Larus* sp.).

Morph A term denoting any one of the different forms of a species population, subject to polymorphism.

Ornithosis A disease identical with or closely related to psittacosis which can produce a fatal pneumonia in humans.

Operation Seafarer A census taken in 1969 to 1970 when professional and amateur ornithologists throughout the British Isles combined to map and count all seabird colonies.

Pyriform Pear-shaped. A term used to describe the shape of some birds' eggs which are tapered towards one end.

RSPB Royal Society for the Protection of Birds.

Scapulars (scapula pl.) Those feathers which cover the shoulder area of a bird, i.e. the area where the upperwing joins the body.

'Splitter' A taxonomist who considers morphological characteristics such as slight differences in measurements, shades of colour, as sufficient to put a bird into a separate subspecies – opposite of 'lumper'.

Taiga A term for boreal forest, found throughout the near-arctic.

Tarsus (Tarsii pl.) Or fully, meto-tarsus. The bone of that part of a bird's leg formed by the fusion of tarsal and metotarsal elements.

Tomium Cutting edge of the bill.

Tubercle A knob-like projection.

BIBLIOGRAPHY

BENT, A.C. (1919)
Life Histories of North American Diving Birds. Bull. U.S. Nat. Mus. 107.

BENT, A.C. (1921)
Life Histories of North American Gulls and Terns. Bull. U.S. Nat. Mus. 113.

BROOKE, R.K. (1978)
Durban Mus. Nat., 11, 295–308.

CAMPBELL, Bruce and FERGUSON-LEES, James (1972)
A Field Guide to Birds' Nests. Constable, London.

CRAMP, S. and SIMMONS, K.E.L. (eds) (1987)
The Birds of the Western Palearctic Vols I, III and IV. Oxford University Press, Oxford.

DEVILLERS, P. (1977) Auk, 94, 417–429.

DYMOND, J.N., FRARAS, P.A. and GANTLETT, S.J.M. (1987)
Rare Birds in Britain and Ireland. Poyser, Calton.

FURNESS, Robert W. (1987)
The Skuas. Poyser, Calton.

GOODERS, John
Birds of the World, Vols I to IX. (Partwork) IPC, London.

GODFREY, W.E. (1926)
The Birds of Canada, Revised Edition. National Museum of Natural Sciences, Ottawa.

GRANT, P.J. (1986)
Gulls: A Guide to Identification, Second Edition, Poyser, Calton.

HALEY, Delphine (ed.) (1984)
Seabirds to Eastern North Pacific and Arctic Waters. Pacific Search Press, Seattle.

HARRISON, P. (1983)
Seabirds: An Identification Guide. Christopher Helm, Bromley.

HARRISON, P. (1987)
Seabirds of the World: A Photographic Guide. Christopher Helm, Bromley.

JOHNSGARD, Paul A. (1987)
Diving Birds of North America. University of Nebraska Press, USA.

LACK, Peter (ed.) (1986)
The Atlas of Wintering Birds in Britain and Ireland. BTO, Irish Wildfowl Conservancy. Poyser, Calton.

MARTIN, Brian P. (1987)
World Birds. Guinness Superlatives, Enfield.

MEARNS, Barbara and Richard (1988)
Biographies for Birdwatchers. Academic Press, London.

NATIONAL GEOGRAPHICAL SOCIETY (1987)
Field Guide to the Birds of North America, Second Edition. National Geographic Society, Washington.

NETTLESHIP, David N. and BIRKHEAD, Tim R. (1985)
The Atlantic Alcidae. Academic Press, London.

PALMER, R.S. (ed.) (1962)
Handbook of North American Birds, Vol. I: Loons through Flamingos. Yale University Press, New Haven.

ROBERSON, D. (1980)
Rare Birds of the West Coast. Woodcock, Pacific Grove.

SHARROCK, J.T.R. (ed.) (1976)
The Atlas of Breeding Birds in Britain and Ireland. BTO. Poyser, Berkhamstead.

ACKNOWLEDGMENTS

I am particularly grateful to Graham Harrison for reading my original draft and for making many useful observations that helped make the text more meaningful. I am indebted to him for casting his critical eye over the proofs. I also thank his wife, Janet, for her invaluable help in sorting out the maps, text and pictures to ensure they all came together in the right order.

I have to thank the many photographers whose work is represented, for it is indeed the excellence of their pictures which hopefully will delight and endear the reader to this book. Their names are listed below against the page number where their photographs appear throughout this volume.

If I may single out any one photographer for special thanks I would particularly like to say how much the late Brian Hawkes went out of his way to help with the north Pacific species and, equally, Doug Weschler of VIREO has been especially helpful in providing material for some North American species.

PHOTOGRAPHERS ACKNOWLEDGMENTS

Front cover
M. C. Wilkes
Back cover B. Hawkes
2/3 C. Smith
7 A. J. Richards
9 A. J. Bond
10 M. C. Wilkes
11 M. C. Wilkes
12 B. Speake
13 G. W. Ward
14 E. Mackrill
15 P. T. Castell
16 D. S. Whitaker
17 D. A. Smith
18 P. T. Castell
19 **top** P. T. Castell
   bottom S. Young
20 R. T. Mills
21 **left** P. T. Castell
   right M. Lane
22/3 G. W. Ward
25 P. T. Castell
26 **top** G. Langsbury
   bottom M. C. Wilkes
27 H. Kinloch
28 **left** H. Gebuis
   right A. J. Bond
29 H. Gebuis
30 B. Hawkes
31 A. J. Richards
32 D. Wechsler/Vireo
33 H. Clarke/Vireo
34 G. Langsbury
35 W. Lankinen
36 W. Lankinen
37 B. Hawkes
38 H. Kinloch

39 R. T. Mills
40 H. Gebuis
41 M. Birkhead
42 W. Lankinen
43 W. Lankinen
44 W. Lankinen
45 G. R. Jones
46 B. L. Sage
47 M. C. Wilkes
48 B. Hawkes
49 P. Doherty
50 C. Greaves
51 A. W. Aitchison
52 W. Lankinen
53 W. Lankinen
54 E. Soothill
55 B. Hawkes
56 J. B. & S. Bottomley
57 E. K. Thompson
58 H. Gebuis
59 P. Doherty
60 R. Tidman
61 **top** E. Mackrill
   bottom H. Gebuis
62 **left** P. Doherty
   right M. C. Wilkes
63 B. Hawkes
65 W. Lankinen
67 **left** S. Young
   right P. Doherty
69 B. Hawkes
70 **top** D. Frost
   bottom B. Hawkes
72 **top** A. Morris/Vireo
   bottom W. Lankinen

73 P. Doherty
74/5 M. C. Wilkes
76 E. K. Thompson
77 E. Mackrill
78 P. Doherty
79 A. Morris/Vireo
80 **top** A. Morris/Vireo
   bottom A. J. Richards
81 P. Harris
82 P. Harris
83 M. C. Wilkes
84/5 B. L. Sage
86 W. Lankinen
87 E. K. Thompson
88 P. T. Castell
89 R. Glover
90 M. Lane
91 R. Maier
92 **top** C. Smith
   bottom W. S. Paton
94 **top** P. T. Castell
   bottom S. Young
95 M. Lane
96 B. Hawkes
97 A. J. Richards
98 J. Cruickshank/Vireo
100 **left and right** A. J. Richards
101 **left** D. Weschler/Vireo
   right B. L. Sage
102 D. Weschler/Vireo
103 B. L. Sage
104 P. Doherty

105 P. T. Castell
106 R. Tidman
107 B. Hawkes
108 G. G. & I. M. Bates
109 P. T. Castell
110 E. K. Thompson
112 R. Mellon/Vireo
113 J. A. W. Jones
114 E. Mackrill
115 M. C. Wilkes
116 S. Young
117 R. T. Mills
118 J. L. Roberts
119 P. Doherty
120 P. Doherty
121 J. B. & S. Bottomley
122 C. Greaves
123 J. B. & S. Bottomley
124 M. C. Wilkes
125 P. Doherty
126 D. S. Whitaker
127 B. Hawkes
128/9 C. Greaves
130 P. T. Castell
131 R. T. Mills
132 B. Hawkes
133 S. Young
134 **top** A. J. Bond
   bottom R. T. Mills
135 R. Tidman
136 D. S. Whitaker
137 W. Lankinen
138 **left** W. S. Paton
   right R. T. Mills
139 M. C. Wilkes
140 R. Villani/Vireo

141 P. Doherty
142 A. J. Bond
143 P. Doherty
144 E. Soothill
145 J. J. Brooks
147 **top** D. Frost
   bottom B. L. Sage
148 P. Doherty
149 P. Doherty
150 M. C. Wilkes
151 M. C. Wilkes
152 P. Shaw
153 R. T. Mills
154/5 A. J. Bond
156 **left** D. Platt
   right A. J. Bond
158 K. Brink/Vireo
159 **left** P. T. Castell
   right B. L. Sage
160 R. T. Mills
161 D. Green
162 P. T. Castell
163 P. T. Castell
164 C. Heyes
165 A. Morris/Vireo
166 A. J. Richards
167 D. S. Whitaker
168 D. Roby/K. Brink/Vireo
169 B. Hawkes
170 M. C. Wilkes
171 P. T. Castell
172/3 B. Hawkes
174 G. Langsbury
175 D. Roby/K. Brink/Vireo
176 D. Weschler/Vireo
178 B. L. Sage

INDEX